D1245383

Lead Us Not Into Temptation

Lead Us Not Into Temptation

Raymond Arroyo Jr.

Library of Congress Control Number: 2010906210
ISBN: Softcover   978-1-4500-9468-9
                 Ebook   978-1-4500-9469-6

This book was printed in the United States of America.

To order additional copies of this book, contact:
Xlibris Corporation
1-888-795-4274
www.Xlibris.com
Orders@Xlibris.com
80724

Proverbs 3:5 . . . 10

Trust in the Lord with all your heart,

lean not onto your own understandings.

In everything you do acknowledge him,

and he will direct your paths.

Be not wise in your own eyes;

fear the Lord, and turn away from all evil.

It shall be health to your navel,

and marrow to your bones.

Honor the Lord with your substance,

and with the firstfruits of all your increase:

So shall your barns be filled with plenty,

and your presses shall burst out with new wine.

ISAIAH 40:31

But they that wait upon the Lord shall renew

their strength; they shall mount up with wings

as eagles; they shall run and not get weary; and

they shall walk, and not faint.

Help us Lord, Help us Lord, amen!

CONTENTS

PROLOGUE

I've written this book not as an author for I've never written anything before let alone a book, but I come as a messenger of God. For it was through one of many visitations I had with the Lord Jesus Christ from whom this book was summoned. Its purpose, concept, and the words aren't mine, but belong to Him who summoned me to write this book, to the Lord Jesus Christ himself. He supplied both the inspiration and the courage for me to come forth and write this book for him. I say courage because for one I am not in the ministry nor have I ever written anything. My English is Brooklyn brogue (I was born, raised and have lived in New York most of my life) and I have never done well with grammar. Two it required that I bear my beliefs and convictions in God, in man and in the world we live in. And finally it required that I bare my life in this book, which I found most difficult to put on paper even though those parts of my past are gone forever and were healed by God, but nevertheless painful when I look back on them. Therefore for the sake of God and for the many people whose lives that will be hopefully healed and mended back together through reading this book I bare the naked truth of myself and all that God has for you. It's imperative that I do it this way to give credibility to all that I have written and all that God has taught me. Therefore I have made the last part of this book titled Jesus and Me, a sort of autobiography of my life and also bear proof that Jesus Christ is the Son of God and Savior of the World. When you read my autobiography you will know of the miracles he did for me, the visitation I had with him and the fact that I live to this day because of his undying love for me to keep me alive.

Writing this book became an overwhelmingly difficult task, as I don't have a doctorate in psychology or any of the other social sciences that would lend more credibility to my written words. My sheepskin is that of a lay person, a bible teacher and lay minister having spent many years in street ministry work with drug addicts and run away teenagers and bringing the word of God to all people with an ear to listen. This as well as many years serving as a visiting minister to and old age home in Ridge, New York and a lay minister at Southside Hospital in West Islip, New York, visiting patients at the hospital including terminally ill patients. Bringing them the message of the Gospel of Jesus Christ and offering them the love of God that lives within me. In addition to this I've counseled and shared the word of God with thousands of people to this very day. Sharing with so many who were down cast and disillusioned and others who had lost their faith brought on by the hard lives they have lived. Bringing them refreshing good news of God's word and of his promises not as the churches teach it, but how God teaches us. For the written word of God is yes and amen and never changes and never alters. We change it and alter God's word to suit our own purposes be it for religious or political gains. Too often we teach the fear of God rather than the love of God. What I bring to you is God's word to lift your spirits, give you new focus in your life and to meet your spiritual needs. For God so loves us and wants us to know he's ready, willing and able to heal, forgive and put back together every life, every soul that confesses to him and says yes father I need you first and foremost in my life. I know for I've been there and was saved many times from the clutches of death by the miracles of a merciful Lord Jesus Christ, who through his love and caring not only saved my life but my soul also.

I've ministered to people from all walks of life and from all religious persuasions, from the religious to the intellectual, from the young to the elderly, to drug addicts, prostitutes, the rich and the poor. It has been a labor of love which I pray I can keep on doing as long as I live and have breath to help someone find their way with God. For my purpose in life as God has shown me is to bring enlightenment to the hearts of man so that all may know and love Him and foremost believe in Him.

My purpose is not to show you a new religion or point you in the direction of any one religion. I will help you find your pathway to God, and he will direct you where you should be from that time on. For we are all his children and he wants only the very best for us and to heal us from whatever problem or illness we suffer from. For we all do suffer in different ways and commit sins through out our lives for none of us are perfect. Yet Jesus who is perfect and is Lord of the earth wants to bring you back onto the path to

God the Father, so that you may have a truly complete life centered in His love. To then become his witnesses on earth of the work and the miracles he has done in each of your lives so you can spread the good news around. Jesus who was given lordship over the earth and all that is on it once said, *that of all which the Father has given me, I shall lose none.* In a world so torn with turmoil, war, poverty, hunger and death it's a prime time for all of us to question where we are in life and what kind of relationship we each have with God and with one another.

This is not a Christian book or a book proselytizing Christianity or any other religious faith. The Lord Jesus who saved me not once but many times will show you where you belong in this world. Christianity is not the only religion in this world and we are all the children of God whom he intends to save. The purpose of this book is to help you to refocus your heart and soul on God as the principal being in your life. Not the one you turn to just on holy days, but everyday for daily guidance, for learning, for help with every situation in your daily life. To consul with him daily and give him praise and thanks and to bring him your beefs of the day so that he may help you through it. Even Jesus said when you pray, pray to the Father which art in heaven. Whether you do this as a Christian, a Jew, a Muslim, a Hindu or a Buddhist or any of the other fine religions in the world is for you to decide with the Lord Jesus Christ. He who saved me and gave me back my faith led me to where I was best needed and where I would be best off and cared for. Where you stand and where you want to go with your religious preferences after reading this book is a decision only you can make through prayer with your heavenly Father. No religion is any better than any other in this world and they all have one main thing in common. They were all created by men and not by God.

Only one caution I give to everyone, know your church, know your religion. No church, no priest, no pastor, no minister or rabbi should preach against another religion. No religion or church leader should preach hatred, bigotry or war, for that could never come from God. God is not the author of hate and confusion but of love. Nowhere in the bible is a religion given for man to follow. We are told to have faith in god and in his son Jesus. We also have one major thing in common and that is we all believe in God, the Supreme Being who created everything that is. We have different names for him, but the same God. Will the reading of this book cause you to convert and become a Christian? The answer to that is maybe yes and maybe no, but what is important is that upon reading this book it will help you to become enlightened with God. To open your mind and heart to centering you life on a new option for life and that is a life centered in God. Will the reading of this book cause you to become a believer in Jesus Christ? I hope so, but again the answer to that is again maybe and maybe not. Through soul searching and prayer with God, you will find the truth and the truth will set you free. He will direct your path and you will know where to go.

For those who don't trust or believe in Jesus Christ, I offer this. He lived and did the wonders and miracles we are told in the bible. He was a prophet of God and much more he was the son of God, appointed the Messiah of the world to save all the souls on earth. He is the son of God but so are you the sons and daughters of God. He never professed a religion to man, but he himself followed the Hebrew faith. He's the only man who has ever lived to have had so great an affect on the world and all the people in the world even to this day two thousand years later. Today about one third of the people in the world believe in Jesus Christ through one form of Christianity or another. Even in the Muslim faith they believe in Jesus Christ as a prophet of God which can be found in the Koran. As Jesus himself said he is the son of man, the son of God. He is not God, but Lord of all on earth with the mission to bring salvation to all on earth, to the Jews and to all the gentiles. After all there are no exclusive clubs. God's desire is to save all citizens on earth. Jesus said (John 6:35-39), *I am the bread of life and he that comes to me shall never hunger and he that believes in me shall never thirst. All that the Father gives me shall come to me; and he that comes to me I will in no way cast out, for I came down from heaven not to do my own will, but the will of Him that sent me. And this is the Father's will which has sent me, that of all which He has given me I should lose none.* This means exactly what Jesus says, his mission on earth is to save all the people of the world for he was given dominion of the world. We may be stiff and obstinate, war mongers, sinners, whatever, but in the long run God will win our souls if not in this life then in the next one.

There's much to read and much to learn in this book. How you deal with it is up to you. My hope for you is that it will open your heart and mind to all the possibilities God has for you and that you find your spiritual awakening with God. If that's all you receive from this book, then my work is truly done. The rest of your life is between you and God. As for me, I'm just one of many prophets of God pointing the way to him and helping to shine a light on the many mistakes and sins we all have made with our lives. Mistakes and sins like hatred, bigotry, selfishness, greed, crime and the abuse of one another. And even more dangerous ones like that of pride and fanaticism, be it religious, political or secular.

A question you might be asking which I already asked God is why use me to bring this message? Why didn't he use the Pope or a famous evangelist or famous television minister or a famous guru in spiritualism to write this book? I believe when you read this book the answer will be clear that everything they have to say has been said in every religious and spiritual manner possible. From the pulpit to the air via radio and television they have preached their sermons in a cadence of religiosity trying their best to bring you into their persuasion. Yet in spite of all their preaching the world still lies in danger of a final holocaust, the Great Tribulation of the End Times. So as I believe it was time for God to pick new voices and none that are caught up in religious or governmental diatribe, indoctrinated by any political ideology. Not proselytizing their religious beliefs to others, but people who would just simply speak and write God's truth. Not a religious truth, but God's truth which is the truth to all people around the world.

So as in the past God once more summons a person no one knows, me a sinner who had no belief in God. A person with a chip on his shoulder from the built in anger for the years he's had to suffer as a minority Latino and Gay person and as one who had to suffer ten years of sexual abuse. It took a mighty miracle to summon me to his service for I had no faith at all. And not just one miracle, but many over the course of over twenty years for there was much to heal in my soul, in my mind and in my heart. The first miracle was a visitation from Jesus Christ that changed my life forever more. He gave me a truth, a real world reality for myself that went beyond all that I had ever learned or was told. It went beyond the churches with all the hate and bigotry they spew against people they know nothing about. It went beyond all that this nation stands for. Here was Jesus Christ talking to me and the message he brings me is this "my son, my son I love you and want you to follow me." I fell to the floor crying my heart out yelling: "Lord, what are you doing here visiting me. I'm such a dirty man. I'm so dirty and filled with so much sin." I couldn't stand in his presence and my tears flooded the carpet as I knelt at his feet. With all the love of the ages, of time in creation, he lifted me and said once more, *my son I love you and want you to follow me.* One important thing I must mention, He never condemned my homosexuality, for it wasn't because of my homosexuality that I was in sin, it was because of the prostitution of my body and that was a sin, and this would be the case whether one was homosexual or heterosexual. I repented my sinful life and promised to follow him from that day on for all of eternity, but cautioned him how weak a man I was and how that I feared falling back to my sins over and over. His response was "whenever you fall I will be there to lift you up again and again and set the pathway straight for you." You just follow me and I will lead you and teach you and make you a precious child in my home. He has changed my life forever and I've never turned back as hard a road as it has been for me at times.

Just like all his disciples before me, God chose the foolish to confound the wise. So here I am, restored from death, washed clean of all my sins and converted to a man of God, a voice out of the wilderness, who has answered the calling of God to write this book with his guidance and inspiration.

Jesus said we must be born again. This was a call to mankind that we must become spiritually enlightened with God the Father. Unfortunately being born again is becoming a mockery as many born again Christians treat their faith with a fanaticism, overbearing and with unloving manners and approaches to other. Many born again Christians are like a cult in the behavior. But having a real spiritual awakening with Jesus, one becomes enlightened spiritually, your life will change completely to that of one of righteousness and you'll be set free from your sinful ways. That is being born again; we die to our old self and rise up a new creation of God. We must all come to understand that the differences in our religions, doesn't change the fact that we all serve and pray to the same God. We don't need to change our religions, which were man made, but to change our attitude within our hearts. In a perfect world there would be no religions, just a love for God. Religions are like nations, they separate us one from another, creating boundaries, bigotries and a disliking for one another.

We cannot change the world nor can we remove the religions in the world, but we can make them better to serve both man and God in a world free of hatred, bigotry, war, and all the many sins that affect our world today. That we must put aside our differences, our hatreds of one another including all the bigotry and recreate the world through God's help into a world of love, of caring and of peace for one another. It is God's message for humanity, or God's final call to man. We're at the crossroads of life, the final curtain has been drawn and we're the last act. What we do from here on end will determine the final destiny of all humanity.

No we can't all be the same nor can we be robots. That's the beauty of man, we're each different from one another and each one unique to God the Father. He cares most deeply for each and every one of us, and wants us all to make it into the kingdom of heaven. After all he is not the God of a select few but he is the father of over six billion children here on earth. We are all his creations, souls that emanated from his soul and consequently his aim is for all to make it. Jesus said that all that the Father had given him, he will lose none. God gave Jesus Lordship over all the earth and all that lives within it. This means everyone on earth past, present and future will get to the kingdom of God through him. He will lose none and he will find a way to reach you if not in this life then in your next life. I will write on this topic later in the book. There is only one way to be excluded from the kingdom of heaven and that is to absolutely reject God the Father in your heart, mind and soul. It's called in the bible the unpardonable sin, for you can't be forgiven by him whom you completely reject and refuse to believe in. Consequently by your own rejection of God, you have chosen to become a lost soul.

It is imperative you read this book with an open heart and put your religious beliefs aside for a moment. For this message is an outreach to each of you as individuals and not an attack on your choice of religions that you each choose to follow and worship God in. Therefore whether you call him Allah, God or Jehovah or the many other names he is given in this world he is always the same God, the Omnipotent One, all knowing and all present. To him goes glory forever and ever, Amen.

Once you do commit your life to him, he is more than capable to pointing you in the direction you should go and where you'll be happiest in worshipping him. Believe me at that junction of your life you'll only be too happy to follow him. I know for I have been there and experienced exactly that personally with Jesus, who did just that for me. If he did it for me, then he'll do it for you. He took me from a lost unbelieving soul and showed me the way to him and to a church I could believe in. So who is this Jesus, he is the intermediary between us and God the Father. He is the Son of God. He is our lawyer who defends each one of us before God, and washes away our sins and faults.

So I will close this introduction with this. Keep your mind and heart open as you read this book and let God work within you and show you who he is. He will show you the truth and the truth will set you free. Happy hunting as you read through the pages of this book, that you become enlightened with God as you conclude your reading. God bless you all.

PART ONE

Lead Us Not Into Temptation

CHAPTER ONE

THE DECEPTION OF MAN

The bible tells us in the Old Testament that in the beginning God created the universe and everything in it. He created all living things and he created man in his image, both man and woman. They were Adam (the first Adam) and his wife Eve and with them began the deception of man.

According to the bible Satan the deceiver came to tempt them and succeeded in doing so, by getting them to eat of the forbidden fruit in the garden. He accomplished this by appealing to their carnal minds filling them with deception, lies and the lust of the eyes until they succumbed to the temptation. In doing so they introduced sin into the world, bringing death into the world and man into a world of darkness. The choice was theirs, to keep what they had which was life eternal in the Garden of Eden, or to choose that which Satan offered, a life of slavery to sin. This was the first deception of man leading to their death and expulsion from the Garden of Eden. For in doing so they gave up both their spiritual and eternal lives and traded them in for carnal lives lived by the lust of the eyes and mind and for a life that would know suffering, bear pain and eventually face death. A life of worldliness and from this point in time sin came into the world and took hold of mankind. Never would the world be the same for no longer could man live in the Garden of Eden. Now man would live in a world of greed and darkness and man would live by the sweat of his brow.

There are other variations to the Adam and Eve story which are accounted for outside of the bible. They were discovered in the bible codes confirming what the great psychic Edgar Cayce saw in one of his prophetic dreams. It one of them it seems Adam and Eve weren't the first people on earth, but they were the first homo-sapiens. The world was still being inhabited with the Cro-Magnon man. In this account of the first sin it was infidelity and not disobedience. In this account Eve slept with another man from the Cro-Magnon race and became pregnant with Cane. Consequently Cane and Abel were only half brothers, Abel being the first born son of Adam. As the story unfolds the first born Abel was then slain by his own brother Cain, who was taken over by jealously and greed. That because his offering to God wasn't considered by God to be the very best he could offer. Not like the offering of his brother Abel, who gave the very best of his flock to God. So strong was his jealously that he killed his own brother and now as he is banished from the Garden of Eden by God, sin began to spread like a virus taking hold of all men. From here man became deceived into committing all types of sins which are all based on the flesh.

Once out of the Garden of Eden, the children grew up joining together with those who lived outside the garden and bore children with them. And sin had its way with man spreading like wild fire consuming the hearts and minds of men. Since then man has lived in the world he chose over the world God had prepared for him. Since then hate, bigotry, wars, famines, lust, pride, hunger and pestilence to name a few has ravaged the world ever since destroying the lives of countless millions along the way. So has it been since the beginning of time until this very day, people living materialistically, choosing to live in darkness and rejecting life in the light of god. The sins of man yesterday are the same ones today. We read and hear about them everyday women being raped, children being abused sexually, the slave trading of men, women and children, drug abuse, murder, and the list just goes on endlessly. Ironically the wars of Old Testament times are with us once again in these modern times. Only now the Middle East threatens to bring the world into World War III and possibly an end to our way of life. Terrorism is the enemy of our times brought on by those who are filled with hatred in their hearts. They call it a religious war as they did back then, but in fact has nothing to do with religion but more with bigotry. For God is the head of all religions no matter what name you give him God, Allah or Jehovah and God never advocated violence towards anyone. And one of the commandments of God is *thou shall not kill.* I don't think the message can be any plainer than that. Yet man is still the same creature of old habits and constantly repeating the mistakes of yesterday, only now his ways have brought the world to the brink of total destruction.

For all the science and technology of man, the results have been broken and false promises. The poor of the world are still with us but only in greater numbers. The numbers of those starving to death runs in the tens of millions each year. Disease still ravishes the world killing people in the millions and the world is no better off than it was one hundred years ago.

Oh yes we see tremendous advancement in the way we live here in the USA. Many countries around the world have also advanced tremendously through science and technology. We have luxuries never thought of before for the working man, yet something is wrong. We're on the edge of the extermination of the human race. Hate has consumed the hearts of man around the world. Greed has separated the ones that have from those who have not. Over two thirds of the people in the world live in poverty, wondering if they will eat one day to another. While the haves of the world wondering if the stocks, bonds or their 401k will rise so they can buy more luxuries and trinkets. I tell you true that the day is coming when the Dow Jones will fall way under 5,000 taking with it many of the largest financial institutes around the world. And then what, panic, suicides, chaos, war to try to solve the unsolvable? Our prisons are filled to capacity with all sorts of men and women who lived by the flesh and were void of any spirituality. Our streets are littered with hundreds of times more criminals than those in the prisons poisoning our citizens with all sorts of sinfulness and destroying our youth.

There is one big difference of today's world from the world in biblical times is that we have the weapons of mass destruction that can destroy the entire world. Nuclear weapons once were only in the possession of the United States government and Russia. Now many nations around the world possess nuclear weapons and other nations are developing theirs. Of this many are third world nations who are not exactly friendly with the other half. Politicians try to convince us how much better the world is today than in anytime in our history and for the one third of the world who has everything that is true and yet the other two thirds of the world it couldn't be worse. Man in all his wisdom is blindly foolish and cannot see the forest through the trees. He cannot fathom why the world is in such a mess, why that war dominates the planet all around the world. Why that people commit such atrocities against one another such as in slave trading of children and women for sex markets or forcing children into slave labor to make sneakers, rugs, clothing for those in the one third of the world that have it all. We've become so blind by materialism, possessions, power, domination, wealth that we can no longer see that we've lost our spirituality and for man their souls. We have lost our way and God is not at the helm of our hearts, our greed is now our god. All the things that we allow to dominate our lives where we give no concern to God have become our god. Try praying to your money or to all the things that possess your life and see if they answer you or fix your problems in life.

The wealthy and the fat corporate leaders tell us how fortunate we are to be living in these times, but the only people benefiting from these wonderful times are themselves. Let them try living on $200-300 a week and raise a family and pay rent and put food on the table. The halls of Congress in Washington D.C. are full of multi millionaires, and yet none of them would give up their Federal salaries and work for dollar a year. No they not only take the fat salaries which they really don't need, but many steal from the public pushing through legislation to create programs and projects no one needs but they get a kick back from. A few major corporations today control the wealth of the world forcing nations to humble themselves before them. Too many politicians humbling themselves before big fat corporations begging to eat crumbs from the corporate table, only too willing to make deals that will make corporations richer than ever before in human history, as well as making them rulers over our lives and our world. Too often political decisions and policy are based on how it benefits the corporate giants in the country.

Consequently the world today is ruled by two types of governments; one being the governments that rule over each nation of the world and the second being the corporate giants of today's global economy that rule over our daily lives and livelihood. For they dictate and control all the science, medicine, technology, food and supplies and finally all the wealth of the world.

As with the serpent in the Garden of Eden tempting Adam and Eve, the corporate world is the serpent of this world constantly tempting us with their delights. Constantly through their science and technology inventing and constantly reinventing all the latest marvels in electronics, aviation, automobiles and newer and more advanced computers to keep man hungry for more and more. Everything from clothes to the food we eat are constantly reinvented with flash, sex appeal and lies upon lies to keep the public dangling on a string hungry to buy more and more of the wares they truly have no need for. Our foods are ladened with chemicals and preservatives, and our minds being brainwashed with advertising making us believe we are eating the very best the world has ever had. Yet cancer, heart disease, diabetes to mention a few continue on the rise out of control, and the death toll rising more and more every year with no cures in site. Hospitals are overrun with sick and diseased patients, doctor's and hospital bills skyrocketing and insurance claims running in the billions just here in the United States. All through out the world tens of millions without insurance or money to pay for their health care. One can only wonder that the master plan of corporations is to keep people sick which makes the pharmaceuticals corporations richer, hospitals richer and doctors richer and all the while bankrupting the working class of all societies.

Man has allowed himself to being deceived since the very beginning and today with all the knowledge and communications we have with one another we're deceived even worse than poor Adam. Imagine with all the education we have today we fall victim to the cheap tricks of politicians, corporate CEO's with their cunning advertisements. We have banks, mortgage companies, lawyers and accountants working hard to defraud the public and all for a buck. Every deception of man through out history was to serve the rich to getting more wealth for themselves. Today the rich are sickening with CEO's making hundreds of millions of dollars a year and looking to invent schemes to defraud the public so they can make more. When Jesus said money the root of all evil, he was absolutely right and I'm sure He meant it more for our generation than any other before it. Greed runs rampant in this world, our politicians are no exception. So what do we do about it? One thing is for sure stop trusting man, government and big corporations to solve your problems. Take responsibility for yourself, learn and educate yourself. There's no excuse not to for answers and information regarding all your problems are available to you. And when you need to put trust in someone put it in God only. Trust no one else for no one will have your best interest at heart but God.

One must also beware of other serpents in the world tempting man to fall. They peddle drug addiction, alcoholism, slothfulness, lust and just a multitude of vicious means to get your attention. Think it could never happen to you? Well it happened to Adam, and he knew God. What's going to save you from you big fall? The answer is Jesus Christ.

Through Jesus Christ man can fight off the biggest serpents of all, the corporate giants and the governments of today. Both are in bed with one another inventing and creating all those wonderful ways to control man and his control his will. On the one hand they build nuclear, chemical and biological weapons of mass destruction and on the other they tell us no country should be allowed to have these weapons. They do the same double talk with all the legislation they pass and then on the other hand fail to pass very important legislation the public truly needs, like health care. Advertising is another prime example of this manipulation of man showering him with all kinds of lustful ads for cars, clothes, jewelry, expensive vacations, homes, credit cards, credit cards and more credit cards, etc. All for the purpose of controlling and subduing the mind of man and finally dominating his will. Thus conquering his individuality and defeating his independent spirit, making him a pawn to the corporate fathers and government leaders of the world. Imagine this that after thousand of years, man hasn't achieved anymore than the first Adam achieved in the Garden of Eden. That is to being deceived by the devil (or in today's world by the corporate and government leaders) into believing and accepting their concept of true life and happiness. All based on materialism and worldliness and void of God. Yes that's the true evolution of man for he hasn't evolved at all, but remains a dupe to be controlled by the forces of darkness. Whether it's Satan, as with Adam or the corporate world as it is today, the enemy of man is man himself, for he lives by site and not by faith. We live by what we can see and feel and not by spirit. And the corporate fathers as we've witnessed laugh their way to the banks with the hundred million dollar annual paychecks, building castles for themselves while the rest of us struggle to pay for the gas to fill our gas tanks with.

If changes aren't made in each of our lives towards a more spiritual life, then the Armageddon or the final war will be upon us and the question won't be will we survive but who will survive. We must remember that we're all responsible for the wellbeing and safety of both our souls and the safe keeping of this planet. All this did God entrust into our hands. As smart as our corporate and government fathers think they are they have not succeeded in finding true peace and happiness for all mankind. Why, because their aim in the end is always in profits and domination and not in our spiritual and mental health. You can see that with the collapse of the stock market this year and the collapse of the housing market with trillions of dollars lost in bad mortgages and tens of thousands of foreclosures on homes across the country.

The country is in a very deep recession heading into a depression and all because of greed running rampant in the country. With banks, investment companies and mortgage companies with their deceptive practices giving loans to people who could never be able to afford the payments. And to really complicate the problem it has become a global issue with markets crashing all over the world. Still think you can trust the government, the banks, and the investment companies to have your best interest at heart? The only thing they have interest in is the money in your accounts and in your wallet. This financial disaster coupled with all the other problems of terrorism, bigotry and hate wars will one day soon explode in all of our faces and World War III will be its culmination.

This will be the final war and promises by the word of God, to destroy two thirds of the world's population through the war, disease and natural disasters that will occur. Jesus says, *that we will know the times for they'll be wars and rumor of wars in diverse places. Earthquakes and natural disasters will erupt all over the world as warnings for the end draws very near. (Matthew, chapter 24:4-8)*

We must awaken and change our ways. We must develop the nature of God in each of our lives if we are to survive and the world is to survive. Bible prophecies are exactly that, warnings of the things to come if we don't change our ways. We must stop giving ear to the world which is against God and be seeking the spiritual truth of God for our lives, forsaking that which is worldly and materialistic for those things which are of God which build you up. Most people today live by sight, by materialism and not by faith and spirit. Choosing materialism or the world over the spirit has made empty shells of us, disbelieving in God, lacking in faith, lacking in love and lacking in compassion towards one another. The consequences of this materialistic life today is beginning to bear it's fruit, the destruction of mankind and his world and it is the enemy's biggest deception on man. We've been duped by our own greed, our lust for power, money and all the baubles we can possess. Satan lost his battle with Jesus when trying to tempt him, but losing the battle didn't mean he had lost the war. For Satan, was well prepared for his second battle and that would be the temptation of all mankind. As the story goes after being baptized Jesus went into the wilderness wandering and fasting for forty days and nights. Satan then came to tempt him three times knowing that Jesus was weak and hungry and it was the opportune time to tempt him into the big fall.

First he tempted Jesus by attacking his weakness as he hadn't eaten for forty days and nights. He dared Jesus to turn stones turn into bread, as he knew Jesus was starving for food. Jesus refused him saying, *man shall not live by bread alone, but by every word that comes from the mouth of God.* Then Satan brings forth his second challenge for Jesus saying, *throw yourself down, for it is written God will command his angels and they will bear you and not let you be hurt.* Jesus again refuses saying to Satan, *You must not test the Lord your God.* Finally Satan, not being a quitter challenger Jesus taking him to a mountain top and showing him all the kingdoms of the world with all the riches and splendors and says to Jesus, *I will give you everything you see if you worship me. Jesus immediately refuses saying: get out of here Satan, for it is written You must worship the Lord your God and serve him only.* The point here is that in every instance Jesus chose the way of God over the temptations of the world. Are we doing the same? Are we making the tougher spiritual choices in life against the more tempting worldly choices that would make life on earth more bearable and more comfortable? Are we the row models we should be to our children and to all children around the world? Or will they just fall in line with what they've learned from us and keep making the same mistakes when it's their time to take over the world. We're living a life filled with lies and disappointments and unfulfilled dreams and a lot of bad karma. Karma is very important to know for it's the law of God. We reap what we sow, the good or the bad it is karma.

The results of this type of living is a life far from the truth that is within us and far, far away from a chance to know God who can only be found within each of us. For life in the spirit enlightened with God can only be found from within and not in the world. Jesus said, *that Kingdom of God cannot be seen, because the Kingdom of God is within you (Luke 17:21).*

You may be thinking, but why does it have to be this way? That is because we are eternal souls that emanated from the soul of God. For it's from God from where our souls come from and it is from God only that we can find the true spiritual life as we reunite ourselves with him. We are all given free will to choose the life we follow be it the world or a spirit filled life with God. Our karma in life will be the result of our choices. Good begets good and bad begets bad results in life. It's from God alone that we can get salvation for our souls, and an eternal life in the kingdom of God. For as I said before, our souls emanated from His soul and it is to Him we each must return.

The one problem we each have is the free will God gave us to choose. It is this free will that causes man to stumble. For this free will allows us to takes our eyes off of God and focus our attention in the world and all its material promises. Thus we have the conflict in man's soul, the light (good) vs. the darkness (bad) creating all sorts of havoc for mankind.

The one thing man never takes into account or into understanding is that a spirit filled life with God doesn't mean poverty and doing without. What it does mean is having God at the helm of you life, guiding you to make the right choices for your life. Helping you to achieve more success in life for yourself and your family then you would have been able to achieve on your own. Does it mean all who come to God, will find prosperity? No, what it does means is that through God you will find all that is there for you to achieve, find the happiness your never knew, rediscover yourself and you hidden talents and most importantly find salvation for your eternal soul. The consummate word being "eternal" as the soul is eternal and where you spend that eternity is up to you.

The problem gets exacerbated when Satan and the world are very busy vying for our attention. Trying so very hard to distract us away from the light and draw us into the darkness, onto the things of the world to cause our downfall. An important point to remember in the creation is that in the beginning there was darkness and nothing existed. And it was from the darkness that God brought out the light. Well we are all a prime example of the same method of creation. We are created souls living in darkness for none of us are perfect and all of us are with sin. Then somewhere in your life comes the challenge to leave the darkness and step into the light of God. So just like God brought the light out of the darkness, if you let Him, He will do the same for you.

Another thing we must all realize is that Satan has no power over man and cannot force us do things against our will, our logic, our common sense and understanding of life. The old saying of the seventies "the devil made me do it" just isn't so. Satin has no power over us. His power is the same as he used against Adam and Eve, and with Jesus Christ, in the wilderness during the forty days of fasting. He presents temptations, lusts for our eyes to behold, offerings for us to get snarled in, but he can't make us do his will. That we do on our own when we succumb to his temptations. And that is the consummate word "succumb." We have to give in to his will, chase after the temptations put before us. And the devil is no fool for he knows just exactly what it will take to get your eyes off of God and onto him. But thanks be to God, who made a way out for all of us. He made a plan of salvation for man to redeem his soul. For as a father, God wants all his children to find a life filled with joy, peace and filled in his Holy Spirit. That plan of salvation is through his son Jesus Christ, who is there for all of us Jew, Gentile, Christian, Buddhist, Moslems, Hindus and people of all nationalities and faiths. Christ was given ruler ship over all of the earth which means the whole human race with the power to forgive all sins, all wrongs to those who repent of the ways and are ready to make the change and become enlightened, a spirit filled life with God or as it is also known as being born again. Many fear the term born again. Yet it simply means that one sheds their old life in the darkness for a life in the light of God. That one takes Jesus into their heart believing him to be the Son of God and their Savior.

This has become a major stumbling block for millions of people around the world who refuse to acknowledge Jesus Christ as Lord over the earth. They choose to believe in their own religious followings and teachings handed down through the ages. So consequently we cannot find peace in the world to this day as man cannot find enlightenment with God. Man insists that Buddha, Krishna, Abraham, Moses or Mohammed is the way to the Kingdom of God. But these men, prophets of God, great as they were, again were just men with a calling for mankind to turn their lives around to God. The same can be said for Gandhi or Sister Teresa. Great servants of God but in each case leaders of their religious followings without the power to unite the world in peace because for one none of them could forgive sins. Only Jesus has the power to forgive sin and bring you into the light of God, but you must choose it. He will never force himself on you. Jesus died for all of us but with one difference He rose from the dead and entered the kingdom of heaven sitting at the right hand of God. There are no bones, no ashes of his remains and why should there be? He is the son of God. Where all the prophets of God died and were buried and their remains turned to ashes. Even the Koran of the Muslim although it only recognizes Jesus Christ as a prophet and a Messiah, but not the Son of God, agrees that it is Jesus Christ who will return in the second coming of the Messiah. So then if it's Jesus who will return as both the Christian bible and the Koran agree then there is proof that He is the Son of God.

We need to finally get beyond our religions, beyond our nationalities and find a way to unite into a world centered in God the Father and in his son Jesus Christ. Unite into a world that is free of hate, free of bigotry and free of wars. A world filled with love and brotherhood for every man, woman and child. To achieve this we must go beyond the religious leaders of the world today, good men as they are. They could never unite the world for their lives will always be shortened by death and will never have the time to complete the work or they don't have the spiritual enlightenment with Christ Jesus, to be able to undertake such a task. And that's where Jesus comes in. He was sent to earth by his Father, to be just that, the one representative that can represent the entire world and all the religions of the world and bring hope and peace to the entire world. But we cannot achieve this enlightenment with God and find true hope and peace on earth if we continue to reject his son Jesus Christ, for he is the forgiver of all wrong and all sin. And God the Father cannot send us his Holy Spirit, until we come to terms with Jesus and deal with our worldly lives and begin a new life of enlightenment. It is the Holy Spirit who teaches us all things and helps us to change our ways, which often are not easy to change.

Today God has become just a word, a thing, a myth past down through the ages that no one can prove. We can't see him, nor touch him, then why believe in him. You hear many people say: I pray and pray, but get no answers. I have all these problems in life, but get no help from God. Or where was God when my mother died or my son or my husband died? Many others say that God has never done anything for them. That the bible holds no more promise for man today than God himself.

The problem is in your prayers and your lack of faith. If for one you don't truly believe in God, then why should he answer your prayers when obviously you don't truly believe in Him? As for most people who profess to be religious and go to church or temple regularly you treat God as most people do in their prayers, as an errand boy, praying only when you have an urgent need or a disaster at hand. I call it the give me, get me and I want prayers. Most people never reach out to God in their daily lives when things are going just right. Remember good times don't last forever and all of us bar none do come upon bad times, loss of loved ones, financial disaster and I think you get the picture. My father used to tell me when I was a young man that life was like a wheel. You'll be on top of the world in one part of your life and then the wheel turns and you're coming upon bad times, hitting the bottom, losing your job, your home or death strikes one of your loved ones and life just isn't a basket full of daisies anymore. It's at these bad times that we remember God otherwise he is non existent in our lives. Worse yet we pray without any faith. We never believe that he hears us, or that he will answer our prayers to begin with. We play at church going to show face but lack the faith and conviction to believe and to take God at His word. We choose worldliness over God for it is easier to believe in what one can see and hold in one's hands. That money, beautiful homes, fancy cars, this is the mark of success that one strives for and can believe in. It pays the bills, spoils the kids and makes everyone happy. The problem is that no one is happy no matter how much they have. If money were the root of happiness then what went wrong with this world.

Following the world's way of materialism has never been the answer for man. It has never brought everlasting peace and everlasting happiness to the world. To the contrary the world has gone through thousands of years of wars, the slaughtering of millions of people all because of greed, materialism, bigotry against their race, color or faith. If worldliness, money, governments and religions were man's answers for world peace, then we have failed miserably as a people. For never once in all the history of mankind has man found everlasting peace and happiness through the world's systems or through any other system away from God. So if nothing else awakens us to the need for having God in our daily lives, this should. For man doesn't have the answers to ending wars and bringing in everlasting peace, nor to an end of poverty and hunger around the world or for an end to bigotry, hate and equality for all mankind. Never has been and never will be without first putting God in the middle to guide and lead us in all things. Just look around and look back at history and you know that I am right. We fool ourselves into always thinking we can do it, but again fail miserably.

Without God at the helm of each of our hearts, we are hopeless to repeat the errors of our ways. In view of all the science and technology today our crowning achievement is the creation of weapons of mass destruction which can only lead us into the Armageddon, the final war, the end of days. Two thirds of mankind perishing in the war, nations destroyed and never again to rise to their former glories. Without God all the fatal prophecies of the end times will come to pass and yet if we all just change we can change the fate of the world.

September 11, 2001 was the attack on the World's Trade Center, one of the blackest days in American history. Terrorism has risen around the globe and continues to threaten the peace of the world, and will one day soon culminate in World War III. Along with this has been a rise in natural disasters from earthquakes, hurricanes and the like that destroys cities, towns and villages, killing tens of thousands of human lives. We have seen the destruction of the killer tsunami in the Indian Ocean. It was a disaster of biblical proportions killing over 300,000 people. Again we witnessed another disaster of biblical proportions with the destruction of New Orleans when hit by Hurricane Katrina and more recently the earthquakes in China again killing unbelievable amounts of people and this to mention just a few. We must take note that they have all occurred during what Jesus termed the end times.

We cannot go on living a godless existence without care and love for God and for one another. That unless we all change and begin a life of true love for God and brotherly love towards our fellow man regardless of color, race or his orientation these end time prophecies will come to pass. Well I guess the only conclusion that can be made is that we aren't making the necessary changes towards God and towards one another and the prophecies of the end times are being fulfilled.

Can there be any doubt that man is on the wrong track. That its time for a new and permanent direction for man to walk in, a pathway that is centered in God and in truth, where worldliness and materialism is replaced with the love for God and for our fellow man.

Failure to do so and the bible codes warn us of a great depression falling on man destroying the world's economy. A warning of a great World War that along with many natural disasters will kill off two thirds of the world's population. This and more will occur between the years of 2006 and 2020. Are we ready for all of this? Do you believe all this will happen? Or do you still doubt? Do you still believe that man can resolve and stop all this from happening? That man is greater than God? My only answer to this is, don't be fooled! Don't let your ignorance be your downfall. God won't be mocked nor denied by man without man paying the consequences, and the proof of that is the fulfillment of the prophecies to date. Do we need any better proof? Another word for consequences is karma. It follows us throughout life squaring off the debts we owe, good or bad according to our deeds.

Karma is nothing new. It is a law of God, better known by man as reaping what we sow in life. Jesus Christ preached it in his ministry. He that does good deeds and gives to others will receive good deeds in his life and more than he gave. For God loves a giver and a good doer. But it goes deeper than that for it applies to all that we do in life. From eating, drinking, working, and playing, everything we do in life involves karma. An example of this is one who eats poorly in life, eating lots of junk food over the years and over stuffing himself when he eats resulting in obesity (a typical American diet). Not only is obesity the bad karma from all the over eating and junk foods, but so is the diabetes one gets later in life or a bad heart condition or cancer often resulting in death. I know for I am a victim to all three diseases and I live only because Jesus Christ performed miracles in my life to keep me alive. Same thing happens to one who drinks liquor heavily in life or does drugs or smokes cigarettes. Down the road you pay the price of those abuses to your body. Again nothing good can come from it. Another way to look at it is if you do the crime then you will do the time. Everything in life involves karma. Plant a new garden with seedlings and new shrubs, fertilize it and feed it regularly. The result will be months later a beautiful and lush garden, good karma. Good karma at work results in pay raises, promotions. Bad karma at work and you get fired. I think by know you get the picture and that is what the bible codes are warning us about. It is God's way of warning us about bad karma coming upon the world. It's payback time and if we continue on the pathway we're on then karma will kick us all in the butt and it has already begun. But it's never too late to change. We don't have to go through World War III and see two thirds of the world destroyed. We don't have to be like Adam and Eve. All they needed to do after the sin was repent and God would have let them stay in the Garden of Eden and the world would have been a different world than what we know today. But no, they chose not to repent and lost the world they lived in which was paradise for a world in darkness, pain and suffering. God is giving us our last chance to choose. Are you ready to repent, accept Jesus Christ into your life? Are you ready for an eternal life in God's Kingdom or will you do as Adam and Eve did, do nothing and lose it all?

We can have everlasting peace here on earth, but we all have to decide that it's time to change our hearts and give our hearts to God. To open the doors of our hearts and let God in to show us the road to repentance and the new journey he has for each and every one of us. He did it for me and I follow the path put before me everyday. When I commit an error on the way and fall to a sin, he's there to lift me up with all his love and put me back on the road he laid out for me. I used to live in hell, my life given in to so much worldliness and sin. He changed all that for me, but I had to be willing to want the change. I was hungry and thirsty for a life better than my miserable one in sin. I knew I was a sinner and I was tired of doing things my way. They didn't work and even in my successes in life I was unhappy. I found myself empty, unfulfilled. God knew this and when he knew my search for a better life was ripe, that I had reached the point even though I was faithless, to receive, to believe a new way, he came into my life. The door to my heart was open and I was ready to hear from anyone who had the truth for me to believe in. I couldn't be deceived anymore for I already knew the road to destruction and I was dying in it. This is when I had the first visitation with Jesus Christ, savior of the world. I say the first for there have been many, many more. But it was that first one, where he washed my sins away with all love. He came to me saying: "my son, my son, I love you and want you to follow me." The sins of my life poured out of me through my tears flowing all over the floor. I repented saying how sorry I was for the pitiful life I had lived, denying him in my life. He then said to me: "my son, you follow me, and I will lead you into kingdom of God." I answered oh yes Lord, I'll follow you through all eternity and I will do you will, but I'm a weak man who will fall again to my sins for I am only human. He said, "don't worry about the falls, no matter how many, I will lift you up each time and set you back on track with your new walk with me." And so it has been since that glorious day. To him goes all the glory, for he saved a very sinful person, when he saved my soul.

Four thousand years after the first Adam came the second Adam, Jesus Christ. This is the spiritual man, filled in the Holy Spirit who conquered sin and hell where the first Adam failed and fell into sin and destruction. This is also the first declaration from Christ Jesus, that he is the Lord and the Son of God. His life is also the first true example of spiritual living we are given to guide ourselves by. Through him we can redeem our lost souls and recapture the truth and rid ourselves of the deception we fell victims too. Through him we find our true reality and the knowledge of our eternal life.

In both the Old and New Testament, no greater stories exist apart from these two. Both events occur at the beginning of each book giving us the difference of a materialistic life in darkness via the first Adam versus spiritual or spirit filled life via the second Adam, Jesus Christ. This has been the clash of humanity since day one, worldliness versus spirituality, darkness versus the light. In part two of this book I will explore and teach you about spiritual living (a spirit filled life), its components and how to develop it for yourself. Hopefully it will help you sort out your own problems in your life and help you to make the right decisions and corrections needed to bring you into the light, turning your life from a material world into a spiritually enlightened life.

CHAPTER TWO

The Rebellious and Destructive Nature of Man

To this day one of life's major problems and what I consider the root of many of our failures as a people to live in peace has been bigotry and hatred. This has existed because of the differences of our color, race, language, sex, culture and religion. It has plagued man since the beginning of time and seems like it will continue to do so until we either find love and eternal peace on earth with one another or we take the worse option of exterminating ourselves from among the living and giving the planet back to the animal kingdom. In man's struggle for power and dominion over others, he needed to create superior classes in society based on wealth, race, religion, class, sex and whatever other crazed standard man could come up with in order to achieve his goals. As societies evolved through out the world so did this standard of separation, breeding more and more hatred and discrimination of others who were different or less fortunate. Consequently here we are at the far end of life's spectrum and nothing has changed. Bigotry and hate are still running rampant in the hearts of men. The powerful steal from the poor and still deny all those who are different by color, race or sex equal opportunities. In the last 60 years of man on earth we've seen the extermination of tens of millions of people because of their race. Hard to believe or to even imagine that in a modern world as we have today that genocide is still happening in the world.

The book of Revelations gives us many warnings of what is to come in the end times. Evil will be the norm and those who believe in God will be arrested and even executed for their faith. The anti Christ will rule the world for three and one half years. No wonder the book of Revelations, the last book in the New Testament, calls it the rise of the second Roman Empire. Do you think God was trying to tell us something? Do you see how humanism and our worldly lifestyles are leading us in this direction? After thousands of years and all the science and technology that we have achieved, nothing much has changed in us as a people! Bigotry and hate being prime examples of the more serious problems we still face in the world today, if not the most serious. It divides the world bringing brother against brother or man against man. Wars and terrorism are raging across the globe threatening to bring the world to its end. We have entered the "End of Days" as prophesied in the book of Revelations, or at least are at the gates of its beginning. It's going to take an act of God to save this world and unfortunately most people don't believe in Him and are to busy with their mundane chores and worldly concerns of their daily lives to even care.

Bigotry and hate is the modern equal of the ancient term in the bible called in-hospitality. In-hospitality was the major sin of Sodom and Gomorrah, which caused their destruction at the hands of God. It was the problem in Persia, Egypt, Greece, Babylon and Rome, empires conquering the world and destroying other civilizations simply because they were different than their own. All of them as great as they were, eventually suffered from the ills of a decaying society filled with their own internal bigotry, lasciviousness, slothfulness, greed, lust, idolatry, and in-hospitality to mention a few.

And yet where are they all today these great empires of yesterday? Today we find them as small nations, defeated long ago by their own self neglect and internal turmoil. These were great and mighty nations that God finally turned against and in doing so removed all His blessings from them. Their power turned into a decadent nation filled with lasciviousness, sloth, greed and other wrongful appetites causing their demise.

How ironic how the great empires all fell through internal decay and waste and sometimes at the hands of a new and stronger nations. But mostly they conquered themselves because they couldn't and wouldn't turn from their evil ways thus committing that unpardonable sin of a total rejection of God. For some reason men have always thought themselves to be better than other men or races and not in need of God or not wanting God, but wanting to be gods onto themselves. For they've had their own truths filled with delusions, whose only interest was and is still to this day in the controlling and dominating other men, to rule with power over them and to control their wealth and that of the nation and of the world. As history has shown us this has resulted in the endless wars man has fought since the beginning of man's existence on this planet without ever finding peace. Their need to purge the world of what was different than they were, be it because of color, race or religion or whatever other madness they used to justify their bigoted actions. Those they didn't kill they conquered and enslaved. But as time marched on God would have his way with them, for they would become delusional, lazy and fat from the wealth they've acquired. Lust, perversion and depravity would enter their lives giving rise to all types of crimes and sinfulness which soon would become the standards of their societies affecting most of its people. Before long the decay of their societies ended up crumbling their empires.

We have seen the crumbling of empires throughout history and more recently with the fall of the Soviet Union, Great Britain, Spain, Portugal and France and some think now even the United States, maybe headed in that direction. Don't think so? The latest bible code findings in 2008 predict a real doom and gloom picture for the United States for 2009 and 2010. It predicts the probable assassination of the next president. That the economy will collapse in 2009 and that the United States will be a destroyed nation in years of 2010-2012, by a series of natural disasters and an atomic attack upon New York City (for those of you who would like more information on the bible codes you can do an Internet search with Google, Yahoo or any of your favorite search engines to get a load of information and codes that have been discovered. There are also quite a few books written on bible codes found in bookstores and Amazon.com). It is a prophecy which means it isn't etched in stone and things could change to avoid those disasters. How you may ask? By people believing in God, asking him into their lives and praying to Him for world peace. The prayers of the people does change things for as the people change so does prophecy and if none of the doom and gloom prophecies come to pass will mean that we Americans in large numbers did change and went back to God and made enough of a difference. What happens if we don't change and everything remains status quo? I will tell you to remember the story of Sodom and Gomorrah which God destroyed. Every one was killed except for Lot's family who were the only righteous God found living there. So he removed them from the city and destroyed every one else. The same happened with Noah. God saved only the righteous and destroyed every one else in the world. The very same will happen here if we all don't start making serious efforts to change our ways and return to God.

Bigotry today continues to rip this country apart as well as most countries throughout the world. This because so many people segregate themselves from those they see or feel as being different than they are. In fact they take it to the extreme by denying people their equal rights both in government and in private life. Thus making themselves superior and in control over the lives of others. Determining what education their children can get, and where they can live and not live. What jobs are open to them for employment and which jobs are taboos because of their color. Don't think things like this happen, especially here in the USA. Then think again! For it happens everyday and it's what bigotry is all about, denying the less fortunate, those of different color or race or sexual orientation or religion their places in the sun. We have ghettos in every city because people are being pushed aside and forced to live in these ghettos because of their color, race or religious background. They are denied good jobs and schooling for their children making ghettos the only way they can live. Even the education their children get is scholastically far less than that given children in white neighborhoods.

Therefore I ask you by whom and when was it ever declared which race white or of any other color was to be the superior one, the one to rule over all others? Where was it written down? Surely not of God for He is God of all creation, white, black, brown, yellow, gay or straight and sees all his children as being equal to one another no matter what. Besides that when we go back to the beginnings of man, we note that he originated somewhere in the Middle East and the African Continent. So from that alone one must conclude that man was first of color before he became white. Who knows the Lord Jesus Christ being a Middle Easterner could very a darkened skinned man. Wouldn't that shock many people?

Then there's the Constitution of the USA and the Declaration of Independence, and no where's is it written in either one that men aren't created equal or that the white man should have superiority over all races in America. For certainly our forefathers founded this country on the principal that all men are created equal and with inalienable rights. Then the obvious question is where did we Americans go wrong? By what or by whose standards do we deem one color superior to another or one religious group superior to any other? By what measure was it determined that the Black man and the American Indian weren't equal with everyone else because of the color of their skin? Or is sexual orientation a justification for such bigotry? Certainly not! And if you think homosexuals don't deserve equality with all other men, then think again. No where will you find it written in the bible but you will find the second greatest commandment of God and that is to love our fellow man as ourselves. He didn't justify it by saying love your fellow man only of the same color, the same race or sexual orientation. He said love one another, as you love yourself.

So the obvious conclusion is that bigotry isn't a law, a rule but an evil born out of the hearts of men. It's a cancer that cuts through the life of a man destroying all that he is. It's a cancer that unless it is cured, will destroy its host and destroy those involved with him also. It also robs the bigot of all their joy and peace, for their hearts' are filled with all this hatred, evil thoughts and evil doings. So much so, that as history has shown us even to this very day, has resulted in the numerous acts of violence, deaths and wars which again threatens our very existence on earth.

Man is the creator of all that is wrong and evil in the world then it's up to man to clean it up and remove his filth and sin from the world. Bigotry and hate cannot be tolerated nor condoned against anyone for any reason, period. To allow even the smallest amount of bigotry in the world even if it's against one person out of six billion, will bring the world to an end and destroy everything. For if you allow it in just that one instance it will fester and grow like a cancer and before you know it you end up with a world like we have today with wars being fought in all parts of the world. A world filled with unrest and at the brink of extinction. Bigotry and hate are the engines fueling the fires in many of the killings and conflicts and wars throughout the world. In the book of Matthew Jesus says, *Go ye therefore and teach all nations, baptizing them in the name of the Father, of the Son and that of the Holy Ghost. Teaching to observe all things whatsoever I have commanded you; and lo, I am with you always, even until the end of the world (Matthew 28:19-20).* God's word, God's blessings and God's salvation is for all people of all nations, all races and all colors. There is no exclusivity but that which man has created.

Here in the United States, we fought a civil war in the 1860's that nearly destroyed this nation. Yet here we are 140 years later and although there have been some improvements for Black Americans, but at the same time much still remains the same. The black man is still denied his equality with the white man and only until recently were black people allowed in private country clubs. This bigotry and hatred has been left unchecked and has festered like a cancer extending itself to the bigotry against women, Latinos, Asians and other 3rd world minorities living in the United States.

We're all the children of God, and as the children of God all equal under God. Our Declaration of Independence declares that *We hold these truths to be self-evident, that all men are created equal, that they are endowed by their Creator with certain unalienable Rights, that among these are Life, Liberty and the pursuit of Happiness.—That to secure these rights, Governments are instituted among Men, deriving their just powers from the consent of the governed.* This country's ancestors, who came to this country in pursuit of equality and religious freedom and yet were only willing to offer it to people of their own color, white. So from the very beginning of Europeans coming to the new world in pursuit of equality and religious freedom they immediately denied the same to the American Indian. The white man proceeded to exterminate over ninety million American Indians, so they could have the country to themselves. Then to put salt in the wound, our ancestors bring in kidnapped and purchased Black Africans to America to serve as slaves to the white man and the atrocities begin all over again as millions of Black Africans are murdered at the hands of white men. It's a miracle this country survived the Civil War.

Today the problem has worsened for we have the Islamic wars with Israel since the birth of Israel in 1948. To this day we can't find a peaceful solution to the bigotry, bitterness and hatred being spewed out against the Israeli people, with some countries vowing to exterminate the people of Israel and all because of racial and religious differences. Now the problem is getting more complicated as the world of Islam is now including Christians as their enemy also. Eventually this hate, this bigotry will erupt into World War III, and the winner will be?

And an important point to ponder is this, when we enter the New World with the Messiah and when we finally make it into the kingdom of God, guess who will be there? If you're answer are people of all races, colors, religions and sexual orientations, then you're right. And none of them will be bigots, evil doers, terrorists and murderers and sinners who refuse to repent, who have denied God in their hearts. Why you ask? For the answer to this question I refer you to where Jesus says, *every kingdom divided against itself will be ruined, and every city or household divided against itself will not stand. If Satan drives out Satan, he is divided against himself. How can his kingdom stand? (Matthew 12:25-26).* So in conclusion only those who are for God and believe in God can enter into his Kingdom.

This is a great country in putting laws on the books for justice, democracy and freedom for all, but in the hearts of too many the opposite is true. There is too much hypocrisy taking place today, people saying one thing but doing another. We're talking the talk but too often not walking the walk and this has been the problem with America from the very beginning. We talk equality and write it into law, but the people were never ready to accept it and so bigotry and hate prevailed in the heart of the land. You see we can write all the laws we want, but you can't legislate morality. It has to come from the heart of man and that can only happen when man is ready to accept and believe in God.

Another point we must consider is that when God created man he created most men of color. Just take a look around the world and you will see that the largest population of people in the world are yellow not white. For the Asian races make out at least 1/3 of the world's population. Then take the Latinos, the Indians and the Black races and what have you got but a world largely made up of people of color. I hope I am hitting a nerve, for it's time for an awakening. The bible says in Romans 3:23 that *we're all sinners and fall short of the glory of god.* The consummate word here being all, for it means white, black, brown red and yellow races and people of all sexual orientation. No one is excluded from being a sinner; we all share equally in sin. God also provided scripture in the bible that shows us the way out from being a sinner. One of those scriptures is John 3:16, where Jesus tells us, *For God so loved the world that he gave his only begotten Son, that whosoever believes in him shall not perish but have eternal life.* Again here the consummate word being whosoever, meaning black, brown, yellow, white or red, gay or straight. An important point to be made here also is that no one, absolutely no one should consider themselves good and worthy of the kingdom of God. For only God can make one worthy and righteous. It begins with you having faith to believe and repent and receiving Christ Jesus into your life. Everyone throughout the world needs to repent their sinfulness and I mean everyone bar none. And I caution you to give up your pride and not think of yourself as a sinner. Everyone from the Pope of Rome down is a sinner. Yes you may go to church every week or even daily, but God is true in his word all have sinned and come short of the glory of God. This is where daily prayer and meditation becomes so important to us. For through daily prayers and meditation we draw near and become one with our soul and in doing so start to draw near to God. Eventually we learn to turn control of our lives over to God and learn to communicate with God. We then begin drawing to the light and become witnesses to the sins in our lives. This alone will lead us to remorse and a desire to repent of those ways and to asking God for daily guidance from that day on. This then becomes the day of your salvation with God.

We're a world rich in the cultures left us by our ancestors who came from all corners of the world of all colors, religions and sexual orientation. This is even more prevalent in America, a nation formed from every race on earth. America is a melting pot of people from all religions, sexual orientation and colors found on earth. This is a nation which has the highest standard of living ever known in all of the history of the world. A standard of living that evolved from the struggle for freedom by people immigrating to this country from all over the world and bringing with them their culture, their minds, their creativity. We took from them a little of each and applied it to the American way and by adoption their cultures have become the web or the foundation of the American culture. A culture so rich in the traditions from: England, Israel, Latin America, Africa, Europe, Asia, and the Middle East. Their foods have become America's foods from hamburgers to tacos, from lasagna to gyro sandwiches, and from Peking duck to the bagel with lox and cream cheese. We're a nation deeply embedded in the cultures of all the nations of the world. In you daily travels take a good look around you. The world isn't white; it isn't black or brown, there is no exclusivity! God created us in different shades, sizes and sexes, and yet he created us all in His image (Genesis chapter 1:26). Think about what that means, in His image. God then must be white, yes? But he also must be black and how about brown and yellow and red also? For all that were created to this very day were created in the image of God. So to reject anyone because of bigotry and hate is to reject God himself for you are rejecting his creations made by him in his image. Get the picture? He's all in all and to all. So don't you think it's time to get rid of this monkey on our backs, and let's all join the human race? That's what God intended when he sent us his only begotten son Jesus, into the world. That through his son we would all unite in the common love of brotherhood and belief in his son, that through his son we would all find salvation and a love that would bind us all together through eternity.

Yes we're a nation of a multitude of religions and faiths, but guess what we all believe in one God. We all pray and hope to get to heaven when our lives are done with here on earth and guess who has to let us in, God isn't it? I mean He was in charge when I last checked it out and whose world do we live in to begin with? His world isn't it? God created it for us to live in but it belongs to him. Do we have to destroy and pollute that which isn't ours? I think not. Yet in his love, God has done all this for us and we deny him and his existence. Why? What would happen to us if he then would deny us because we denied him? No heaven for us, then what's left, hell? Think about it, if you expect God's best for you and you expect to make it into heaven shouldn't you then give God your best. Believing in him and turning to him everyday for hope and guidance to living your life the best way you can. It's time we put him first into our hearts and souls and teach our children to do the same. It's time to communicate privately with ourselves deep in our own closets and invite God in also to communicate with us. It's time to explore our minds and spirit and ask ourselves what do we really want in life and how can we pursue it. It's time we let our own spirit come forward and speak to us and reveal to us who we really are and what we should be pursuing in life to achieve the happiness that not only will satisfy us but stay with us.

Violence, hate and bigotry aren't new. All that is good and all that is bad or evil has been in this world from the very beginning of man on earth. Going back to the very beginning of the bible in the book of Genesis, in the beginning there was darkness (evil) and God created the light (that which is good) out of the darkness. So from the very start there was bad and there was good. The best part of that scripture for me was always that in the beginning there was evil darkness and that from that darkness, God created the light, and that which is good. So always keep that in mind that no matter how off track your life has become there's hope and there's a cure for those who seek it. God is always ready to heal and forgive everything if you are ready to make a real change in your life and come to him for that help. More than you can ever know your spirit is ready and has been waiting for you to come to that reality. For it's there in your spirit that change comes to its fruition. You can't change yourself on your own, for man works by his senses and temptations, greed, lust and so many other carnal attitudes always get in the way. But in your spirit, in your soul that's where the rubber meets the road. That's the true and real you and it's the place where you make all the needed changes to your life. Science, doctors and all the technology in the world can't do one iota for you for they can't give you eternal life only God can do that. For only your spirit is in touch with God and only your spirit is the true and eternal part of you. The rest of you is temporal, the flesh and bones which someday will die and be buried to waste away in the ground. But the spirit of man, that's where all the real power within you lies. For if you understood the power of your spirit faith would come alive in you. You would then truly know God within you and the power that exists in you to do and achieve all that's there for you in this world. God will fill you with wisdom, knowledge and understanding that will revolutionize your life forever more. Once more I must remind you that the kingdom of god is within you.

God isn't a messenger of hate or of death sending His children out to kill one another. God loves all His children all over the world no matter whom they are or where they're from. Terrorism isn't an act of God or Allah. For evil cannot exist in God or Allah or Jehovah or Jesus. Evil cannot exist with good, or the house would crumble in ruin. Jesus said it best, *Every kingdom divided against itself is laid waste, and no city or house divided against itself will stand. If Satan casts out Satan, he is divided against himself; how then will his kingdom stand? If I cast out demons by Beelzebub, by whom do your own exorcists cast them out? Therefore they will be your judges. But if it is by the Spirit of God that I cast out demons, then the kingdom of God has come to you (Matthew 12:25-28).* So my message to all evildoers, murderers, extremist, cultists and terrorists, your acts are of your own evil doing and not of God and never can be of God, for no evil can exist in God who is perfect love. Therefore judge yourselves by your own deeds from within your own hearts and see whom it is that you truly are serving. For if you kill, cause harm and do destruction to others it is not by the Spirit of God or Allah but of Satan that you act.

Terrorist, extremist and cultist acts of violence and murder are committed by those who have been led astray by false prophets of radical religious groups and by political extremist groups. These terrorist acts are born out of bigotry, breeding hatred until it ferments into the evil we see in the world today. It only takes one to start the evil thoughts and before you know it he has a multitude of followers. As Jesus warns us in Matthew 15:14, *if the blind are led by the blind both will fall into the ditch.* If you give ear to voices preaching out of the darkness not seeking the truth yourself then you will fall victim to their treachery and become like them. You will believe you are acting in good faith to God or Allah, but in fact if you truly checked it out you would find you are serving the devil himself. Beware of false prophets; test every spirit for if it's of God it will produce only good. Jesus again warns us, *Watch out for false prophets. They come to you in sheep's clothing, but inwardly they are ferocious wolves. By their fruit you will recognize them. Do people pick grapes from thorn bushes, or figs from thistles? Likewise every good tree bears good fruit, but a bad tree cannot bear good fruit. Every tree that does not bear good fruit is cut down and thrown into the fire. Thus, by their fruit you will recognize them (Matthew 7:15-20).* When man lives a spiritual life in unison with the Holy Spirit of God he will do no evil for God is with him. God will lead him through the still waters restoring his soul and making him to lie down in green pastures, his cup will overflow. Only goodness and mercy will follow this man all the days of his life and he will dwell in the house of the Lord forever more, amen.

I couldn't see then the wisdom of God as I see it now looking back at those years. The way out of the ghettos of the world isn't by wars or by murder or by teenage gangs, or by violence or hatred. It isn't returning blow for blow, insult for insult. It isn't an eye for an eye, but it's in believing and having faith in God, and getting oneself an education, for only in acquiring knowledge, understanding, wisdom and a good education can you put the ghettos of the world behind you. To free oneself of the bigots of this world, one must empower oneself with the tools of knowledge, wisdom and understanding through both faith in God and in yourself. You can't be taught what you refuse to learn. You must desire good, fight for it and accept no less than god's best or you and you will then find a willing heart to learn. For only through education can you leave the ghetto behind you and become the young man/woman with a great career before you. You must also stay in control of yourself, keeping you flesh under submission and sure footed allowing your spirit to take control of your life and guiding you always in the light of God, to always be one with God. How do you take control, how do you empower yourself? It was best written by Paul in Ephesians 6:12-18: For we are not fighting against flesh and blood enemies, but against evil rulers and authorities of the unseen world, against mighty powers in this dark world, and against evil spirits in the heavenly places.

Therefore, put on every piece of God's armor so you will be able to resist the enemy in the time of evil. Then after the battle you will still be standing firm. Stand your ground, putting on the belt of truth and the body armor of God's righteousness. For shoes, put on the peace that comes from the Good News so that you will be fully prepared. In addition to all of these, hold up the shield of faith to stop the fiery arrows of the devil. Put on salvation as your helmet, and take the sword of the Spirit, which is the word of God.

Pray in the Spirit at all times and on every occasion. Stay alert and be persistent in your prayers for all believers everywhere.

Also know that stress, depression, confusion, mental anguish and similar problems will no longer exist in your life. For in God you will receive not just His blessings and His guidance for your life everyday, but also His peace will reign in you and the assurance of your son ship with Him. For God is not the author of confusion, but of a sound mind.

So there you have it, in your own hands all the power needed to free yourself of the bigoted and violent nature, the hateful nature that's in you. God has indeed always provided a way out for you and me from the frustrations and chaos that happens in our lives. And don't just take my word for it for God has promised it to us in is word. See I Corinthians 10:12-13 which says, *If you think you are standing strong, be careful not to fall. The temptations in you life are no different from what others experience. And God is faithful; He will not allow the temptation to be more than you can stand. When you are tempted, he will show you a way out so that you can endure.*

Whether you're a bigot, a terrorist or one lost to drugs, immorality, violence, crime it is not the end God has made a way out for you through Jesus Christ. Maybe you're consumed with greed, money, power or you abuse others you too can be healed and changed through God. But the buck stops at you, you must make the first move to heal yourself and the rest lies in your faith to trust God for all. You must want to stop and begin the fight to winning back your life from the dark side of you. We have God's son Jesus, to lead us out of the mire and we have available to us (every one of us on this planet) all the armor of God, to take it and to do the battle not just to win back our lives, but to keep it free from all pain, from all sin and from all unrighteousness. We don't have to stay slaves to sin, to pain, to hate, to bigotry, to misery and misfortune and unhappiness. We can have victory everlasting, but we must acknowledge our need and our faults and begin the journey to saving our souls through God. For here in the soul of each one of us lays the truth, all the hurt, all the anger, all the misery, the hate, the bitterness and misfortunes of life. We must face it and deal with it and give it to God, and in return fill our souls with his mercy, love and caring for our souls. No one else can save you and no one else can heal you from the pains and sorrows and miseries of your life, only God. All the churches and religions cannot save you, nor can the doctors of this world, nor all the worldly wisdom of this world or its governments, but only you can through God and God alone.

Sounds weird or hokey you may think, but believe me it's not. I am proof for I was dead in my darkness and Jesus came to me and took me out of the darkness and gave me His light, His blood and eternal life. I live with the blessed assurance that I am a child of God, and He has reserved a place for me in the kingdom of heaven. It took a whole lifetime for me to learn that, which is why I'm writing this book. To help you through the pitfalls of life and help you find your pathway through it sooner and a pathway much less painful.

I don't want you to think you can avoid problems in life, for you can't. We all have problems at one time or another for its part of life and living in the world and part of the growing process. It's God's test on each of us to see how we do through those tough times. It's where one acquires lots of wisdom and understanding from him. So don't waste all those precious years pointing the finger and blaming others. Take the bull by the horn and go do it for yourself and do it one better. Put God at the head to manage your career. Man it works and God is only too willing and able to help you all the way. Remember this and remember it well you're not only cheating yourself out of a relationship with God but with your own spirit also. You are cheating yourself and denying yourself every chance to being successful as well as happy in life. For if you deny your own spirit and you deny God, all that is left are the things of the world which are temporal and fleeting. And what you have today will surely be gone tomorrow but a person grounded in God and in their own spirit will achieve success and happiness beyond the grave. For they have lived a life in the spirit and have fed their spirit wisdom and understanding and knowledge to take with them throughout eternity. And that my friends, is the optimum word "eternity".

For whatever reason bigotry still exists in the world, it must come to and abrupt end or as surely as I write this book our world will someday soon come to its end! We can't afford to wait any longer for the signs of the times are vividly clear and to wait any longer can be and will be suicide for us all. This is one of the major factors in all of the history of the world that has been more damaging and threatening to man's survival.

Soon people will be at a serious cross road in American life being forced to deal with the new reality of the minority becoming the majority. In a short distant future, the Latinos will be the majority race in this country and coupled with the Blacks and Asians will definitely make the white man a true minority in the United States. We will be confronted in having to deal with one another in a new way and bigotry must go by the highway or else what, civil unrest, killings and mayhem? I don't think America will be able to withstand all that. If we don't end bigotry once and for all and make this country a country for all people then there will be a backlash so great it could bring this nation down on its knees. God forbid, for that would surely tear the fabric of the nation apart and could darn well destroy our democracy.

Remember retribution or karma doesn't always come when you do the wrong to someone else. The bible is testimony to this. God took retribution only after many years of abuse and sin in hope that the people would awaken and repent from their sinfulness. Finally when God saw that man had become reprobate and would not repent of his sinfulness was retribution brought upon man as was in the days of Noah. Not to destroy man but to awaken him to his sinfulness just like a father correcting the wrong doings of his child. Maybe that's why we get so many tornadoes and hurricanes and earthquakes today. God is speaking to us but we're not listening, it may be the beginning of the big pay back. Remember the end time prophecies for this world and remember God once before destroyed the world because of its sins.

There doesn't have to be an Armageddon? That prophecy in the bible is what is called a contingent prophecy. It will happen only if we persist to live the course we're living and not change our ways. God is allowing us to see ourselves for who we are and to where we are headed. We can change it says God, we don't have to have an Armageddon. We don't have to suffer the Great Tribulation of the bible. To avoid all these catastrophes we need to do change our ways and turn our lives around from the materialistic to the spiritual and back to God. All of us must do it throughout the world, no exceptions we must unite all in brotherly love and remove this blight from the world called bigotry, a world called hate.

Life is simple, pure, logical, perfect and completely filled in love and truth. We know this from our creator God himself in the book of Genesis 1:31, where it says, *God saw everything that he had made, and indeed, it was very good.* Yet man to this day suffers so with it because in his selfishness and pride he became dissatisfied with what God did and allowed himself to depart from the goodness of life and from the truth of life to develop his own ways and his own truths. Thus recreating the world from the beauty in which God gave it to us to that of one which is viewed not by the heart but by the eye, not viewed with brotherly love but a world filled with greed, lust, selfishness, violence, hate and bigotry just to mention a few. Man exchanged we and us in brotherhood for me, I consciousness. This being a self centered and egotistical give me, I want attitude. And what's amazing about this is that we think it's a great world that man has recreated. We deceive ourselves by calling it God's world, but fortunately for us it will again someday soon be God's world. But today we live in man's big deceit. A world of lies and deceptions, where the success of life is measured by how much you acquire and by the power you attain in life over others and not by the quality of your life. Never has man been concerned with his spiritual self but only with the feeding of his flesh. Seldom has man been concerned for his fellow man, but usually his concerns are with his own selfish needs. Only in a few exceptions in history has man intervened to help his fellow man that when the safety of the world was at stake as in World Wars I and II.

We've exchanged the truth taught to us by God for a truth fabricated by man. Man uses his truth to gain power and wealth, to lord it over the less fortunate and to subdue the weak, creating for himself kingdoms for him to rule over. We've gone even further trading the perfect for the imperfect. Giving up the spirit filled love of God for a love that is by sight and unfulfilling. A love that satisfies the senses but not the heart, leaving one's heart filled with discontent and wanting, as the need of the eyes cannot be satisfied. Creating bitterness, greed, envy, hatred, for the desires of the flesh cannot be satisfied. As a result of this way of love many have become bigoted towards others, violent and filled with anger towards one another always in a quest to conquer and control other people thus being the cause for many wars fought by men. Love by sight produces no good reward but brings with it an endless appetite for more as the needs of man can never be fulfilled this way. Consequently to this very day man has been plagued with a world in conflict, always at war, filled with famine, poverty, disease and the innocent slaughter of millions of innocent people all lost because of this way of living materialistically.

In spite of all this we profess to love God and to love one another, and that my friend is the big deception of man. For love by sight and the senses has been the ruination of man and has brought us to the edge of extinction. Living by sight and the senses has only led men away from the one true God and to the creation of new gods for man to follow and worship by. Today we have a multitude of gods in control of the lives of our people throughout the world. You know these gods like for example: money, power, lust, drug addiction, fornication, alcoholism, and the list just goes on and on. Man has no limit to the gods he will create to try and satisfy his empty soul, but refuses to turn to the one true God who gives true satisfaction to a hungry and thirsty soul and complete fulfillment in life.

Man's pride has always been his one major problem in life just as it was for Lucifer, the fallen archangel of God. Man was never satisfied with the world God gave him. He always wanted to do it his way, by the flesh, based on fleshly desires. Man never understood (for he was void of spiritual love living by the flesh and for others was the desire to be as great as God and have people worship them) that God didn't want to control man but to help him create an eternal world where all men would be equal. To create a world where man would be just as creative and industrious as he is now using his mind and soul to his fullest in the all the sciences and technologies. God was never against man doing great and wonderful things with the creativity of his mind. After all it was God who gave man a mind to think with, communicate with one another with, to create with and build things with. Otherwise we'd be like all the animals of the world. It's obvious or it should be obvious to all of us that God didn't want mindlessness or puppets just doing his beck and call. He wanted a people who would worship him freely and take the world and build it with all their abilities into a beautiful and eternal place for all men to live in love and peace.

Today the world is in turmoil and on the brink of destruction because man can't live with his fellow man. This is the evolution of man's six thousand years on earth, the brink of extinction, this because man has refused to believe in God and to allow the love of God to fill his soul. So he made his own gods and now we're all paying the price for this denial of the one true God.

The Middle East is exploding like an atomic bomb and the War of Armageddon seems like only a few years away. Madness you want to call it? Absolutely, for the cure is so simple it escapes the minds of all the leaders of the world, it escapes the minds of the intellectuals and the scientific community as well as the financial wizards of these times. It is so simple that bigots can't see the forest through the trees. What's the simple cure? Its love, plain and simple and it is spelled God. You can't separate them, for they are one, God is love and love is God. For man to stop the madness he must find love and to do so he must make his amends with God, for only through God can we truly find lasting love, a love in the spirit and not by sight. We must also understand the attributes of love and what love is. For love is mighty and love is powerful, yet gentle and kind and all giving. So how do we understand this thing called love? It's God, it's the mind of God, the heart of God, all merciful and all forgiving and full of grace. God has given us a guide for love and the best place to find this is in the book of 1st Corinthians 13, which states, *If I speak in the tongues of mortals and of angels, but do not have love, I am a noisy gong or a clanging cymbal. And if I have prophetic powers, and understand all mysteries and all knowledge, and I have all faith, so as to remove mountains, but do not have love, I am nothing. f I give away all my possessions, and if I hand over my body so that I may boast, but do not have love, I gain nothing.*

Love is patient; love is kind; love is not envious or boastful or arrogant or rude. It does not insist on its own way; it is not irritable or resentful; it does not rejoice in wrongdoing, but rejoices in the truth. It bears all things, believes all things, hopes all things, and endures all things.

Love never ends. But as for prophecies, they will come to an end; as for tongues, they will cease; as for knowledge, it will come to an end. For we know only in part, and we prophecy only in part, but when the complete comes (the Lord himself), the partial will come to an end. When I was a child, I spoke like a child, I thought like a child, I reasoned like a child; when I became an adult, I put an end to childish ways. For now we see in a mirror, dimly, but then we will see face to face (the Messiah when he returns). Now I know only in part; then I will know fully, even as I have been fully known. And now faith, hope and love abide, these three; and the greatest of these is love.

Are we living this example of love in our lives? Is this the basic foundation in each of our hearts? Obviously not and we should all be asking the question why NOT? What's missing in me that I don't have all these attributes operating in me? What went wrong making me the person that I am, instead of the person God would love to see me become? Unless we all begin to do this soul searching within ourselves and seek God's help to change in us that which needs to be changed, we will be doomed to destruction. We are all different each and every one of us. Our capacity to love and hate varies in degree with each and everyone and no two are alike. Yet there is a common ground that God seeks in each of us. A universal and spiritual ground founded in love. Its basis is not in religion but all religions should be based on it. They are the two greatest commandments of God, which Jesus gives us in Matthew 22:37-40, and they are, *Love the Lord your God with all your heart and with all your soul and with all your mind. This is the first and greatest commandment. And the second is like it: Love your neighbor as yourself. All the Law and the Prophets hang on these two commandments.* Imagine that, all the law and the prophets hang on these two commandments. That's how important love is. Without love each of us are doomed to destruction. Without love we can have no place with God or in the kingdom of God. God is perfect and his kingdom is perfect and that which is imperfect cannot exist with that which is perfect. Everything created by God was created out of His Love, and nothing is, that love wasn't the basis for in its creation including man. And man in all his imperfection and sinfulness can be made perfect again through the love of God.

The madness we live in must come to an end and can only end through perfect love. If not then we all lose and we will come to the end. These are our choices you can't reason them out or try to justify them in any other way either by politics, religion or intellectualism. We've already have had six thousand years of doing it our way, following in the foolishness of man and his error filled ways. This is the last call to man to repent of his worldly and evil ways or the end of this world is well at hand. We've spent the past millenniums living our lives separating God and love as separate entities in our lives. We've created religions all over the world to box God into and filled these religions with doctrines, rules and regulations created by man. Man creating God in his own image rather than accepting the fact that we are created in the image of God. We polluted the truth of God with the truth of man and called it religion, politics, government or the way things just are. We accepted the dark side of life as the norm and have long departed from the life in the light of God, the spiritually filled life. We've failed miserably doing it this way, man's way. We have always failed to realize that they are both one. God is love, love is God and the two cannot be separated no matter how we try for the methods used are always secular which are already void of God. For to search for God and love one must do so in the spirit for only the spirit reveals the truth of God and the truth of love.

In the books of Daniel, Ezekiel and the Book of Revelations, God tells us that if we continue in a world without a spirit filled life, filled in true love then the human race will become extinct. The answer to world peace and goodwill for all men lies within each of us and can only be done through a spiritual life and not a secular one. Six thousand years of secularism has only begotten us death, hate, wars upon wars to the point where we find man today at the brink of total annihilation.

The problem with man has always been in searching in all the wrong places for an answer when the place to start the search is within oneself. That's right the buck does stop at you, and at me, and at each and every one of us. The best place to begin is to search within our inner soul. We have the power in each of us to change the world around, but don't stop to take the time to become aware of it. Our hearts tell us the truth, but our flesh wars against our hearts, filling our eyes with foolish wants, lust and greed, blinding us from the truth. This constant deception of man has plagued man from the Garden of Eden to today and nothing has changed. Just like Adam and Eve, we've been deceived by the devil to eat the forbidden fruit and so has it been with man all through the ages, choosing with his eyes and not his heart. Always putting self before all things and always casting a shadow on life causing a life lived in darkness rather than living in the light.

We profess to love God, but how many of us really love God or read his holy word? How many of us bother to know Him and commune daily with him from our hearts? Too many of us have taken the cheap way out by accepting only what is preached at the altars of the churches across the world as their knowledge and awareness of God. These ministers, priests and rabbis and other men of God, all mean well but cannot replace your own obligation to yourself to knowing God personally and knowing his word. They can preach and teach you of God but it falls on deaf ears to one who's unwilling to have a relationship with God. And only you can do that. Just like you keep friendships and communicate with other people and with your relatives and care for them, you should be maintaining the same relationship with God. We each must communicate with God and show him how much we do care for Him, love Him and want to follow him and be an example of him here on earth. This alone is one of the most important things a person can do is be an example of God on earth extending love and peace to everyone. It becomes contagious and before you know more and more people will begin to change their lives and do the same and we can someday soon save our world and all that live in it.

We each need to be seeking God's perfect will for our lives and follow the pathway He lays out for each of us. You say you don't know your pathway you must take in life or the will of God for your life? Then you haven't been praying and communicating with God. You hear not for you seek not. Jesus said it best, *Therefore I tell you, do not worry about your life, what you will eat or drink; or about your body, what you will wear. Is not life more important than food, and the body more important than clothes? Look at the birds of the air, they do not sow or reap or store away in barns, and yet your heavenly Father feeds them. Are you not much more valuable than they? Who of you by worrying can add a single hour to his life?*

And why do you worry about clothes? See how the lilies of the field grow. They do not labor or spin. Yet I tell you that not even Solomon in all his splendor was dressed like one of these. If that is how God clothes the grass of the field, which is here today and tomorrow is thrown into the fire, will he not much more clothe you, O you of little faith? So do not worry, saying 'What shall we eat?' or 'What shall we drink?' or 'What shall we wear?' For the pagans run after all these things, and your heavenly Father knows that you need them. But seek first his kingdom and his righteousness, and all these tings will be given to you as well. Therefore do not worry about tomorrow, for tomorrow will worry about itself. Each day has enough trouble of its own (Matthew 6:25-27).

Then in Matthew 7:7-12, Jesus goes on to say: *Ask and it will be given to you; seek and you will find; knock and the door will be opened to you. For everyone who asks receives; he who seeks finds; and to him who knocks, the door will be opened.*

You hear so many people always complaining that church turns them off with the constant preaching of don't do this and don't do that. And that's because that kind of preaching is no better than the way most of are living. It is void of spirit however well intentioned. It's like a teacher scolding you in class, telling you not to do this and that. So consequently what happens here is that we have two people in conflict with one another for both are lacking of the truth, the love and the spirit of the word. The preacher lacks the conviction of what he teaches for he himself doesn't live his life in the spirit and is also void of love himself, so his words are empty, like a clanging bell annoying your senses. He also lacks the faith to trust God to do the work God needs to do in your life. So these ministers create laws and doctrines for man to live by and by doing this getting in the way of God and blocking you and God from reaching one another. Or it's the reverse and you are the one whose life is void of the spirit and lacking in love. You believe and are very religious and go to church or temple regularly but the word of God falls on empty ears. You hear, you feel and yet when you leave the building what you heard departs from you just as quickly as you left the building. Why? For without love, the word of God falls on empty ears and preoccupied hearts. You are in church, but your mind and heart are elsewhere. Your mind and your heart are with your worldly concerns and with your worldly gods. Consequently even in church the word of God falls on empty ears and empty hearts.

Jesus Christ gives us an example of this in one of his parables when he said, *A farmer went out to sow his seed. As he was scattering the seed, some fell along the path, and the bird came and ate it up. Some fell on rocky places, where it did not have much soil. It sprang up quickly because the soil was shallow. But when the sun came up, the plants were scorched, and they withered because they had no root. Other seed fell among thorns, which grew up and choked the plants. Still other seed fell on good soil, where it produced a crop-a hundred, sixty or thirty times what was sown. He, who has ears, let him hear (Matthew 13:3-9).*

In verse 13, Jesus says, *though seeing, they do not see; though hearing they do not hear or understand. So in them is fulfilled the prophecy of Isaiah. You will be ever hearing but never understanding. You will be ever seeing but never perceiving. For this people's heart has become calloused; they hardly hear with their ears, and they have closed their eyes. Otherwise the might see with their eyes, hear with their ears, understand with their hearts and turn and I would heal them.*

In verse 18-23, Jesus explains what the parable of the sower means, *When anyone hears the message about the kingdom and does not understand it, the evil one comes and snatches away what was own in his heart. This is the seed sown along the path. The one who received the seed that fell on rocky places is the man who hears the word and at one receives it with joy. But since he has no root (is not living a spirit filled life), he lasts only a short time. When trouble or persecution comes because of the word, he quickly falls away. The one who received the seed that fell among the thorns is the man who hears the word, but the worries of this life and the deceitfulness of wealth (worldliness-materiality) choke it, make it unfruitful. But the one who received the seed that fell on good soil is the man who hears the word and understands it. He produces a crop, yielding a hundred, sixty or thirty times what was sown.* The seed is the word of God, planted in your heart yielding the first fruit. The harvest of one hundred, sixty or thirty times are the lives that find God and his truth through you the first fruit which then yielded one hundred, sixty or thirty. If we each would hear the word of God and let God plant it permanently in our hearts you can see the effect it would have on the world when we each yield one hundred, sixty or thirty more. It wouldn't take long to save all mankind.

How do we begin in getting the word, by first going before God and repenting of all your sins asking him to help you to change what has been impossible for you to change. Then ask him saying Lord please come into my heart and live with me forever more as my God, my Savior, my Friend and my Teacher. The next to do if you don't own one is to get yourself a bible to keep in your home so you can read the word of God daily or as often as possible. And be aware that there are many new translations of the bible to suit your understanding from the King James Version to modern English versions more easily understood. Even just ten, twenty minutes a day for starts is great. You need to pray and practice meditating and communing with yourself in the quietness of your soul. You will find that in your soul lies all the truth of you good, bad and indifferent. No matter whom you are or what lies or sins you have, your soul is only too anxious to reveal all truth to you and lead you to God, where there is forgiveness, mercy and grace for all. Through prayer and meditation, your own soul shows you the truth and the need for changes to be made in your life. Your soul will also show you the errors and failures in your life as well as the successes of your life. You will see your sins before you as well as the good you have done and you will be broken when you understand the truth about yourself. This is the beginning of your new life when you come to the understanding and acknowledgement of your sinfulness. It's at this point you are ready to give it all to God and repent of your ways and ask God for your new life in the spirit. If it's a new and better life you seek then you will begin to see the light and start making the changes needed in your life. If its truth and love you seek, your soul will reveal it to you and show you the way. And it's here in your soul where one will always find your pathway back to God. For here in your soul lies the kingdom of God. Yet we spend our entire lifetimes seeking God, love and truth in all the wrong places. It's in us, in our souls. We must turn within to find all the wonderful answers to life's mysteries. We must turn within to find the truth of ourselves, and of our need for God in our lives. In Luke 17:21 when asked about the kingdom of God, Jesus replied, *Neither shall they say, Lo here! Or Lo there! For, behold, the kingdom of God is within you.* Then when you go to church or temple and hear the word of God and the do's and don'ts preached from the altars, they will not go against your spirit for you know the truth and the truth has set you free.

Also think of this, God in his total love for us and concern for our well being, inspired numerous prophets and apostles to write books and epistles through a span of thousand of years. This to be compiled into one holy book called the bible, for all of us to read and use as a guide for living, for knowledge, understanding, wisdom and for getting to know our creator. It is the only thing in the world that has remained constant through the ages. For the word is from God and the word is God and God is the only being which is always the same yesterday, today and tomorrow. The one we can all always depend on. Yet few have ever bothered to read the word of God. If as many people who read fiction books, non-fiction books, magazines and newspapers daily around the world, read the bible, the world would never come to an end. For surely God would reach the hearts of man through out the world regardless of his religion and the world would turn around from its dark side and step into the light

Ever wonder why you receive no blessings or few blessings and no miracles in your life or the life of your loved ones? Well how can God bless the absentee? Don't you think you'd need to be with him in order for him to reach out to you? If you dedicated your whole life to worldliness, a life where God doesn't fit in or you just have no time for God or you don't want anything to do with God. Then there's your answer, you have reaped nothing for you sowed nothing with the Lord. You've chosen the world and the things in it as your god and thus God himself is of no consequence in your life. Thus the blessings and miracles you seek can only come from the god you worship be it the world or whatever thing in the world that has stolen your heart. Fat chance you'll ever get anything from the world you say. That's right it's like playing lotto your chances are one in the tens of millions. In Mark 10:27, Jesus said it best, *With men it is impossible, but not with God: for with God all things are possible."*

Also we must remember that principle of life given to us by Jesus, and that is that we reap what we sow, it is the law of cause and effect, God's universal law. So if you sow everything to the world then the world is your blessing for whatever you can get out of it and that is always temporal for in the world nothing is eternal. But with God, all his blessings are everlasting. Kind of makes you think who got the short end of the stick doesn't it. We put all of our apples in that worldly basket and for what a cheap thrill. To gain that which soon will corrupt, rust and waste away. This has been probably one of the biggest deceptions of man, chasing after vain glories, and putting all his trust only in that which he can see, the world rather than God whom he can't see, thus believing only in that which can be seen or held or possessed. Just like the apostle doubting Thomas, Jesus told him, *you believe because you see me, blessed are those who believe and haven't seen me (John 20:29).* Wouldn't it be wiser to chase after the prizes that last forever? Things that can heal you, rebuild you into a smarter and better person full of wisdom and understanding.

I bet many of you shun God, because you feel that God will only bless you in terms of healing, love, extending mercy and mending a broken heart to name a few. And the answer to that is yes, but my friend God does much, much more. He rebuilds shattered lives, he restores wealth and prosperity to those He sees in need. God can and will to those he chooses to bless, help them in their business, work, school or whatever needs you have that God feels is worthy of his blessings. Remember this well not all of the prophets of God were poor men. Abraham was one of the richest in the world in his time, and King David was no slouch. Job who lost his family and all his wealth was later blessed by God with a new family and wealth seven times greater than that which he had lost. And remember that the world and all that it contains including all its riches and glory nor all your deeds good, bad or indifferent can save your eternal soul. Just like you can't buy your way into heaven, neither can you buy a blessing or a miracle from God. God gives them freely just as he gives us salvation, by his grace and not by our works so that no man can boast (Ephesians, 2:8-10). Folks you can't earn it, pay for it, beg for it, that's another of the deceptions of man. Man always feels if you work hard and do good you are saved and will be blessed of God. No way, for if you do all those good and wonderful things but have not faith in your life you are still a lost soul. You must have both working in your life, faith in God and your good works. Galatians 2:16, Paul says, *yet we know a person is justified not through the works of the law but through faith in Jesus Christ. And we have come to believe in Jesus Christ, so that we might be justified by faith in Christ, and not by doing the works of the law, because no one will be justified by the works of the law.* Then in James 2:17, James goes on to say, *So faith by itself, if it has no works, is dead. And again in James 2:21, in his teaching that faith without works is dead, goes on to say: "Was not our ancestor Abraham justified by the works when he offered his son Isaac on the altar? You see that faith was active along with his works, and faith was brought to completion by the works. Thus the scripture was fulfilled that says, Abraham believed God, and it was reckoned to him as righteousness, and he was called the friend of God. Therefore justification is by good works and faith and one's faith is made complete by one's good works (verse 22).*

But let me take it one step deeper so that we all can have a better understanding of this law of God. Faith is a free gift of God, but if not used it is good for nothing. For like a muscle in the body, we must exercise it if it's to be of any good use. And faith without good works is a muscle not being used and suffers from atrophy and eventually becomes useless. Look at us, at our world and at the universe itself. Nothing that is including us could be without the faith and the works of God. And what did it take for God to do all this creating, a simple thing called love. That's the deeper part of faith and good works. We must have love for without love everything comes to naught. For without love there could be no universe, for God created the universe by His faith (He believed that He could), by his works (He spoke it into existence and he was thus exercising His faith) and by love thus making perfect all that he created, thus all that God created is everlasting and the universe is God's best example. It's been around for tens of billions of years. Another good example of God's works is the verse in John 3:16 which states, *For God loved the world so much that He gave His only Son, so that everyone who believes in Him may not die but have eternal life.* Over and over again we see the principles of God at work in perfect harmony: faith, love and good works. In 1st Corinthians, St Paul tells us: *and now these three remains: faith, hope and love. But the greatest of these is love.*

Jesus teaches in Matthew 5:13-16, *You are like salt for the whole human race. But if salt loses its saltiness, there is no way to make it salty again. It has become worthless, so it is thrown out and people trample on it.*

You are the light for the whole world. A city built on a hill cannot be hid. No one lights a lamp and puts it under a bowl; instead it is put on the lamp stand, where it gives light for everyone in the house. In the same way your light must shine before people, so that they will see the good things you do and praise your Father in heaven. Again we see here the operations of God's perfect law: faith, good works and love and the three cannot be separated. They are the forces that work from within us, the forces that come to us from with God Himself. That's why we must begin a life of meditation and communion with our souls for it's here that we discover this truth for ourselves and we discover God Himself operating within us.

You see how God went through all this trouble of leaving us His legacy, his holy word that would be used by us to learn of Him, find faith in Him, and learn of His ways and to adopt them into our own lives as our ways. Men copied it down, handwritten and past it on for thousands of years until man invented the printing press. We have since then printed the holy word of God, millions upon millions of times for the people of the world to have and get to know God. It's available in every bookstore across the land and around the world. It comes in every language and every religion has its version of it. Whether it's the Holy Bible, The Koran, The Vedas of the Hindu Faith, the Teachings of Buddha, etc., they are the word of God. We have come as far as acknowledging its existence and accepting the fact that the bible is the holy word of God. Yet most have managed to avoid it and have never read it, relying simply on what is told to them at the services of churches and synagogues all over the world. Treating God as a once a week ordeal at a local church or temple as if it was a painful experience to know God, and that for those who actually go to church, for the majority of people don't, and far too many others not caring at all for the word or the spirit of God.

One of the deceptions that also contributed to the fall of man is his idolatry. Since man first put his foot on earth, he's tried over and over to recreate God, in his own image. He's conjured up his own images of God, translating those images into carvings of stone, wood and gold. He's pushed God aside and made gods of these images he created and began to worship them. Worshipping dead, lifeless, empty images until man became filled with delusions and began creating religions of his own wild imaginations perverting all that was good and holy to that which was corrupt, lethal and perverted. Making human sacrifices and performing sexual orgies of all kinds at the altar. As time past, man came to believe only in his works and his religion. To this day most believe more in their religion than in God himself. Most people feel all they need is their religion, their rituals, their ministers or rabbis and this is enough. Well not to bust any bubbles, it isn't enough and it has nothing to do with God. God isn't about religion at all for if he had been he would have given us one in the bible to follow.

God is about faith, believing in Him above all else and allowing Him into our hearts so that he can teach and direct us. He is universal for all the people of the earth, not for a select few. I think this is one of the most important points about God; he is universal to all men, to Jews, Christians, Muslims, Hindu's and so on. To quote Jesus himself in John 3:16, *For God so loved the world that he gave his only Son, so that everyone who believes in him may not perish but have eternal life.* No mention of religion here just pure faith in the Lord. Does this mean that I condemn religion, absolutely not? For the religions of the world although different from one another as they are, do a service for all of us. They provide us a place to gather in fellowship with one another. To worship and pray in a united body, teaching and learning from one another about God and all that he is doing in each of our lives. Like prayer and meditation, the church fellowship we have with one another is priceless and is also a pathway to God. But we must learn that religion by itself isn't enough and cannot satisfy nor save the soul. We each need a personal relationship with God, and that can only come from within and with a commitment, a total focusing on each our parts to accept nothing less in life than a relationship, a fellowship, a walk with God everyday of our lives.

We each must make it our duty to know God and to turn our hearts to Him and receive His salvation and blessings for our lives. We each should open the word of God and begin reading it as often as possible, daily if possible to learn of God. Imagine what you could achieve if you gave God 30 minutes a day to get to know him both in prayer and in the reading of his holy word. Just taken a moment and try to picture in your mind an average day in your life and all the things you normally fit into that day. I'm sure that at least half of the things you normally fit into your day aren't important but pleasurable none the less. You fit them into your schedule to relax, enjoy and to share such as going to a movie, watching television or having friends or family over. Yet most don't have time and won't make time for the one being that should be the most important in all of our lives and that is God.

We can make time for almost anything on earth but can't make time for the one being that is most important to us, our creator who gives and takes life away. And if we won't make time for God be it in prayer or daily conversation, then what chance is there that any of us would bother to read his book. As so often we hear people say, it's too hard to read or I just can't understand the bible. If you truly feel you don't understand what you're reading then pray about it asking God for clarity in His word, and the Holy Spirit will guide and teach you the word of God. Or go and buy yourself one of the modern translated bibles into modern day English, Spanish, etc. Sounds foolish well trust me it works if you just open your heart and believe. For when I was illiterate and had very little comprehension in reading God opened my heart, my mind and my eyes to understand his holy word. Of all bibles to start with I began with the King James Version. Believe me when I say that when I first started reading the bible it was truly like a foreign language to me. I understood nothing but I prayed with my heart for a real help, a real understanding of God's word and He opened my mind and heart to understand His word.

It's easy to be religious or pious. It's like playing politics, anyone can talk the talk, but can you walk the walk. Matthew 15:8-9, Jesus is quoting Isaiah, from the Old Testament and says, *This people honor me with their lips, but their hearts are far from me; in vain do they worship me, teaching human precepts as doctrines.* He goes on to say in verse 11, *it is not what goes into the mouth that defiles a person, but it is what comes out of the mouth that defiles.* And then finally in verses 17-20, he says, *Do you not see that what enters the mouth enters the stomach, and goes out into the sewer? But what comes out of the mouth proceeds from the heart, and this is what defiles. For out of the heart come evil intentions, murder, adultery, fornication, theft, false witnesses, and slander. These are what defile a person, but to eat with unwashed hands does not defile.* The mark of a child of God, on the other hand is the one who can walk the walk, and who takes the word of God and applies it to his life. The one who believes in Christ, in God although never having seen God, but believes in him by faith, repents and receives Him into his heart. Thus in doing so becoming one with Christ, with God and receiving the Holy Spirit of God to guide one through life, thus beginning a new life living in the spirit and no longer being controlled by one's flesh or by worldly desires. You'll enjoy life more and to the fullest and your career will soar to unparalleled heights and you'll find most of the stresses of your work that so often brought you down coming to end. For now you have gained something new into your life and that is the peace of God. I know it sounds all so utopia, the perfect life and it can be for everyone who makes the effort to go it one further for themselves. Not to accept life as it is, but how it can be through God by simply stopping and taking hold of your life. That by making a commitment to yourself, that you want to make a change and get to know yourself truly from within your soul and to know God and that He's there for you.

So these are our choices and they are only two. To choose the way of God, the light of man for our walk or to cling to the dark side, living always in sin and leading us always unto to death. So it was for Adam and Eve, in the garden and so it is for all of us today. The devil didn't make them do it, but Eve beheld the fruit with her eyes and saw that it was good and took and ate and gave to Adam who did the same. They lusted in their hearts for what they saw with their eyes and were led by their own flesh to commit the sin. Remember what Jesus said, it wasn't the fruit that caused Adam and Eve, to sin for that was outside the body, but it was what emanated from their hearts that caused the sin and that was their evil intentions. A child of God, living in the spirit is working in unison with the Holy Spirit, who teaches you all things and raises you up to be a child of God. In doing so you eventually drop the chains of bondage that had you bound to sinfulness and emerge a free man of God. One who's traded in his mortal sinful life which was leading onto death for an eternal life where death has no dominion, to live your life under the guidance of the God and his Holy Spirit. Do you love God, yourself and you fellow man (this includes all men including your enemies)? Do you see all men in your heart as created equal? Are you faithful to your spouse, your family and friends? Are you honest and truthful, your yes is yes and your no is no? This and much more are the values God looks for in us. This is the real circumcision, the circumcision of the heart and not of the flesh. What good are all the religious rituals and sacrifices and doctrines that one does and obeys if they are not of the heart and of God? And the only way they can be of the heart is evidenced by a changed life. And who needs a change of heart, a changed life? All of us, for salvation is of God, and it's free to all who believe, repent and allow God to change their lives around. For we're all sinners, all bar none except Jesus Christ, the only man to live a life free from all sin. It says in the book of Romans, chapter 3, vs.23, *all have sinned and fall short of the glory of God.* And for certain we are all in the last days of man, the End Times. We are running out of time in which both we and our planet can be saved. The time to act, to open your heart to God, to become a believer in all that God is, is now, today! Sense it and feel it in your heart and in your spirit. Don't lie to yourself and don't cheat yourself from the truth which is God. I'm not writing this for myself, but for you the reader who in the course of your life lost your way from God. God intended for you to read it so that He may touch your heart and open you to His truth. I have no church of my own to send you to so this isn't for any gain on my part.

Listen what I offer you is that which God gave me. I was a very lost soul, living deeply in the dark side of the world. I had no faith, hated my life and the circumstances of my life. Nothing good ever came to me in this world until I was thirty-eight years old. I've suffered much; bore much pain and sorrow which in turn became a way of life for me. I lost hope and faith along those darkened corridors of my soul, love had deserted me for I had exchanged true love for the passions of the flesh. Life for me was a paradox being hurt by people I trusted and me hurting others who loved and trusted in me. It was a vicious cycle with no cure, no happiness and no end to the pain one had to live and bare in life. The friends I cherished all have passed away from this world. Death claimed them so very painfully young; some from AIDS, some from drug abuse and some from alcoholism. All in all they surrendered to the darkness, loneliness and rejection had consumed them and in the end death claimed their very souls. I am the sole survivor of all my friends from my youth. I can never forget them and talk of them often in my conversations from day to day. They were all so beautiful both within and without, but they couldn't see it for darkness had blinded them from the truth. They were deceived into believing a lie, and surrendered their lives for they all lived with substitute gods that had no power to heal and to save a dying soul. Fortunately for me I was one of the lucky ones to survive. For unbeknown to me was that on a wonderful day in October, 1980, Jesus Christ stepped into my house to visit with me and with his love turned my world around. When I say he came into my house I mean that literally. Jesus Christ has made over 20 visits to me over the past 22 years. He helped me out of the dark side of life and brought me into the light and made me a child of God. He turned all my failures into one success after another. He brought me out of bankruptcy into prosperity. All that he promised to do for me was done exactly as promised, to the date. He's blessed my life my miracles upon miracles as he put together the broken vessel of clay that I was. He's made me whole and my cup is overflowing with love. For when I was hungry Jesus fed me. When I was blind Jesus gave me new sight. When I had lost all hope he restored hope in my heart. Where there was death and despair Jesus, gave me faith. Thirty eight years of tragedies and pain wiped away with his spoken word and comforting arms. When the world had forsaken me as I no longer had value to the world, Jesus came and made me his treasure. Even when all hope had left me and death had won me Jesus came and fought the good fight and won my soul. I was dead, overdosed from alcohol when Jesus sent three warriors to save my life (he sent three dear friends of mine who believed in God). That was the darkest day of my life for death had consumed me, but God had other plans for me. God drew his might sword, his word and called forth angels and warriors to restore my soul and breathed new life into me. I am in a word a resurrected man, brought back from death by the power of Jesus Christ, who refused to lose me to the darkness. You think miracles no loner happen in the world today or that God doesn't hear us. Well I am proof positive that God is alive and well and doing his mighty work everyday in the world. I'm one of his mighty works which I must say still needs work. I'm not quite a polished diamond yet, but well on my way. With all the love and strength I possess I pray you get this message and plant it deep in your hearts for what God did for me, he wants for you. To save you from a darkened, meaningless life of death and bring you into his light where there is truth, love, peace and life everlasting.

Remember there is a fine line between love and sin and guess what we all know it. But we make excuses after excuses until the day comes when we believe the lies as truths and turn sin into an acceptable way of living. What we can't change or don't care to get involved with we find a way to justify it away. We've prostituted away our nation's morality, its integrity, its pride and exchanged it for lies, cheap thrills and self indulgence. We've replaced God with new gods like money, power, fame, delusions of grandeur, and pride. For others their god is a drug fix, bets at the track, sexual perversion and fornication, and the list goes on and on. The concerns of most people have today are the Dow Jones Average, and how it's building up their 401K's or portfolios. With others is how fast to spend it all and drown oneself in all the luxuries of life. We are so brainwashed into a materialistic life that it's become the norm when we consider what success in life is. We measure success by how much we've accumulated in wealth, and material possessions. We've become obsessed with labels, gadgets and anything that exhibits power and success in life. We're so caught up in ourselves and in selfishness, that the name of God is never mentioned unless we have a problem or dire need. Otherwise God is never a part of our daily lives. So many say oh but we go to church, to synagogue, to temple and pray to God every week. Hypocrites all, for God isn't interested in religious people but in people with faith, who believe in God and are obedient to Him. Sounds like the Charlie the tuna commercial, but it's true.

Many have become so pious and self righteous thinking themselves the exclusive club of God, that they act as if they had a God given right to consume, take and devour everything leaving little or nothing for the less fortunate or down trodden. And when I say a people I include whites, black, Latinos, Asians, all people of all races and color are included in all this, for all are guilty of this sinfully worldly lifestyle. We live by sight and not by faith. We live by the senses of seeing, feeling, hearing, touching and smelling having long squashed the most important sense that of the spirit. Most people having centered their lives on things temporal and not eternal. A life ruled by greed, lust, pride and selfishness. What we need to do is awaken to the sixth sense, the spiritual side of us, and the eternal side which doesn't pass away when our bodies die. For the body, the flesh does dies and goes back to the earth but the soul lives on forever.

Many in America and in the world today have become the Sodomites of today as in the days of Sodom and Gomorrah. Becoming the in-hospitable ones, slothful, selfish and caring only for themselves and their self-indulgences. They are the fornicators and idolaters of the times that we live in. It has been and still is today a "me generation." They want it all and take it all leaving little or nothing for others. They set the pace, the standards, controlling the socialism and politics of the world by the money and power they control and yield in the world. They determine the programming on television, in the theatres and movie houses around the world. They control the news we see on the air or hear on the radio or read in newspapers. They yield so much power that too many have become brains washed, making robots of those who lacking wisdom and unknowingly respond predictably as the powers would have. Using mass media advertising and programming on television as to control our thinking and decision making process. For as time passes on, we each begin to lose our individuality and become hysterical and fanatical believers in the world. Worldliness then slowly begins to replace God in the hearts of man becoming mans' new god. We become robot like, automatically doing what we're programmed to do by television, movies and massive commercial advertising campaigns both on the air or almost everywhere we turn if life. Thus we buy things not needed but are what's trendy and in fashion flashing their labels at all the world. We do this to compete with the Jones' as the old saying goes flashing our labels at the world while the debts we create in our credit cards reach bankruptcy proportions. We eat mostly all the junk and fried foods advertised on TV then wonder why Americans are becoming so fat and diabetic reaching epidemic proportions. We march to the beat of the Madison Avenue drummer. That's who America is today, the loyal subjects of the Czars of Madison Avenue, television and Hollywood films, who control the airwaves, newspapers and all communications available to us. Without realizing it we fall in line and do as we're told to do. Buying and believing all the lies put to us. We're inundated with so much news, gossip, scandals, advertising to buy and buy and buy that we become loyal soldiers and do as we're told without realizing that we've become hypnotized or brain washed into this behavior pattern. And the question becomes why does it have to be like this? Why have we allowed ourselves into this false idolatry where we've replaced God with materialism and worldliness allowing man to delude our minds with untruths, trinkets and materialism so that he and not you can control the wealth and power in the world?

None of us seem willing to admit to this truth. It's so much easier to deny it, ignore it or just run from the truth. Or even better we avoid the truth and pretend it's not there so that we don't have to admit to what we've become. And unfortunately as we keep running from the truth that is in all of us, we also fail to embrace the one thing most important to us all in our development as human beings. That most important thing being the cornerstone of all of our lives and that is "love". We are missing this simple ingredient in our foundations and because of this omission, our countenance is fallen, our spirit is dead and we are lost to God. Our lives have become empty and meaningless, lacking all the necessary ingredients for a sound and righteous life. Righteousness not as we perceive it, but righteousness as God makes us righteous.

Because without love it is impossible to love God or your fellow man for God is love and love is the essence of God. They are one and they are inseparable. This how God loves us "unconditionally!" Why not give that same love to one another. It's in all of us to do so if we want. We need only tap into our soul and find ourselves spiritually and then find ourselves with the Lord himself. For its here in your soul that God dwells and is searching for you. We need to stop living one-dimensional lives affected only by the world we live in. We each need to develop ourselves into multi dimensional people, searching the deep places of our souls to get acquainted with the true person that lies within each of us. We each need to take time out each day to meditate and pray for its here where we find out what really makes us tick deep within. Discovering who we really are and what we truly love and hate. Finding out where we ourselves stand in relationship to believing in God, and if we find that we don't believe then, why not? What and when was God driven out of our hearts and hardened us to the worldly ways of believing only that by which we can see and touch and receive gratification from. It is in prayer and meditation with ourselves that we can face the ugliness that we may have become and be able to face it in all its truth. For only in facing the truth of ourselves can we then commit to making the changes that will make us a more loving individual to all.

It's in meditation and prayer where we each will meet God who in turn gives us His Holy Spirit to teach us and guide us through life. For in meditation we focus our minds into a deep meditative state and in prayer our hearts talk to God. And as we begin our daily journeys of meditation into our souls we will find God waiting for us to help us with our journey back home to the true person that lies within us. This is where not only do you make this wonderful discovery of yourself but make yourself right with God, seeking his best for your life. It is here that when you accept the Lord into your life He sends you his Holy Spirit, to guide and teach you bringing happiness, fulfillment and success throughout the rest of your life. It is here when you accept the will of God for your life that he will make you his own and fill you with his Holy Spirit, making you one with him and him with you. You'll be then living your life in the spirit and no longer in the flesh and thus able to communicate with him, the Father. It is here where you will receive God's word for your life, for your family and where miracles take place. For without God there can be no miracles, I know for I am a receiver of numerous miracles from God, miracles that my family and friends once laughed at until they saw the fulfillment of the promises of God for my life. For when my family and friends were witnesses to the miracles being fulfilled from the promises God have given to me they too began to believe. Today all my friends and family take seriously whenever I say that I've received a word from God, for surely as I receive it so it is fulfilled according to the word of God given to me.

This is a tough world and an expensive world to live in, and to raise one's children in. We're bombarded with the ways of the world. Exposed to its constant sins of lust, greed, envy, strife, hate, bigotry, selfishness and too many are falling victim to it all. Especially the children and there seems to be little hope even for the faithful. So I remind you that we must remain focused in our lives with the way of God, the things of God, putting worldliness aside. Sure we must live in the world but we don't have to be a part of it and become a slave to it, making it our god. But pray and do the exercise given to us by the apostle Paul, in the New Testament. It is found in Ephesians 6:11-18, this is the best assurance that God will keep us in the face of all that is evil. St Paul says, *Put on the whole armor of God, so that you may be able to stand against the wiles of the devil. For our struggle is not against enemies of blood and flesh, but against the rulers, against the authorities, against the cosmic powers of this present darkness, against the spiritual forces of evil in the heavenly places. Therefore take on the whole armor of God, so that you may be able to withstand on that evil day, and having done everything to stand firm. Stand therefore, and fasten the belt of truth around your waist, and put on the breastplate of righteousness. As for the shoes for your feet put on whatever will make you ready to proclaim the gospel of peace. With all these, take the shield of faith, with which you will be able to quench all the flaming arrows of the evil one. Take the helmet of salvation, and the sword of the Spirit, which is the word of God. Pray in the Spirit at all times in every prayer and supplication. To that end keep alert and always persevere in supplication for all saints.*

If your raise your children with the love and respect for God and they do depart from you guidance and take to a sinful life. Don't waste your time wringing your hands and having a pity party over it. Take action and bring your prayers before God lifting that child everyday in prayer to God. Don't stop no matter how long it takes, even years. You see your prayers availeth much in the kingdom of heaven, especially the prayers of the parents and God will go and find your children and bring them home. Somewhere along their path in life God will find a way to their hearts and bring them back into the fold. I know for I was one of these lost children and as I wrote before at the ripe old age of thirty-eight, Jesus came into my life and turned my life around. Proverb 22:6 states, *Train a child in the right way, and when old they will not stray.* Today I'm very happy and have a wonderful marriage and a fulfilled life in Christ. Now God through another visitation to me has given me the opportunity to write this book. To spread his message that he gave to me to give to others, that they might find the love of God, the healing and the salvation that I found in Jesus Christ, my Lord and Savior.

We've allowed ourselves to become a spoiled, selfish and bigoted society in a world where over half of the world's population lives in poverty and is starving to death. We're living in a world where millions of children die of starvation every year and about as many adults. Yet about one third of the world's population controls all the wealth and power in the world and dictates what the rest will get as their piece of the pie. We're living in a world where more than enough food is grown throughout the world to feed the people of this planet numerous times over and yet we don't. Why do you suppose? Obviously because there's no profit in feeding the starving mouths of the world, where is the profit in that? Or even better where is the love in all this? Where is the God that should be in all us? If all believe in God as most of us profess to and hope in God, then how can all this death and poverty and hunger exist? All too often we hear the same old excuse of people blaming God for all the suffering in the world. How can God allow children to starve to death, how can God allow Cancer and AIDS kill so many. But my friends it isn't God who allows these things, it's us. We, you and me and everyone in the world since Adam and Eve, we're to blame not God. We've turned our backs on the children of the world; we brought AIDS into the world not God. When your children are hungry, don't you feed them? When you were hungry your parents fed you? Well we have our brothers and sisters all around the world who have little or nothing to eat, no clothes to wear let alone proper shelters to live in and clean water to drink. How can they hope in God in a world that has rejected and forgotten them? And yet many of them do. On the other hand we who have everything have made God a statue, a religiosity, a word we mention in church, an idol of stone and tablets and empty words. Some pray repetitious prayers, others chant, hum and shout praises onto God in their churches, temples and synagogues, while others dance and sing in their services, all very religious. Yet after the services are over they go back to their worldly gods known as the almighty dollar and what it can buy them by way of possessions and power and esteem. Yet we all expect to get into heaven, but I wonder who will God honor into heaven and who God will reject, what do you think? Listen it's never been about how religious you are but what is in your heart, for that is where God examines us for that is where your true person is revealed. Whether you are a good person believing in God and living for God or a sinful person, the heart reveals all to God.

The corporate world is on a runaway train in the world, controlling all the wealth, economy and goods available to man. They have become more powerful than most of the governments throughout the world. At some point in our future as the population of this world continues to multiply and double itself we will run into a dangerous crossroads. Too few controlling too much and the masses left out in the cold. This has the making for a worldwide revolt that could and probably will bring the fulfillment of bible prophecy of a new global world war, the end of all wars, the Armageddon.

It's nothing new, nothing that we haven't heard before. We've all been warned about it in the book of Revelations, in the New Testament in the Bible. We've heard church leaders and scholars speak of it, warning us that it's the end of all life on earth when it comes. Yet man in all his greed for power, money and control, cannot and will not contain himself, it is as if possessed by some evil spirit marches on to the fulfillment of this prophecy. So now we've arrived in the new millennium and we are facing the End Times as predicted in the bible. All prophecies point to the years 2005 to 2015 during which the Great Tribulation will take place culminating in the War of the Armageddon. The prophecies of the bible codes regarding these times all fulfilled. Prophecies concerning President Clinton's presidency, the World's Trade Center destruction on September 11, 2001, the election of President Bush over Gore and the close election all fulfilled. Prophecies concerning Israel and the conflict with the Palestinian people and Arafat, all fulfilled. Every major event in the past twenty years fulfilled exactly as prophesied. Every major event in the world for the past three thousand years all fulfilled as prophesied and saved for today for us to have. Why, must we know of the fulfillment of all these prophecies of God?For we are the last generation of man on earth that will endure World War III, the terrible earthquakes and natural disasters predicted in the bible and finally the war of Armageddon. We are the generation that will see the Second Coming of Christ, but only after two thirds of the world's population have been killed in all these disasters and wars. God saved the message of the prophecies for our generation, for it pertains more to us than any generation of man in the entire history of the world. It concerns us all today. It's God's last call and testament to man, to awaken from this darkness we all live under and for us to come into the light and rid ourselves of all the sin letting God save us and our world.

When the World's Trade Center was destroyed by terrorist on Sept 11th, we were all outraged by this barbaric and wanton act of terrorism killing so many thousands of people. We immediately took military action and went into Afghanistan and Iraq, and took revenge and defeated this evil enemy and rightfully so. Yet we have millions dying every year from neglect, starvation and abuse but because of government sovereignty we can do nothing but to let the abuse go one. Who intervenes for the citizens of the world who are dying and suffering from such blight? Do we really care or is it that talk is cheap? We must one day all stand up and put an end to all that is wrong and unjust with the world no matter who the government. If we went to war over the World's Trade Center attack, then who defends the starving children dying by the millions every year and the many more millions of adults dying also. Why doesn't that outrage us? Could it be that they live in countries bearing no importance or profit for the rest of the world? They produce no oil, no danger to the stability of the world. Yet the atrocities in countries in Africa and South America are no less worse than those we've seen in Iraq, Afghanistan or the Baltic's.

This one thing I know, it grieves the heart of God, and one day without warning the Lord will return. He'll take back control of his world for man has failed miserably in running the world and unless he returns, we will exterminate every living being and thing on the face of the earth because hate and evilness rule the hearts of man in these times. Even having all the Bible prophecies available to all of us and knowing how over half of the prophecies have been fulfilled with the remainder yet to come. We continue to march on in the path of destruction only to willing to fulfill all the prophecies of the Bible. The good news of all this is that the Lord Jesus Christ does come in the end to save us from ourselves. At least to save those who are left after the big war of Armageddon.

You must realize that God cannot be mocked. If you won't love and help your fellow man, then God will measure out to you the same as you measured out to others. We all are subject to this law of God and that is that we will reap what we sow, the law of cause and effect. You sow selfishness, uncaring, hate, bigotry and so forth and you will reap the same in return. You expect to enter the kingdom of heaven. Then you must come to a reality with yourself and open up your heart to God. You will need to repent and receive Him into your heart and begin changing your life around and allowing the Holy Spirit to teach and guide you through your remaining life on earth. Begin to love all especially those you most disliked in your old life and help those you can help when it comes to you. Easier said than done sure, but you know what? All good things take some work, some effort and time to produce good fruit and God has the time to work out a good thing in you. All you have to do is say yes Lord Jesus, I've been a sinner all my life and I'm sorry and do repent of it all. Help me to turn my life around. It's that simple and yet that tough to do, for you must mean it with all you heart for God sees all and knows the truth in your heart.

I know this is a tough message. But it has to be if it's to do some good. We are living in stressful and difficult times. Times made more complicated by the onset of computers and the Internet and how they have changed our daily lives. For all the benefits we get from the Internet, we have now discovered how so many use it to spread sin, greed and ways to cheat one another with. Its a tool intended for so much good and now has also become the tool of darkness spreading poison to the children of the world. It spreads its perversions to all and is beginning to have some devastating effects on our children.

The computer is also an instrument intended to be the be all and end all for man, yet eventually becomes the downfall of man. For today we live in a computer controlled world that promises to take on more and more of the work that people used to do. Creating more and more unemployment, as the displaced find it difficult to find work and often when they do its minimum retail type of work. Very hard to raise a family with retail type of jobs paying minimum wages wouldn't you say? So quickly we have advanced into the age of computers that they control the food and goods we buy which are inventoried and sold by computer equipment from scanners to computer type cash registers. Soon we won't have need of money for today in America we can buy virtually anything with debit or credit cards, all part of man's computerized world. So advanced have we come that today that many third world nations now are working on developing nuclear weapons for their defense or for the terrorism they want to impart on the world.

We need to take stock of ourselves and see what kind of person we're each evolving into and what kind of future we want and world we want to live in. Be honest, search deep in your soul and be truthful to yourself. Don't cheat yourself, but be totally honest. Do you think it can be achieved without God on your side? If you do, then think again for man has failed miserably since the dawn of man on earth without God. If you want God on your side you're going to have to do something and that my friend is by putting yourself in the hands of God and surrendering your will to Him. Then can the will of God for you life be your direction in life and can God begin to bless you all of the rest of your days on earth. Then and only then when man surrenders his will to the Almighty, will man find peace on earth. For only then will his kingdom come to us on earth. As the Lord's Prayer says; Thy kingdom come, Thy will be done on earth as it is in heaven. We must surrender our will to God and allow ourselves to live by the will of God and then we will all find true love and true peace on earth.

Are you all that you can be or want to be? Do you have a daily walk with God, living your life in the spirit? Do you truly love you family, your friends and neighbors? The people you work with? How about your enemies, do you love them also? Anyone can love their friends and family, but to love your enemy is an act of God. If we each don't make a point to love our fellow man, how can we expect to receive his love in return or for him to give his love to others? How will we put an end to all wars without love? We wouldn't have wars if we spent our time caring and loving one another. Do you really give a damn or even give thought to those who don't have a blessed thing especially food to eat? And I know the old clichés that say "what can I do or they say but I'm just one person." Or we get so wrapped up in our little worlds that we don't stop to notice the injustices all around us. But one person does count and can make a difference. And if one person here does something about something and someone else over there does the same. It begins to take notice among others and the others start doing the same and it grows and grows and before you know it doing good deeds becomes contagious. Well that's how we can eventually cure the ills of the world if we just stop to give a damn and give your brother a helping hand. He's not your concern you say. Think again, for whether we like it or not, we are all our brothers' keeper.

I know that these words aren't applicable to all of us. There are some mighty fine people in the world doing all the right that they can and loving God with all their might. They live a life in the spirit and are enjoying a full and complete life down here on earth, but they are the true minorities on this planet. It's the rest that I'm addressing in this book. You cannot live your whole live divorced from your spirit and from God. Your flesh cannot bring you everlasting happiness nor can it save your eternal soul. All that is of the flesh is temporal and comes to an end, and then before you know it your hungry for more for the flesh cannot be satisfied. For life by the flesh (by what one can see, touch and possess) is a life of greed, selfishness and lust. Thus it keeps you always on the prowl, seeking, lusting and desiring only those things in life that will enhance your status, your fame, your power among your fellow men. Chasing after materiality's in life that satisfy one's soul for a little while, and then your hungry again seeking more and more until you'll settle for no less. Always demanding, give me, get me, and I want. Always for me, acts of selfishness without regards for others. It's what the world has lived by since man first stepped foot on earth. It has only led man into the world of the dark side, a world of Godlessness, a world of hate, death and destruction and now culminating with man arriving at his ultimate destiny, the End Times for man. It is said in the bible that two thirds of the world will perish in the End Times from wars, natural disasters and diseases. Only one third will enter into the new millennium with Christ Jesus. When death comes to you as it does for everyone for it's a law of God that from dust we came and to dust we will return. You will die miserably and lost forever being permanently separated from God, for you chose not to love God but to love the things of the flesh: money, power, booze, drugs, whatever it was that stole your heart away. They became your true gods, but they were all temporal gods and upon death they were gone forever. Also note that no amount of accumulated wealth can buy back you lost soul. You lived by the world and all of its materiality all of your life. Now pray to the world, to the material god you served all those years to save you and your lost soul. You will come to a very hard and sobering conclusion, that you blew it. No one is there to hear your cries and offer any help. Consequently then you remain lost forever. Now that's what I call a true "bummer".

So don't wait until the going gets tough and your nerves are shattered or you've reached the end of you line. Don't let disaster so fall upon you that your heart becomes so embittered that you never find you way back home to God. Start today to begin a new daily routine in your life to take time out each day to meditate with yourself and pray to God, doing it as if your life depended on it and you what, it does? Talk and meditate within your soul and sort your life out, yielding control of your life over to your soul who is more enlightened than your flesh (your carnal mind). Remember this that many problems if not all problems in life can be resolved in prayer, the mightiest tool put in our hands. Why do you say? For it is our telephone line to God. He answers prayers to those who truly believe in Him and trust in Him with all their hearts. How much more when the one who brings the aid is the one who suffered and gave his life up on the cross. The one who suffered the excruciating agony of being nailed to the cross, only then when the cross was lifted up to feel all his muscles and bones ripped apart from their sockets. The weight of his destroyed body causing him to eventually suffocate unto death. It is the same Jesus, who resurrected after his death conquering hell, death and he lives forever more. He is the same Jesus Christ, who sits at the right hand of God and answers our prayers to those who believe in him, for they know he is a living God. What good are prayers when given to a statue, a stone, to objects of gold, to animals, to the sun or to past prophets or saints who are dead and buried? None of these can answer you, or do anything for you. They can't heal the sick nor raise the dead back to life, but there's one who can. The one who conquered hell and death, the one called Jesus Christ, the Son of God. He is the Messiah of the world, not just of the Jews, but of the entire world. Pray to him and see results. I know for He's blessed my life over and over again with miracles, prosperity beyond my wildest imagination. Whenever I pray, he answers me. Whether it's to give me what I prayed for or to direct me to his will, which will have better results for me then that which I was praying for. I'm never left alone, he is with me everyday of my life. He's my God, my Savior and much more that that. He became my father, my brother and my best friend. He is a part of every part of me. Flesh of my flesh, blood of my blood, heart of my heart, soul of my soul, we are one for I am one in Christ and He lives in me. This is the true faith; this is the way of God and the way to know God. He becomes one with you and you with him. This is what this book is all about, to bring you to God and restore your soul in oneness with Him. It's not a call to join a church or a new religion. It's a call to Jesus Christ, who can help us when everything else fails us. When our money can't buy relief, he can give relief. You'll never forget the incident that caused you pain but you'll learn through him to endure the suffering and how to get through it giving your pain to him and moving on with your life. Never forgetting but forgiving, never judging or avenging but being merciful. This is where healing begins for all especially the broken hearted and why living a spiritually active life with God is so important. He can only help you if you believe he is and is there in the very day of your need. Every need in my life over the past twenty-two years has been taken care of, since the first visitation by the Lord. Every pain lifted from me, every suffering healed, heart disease cured without surgery, brain tumor operated to a complete success. Every final disaster, every emergency met by God with complete success for me. Even every financial disaster I faced in the past 22 years, gone with His blessings. He's not a God who is dead and buried, found only in the history of the churches. He's here today and very much alive. He is I AM, he is now he is today a living God ready to help each and every one of us. When Moses asked God, who shall I say spoke to me? God told Moses tell them that *I am that I am.* When Jesus when challenged by the people as to his validity said, *Verily, Verily, I tell you before Abraham was, I am (John 8:58).*

So there's the answer "I am". He didn't say I was the God or I will be your God, but "I am your God" today as well as yesterday and tomorrow. Today is the day to call on me the Lord your God and I will be there in a very present time to help you. To be able to reach God, you must first believe that there is a God, and then turn to him and pray expecting in your heart of hearts for an answer. Put all your worldliness and intellectualism aside and become as a child, believing with that simple faith that God does hear you and will help you.

I think this is probably the hardest thing for man to do, to really believe that God is, nothing more and nothing less. That God is the "I am," as he told Moses. The God of now, this very minute and not just the God of Moses, a historical god or a god you will see someday in heaven. But he is the God of you right now this very moment. It's not just a name tossed around in prayers in churches and temples, a myth, a fantasy that we gather in churches to pray to but yet not really believing in our hearts. I mean why bother to pray if you really don't believe God is there, or that he hears you, its empty prayers, empty words with no foundation, no meaning, and with no expectation. Why pray to God if all you believe he is there for is for you to get to heaven after you die. That makes less sense. For he is not just the God of you future when you die for chances are you would die with a lost soul not having known God in your lifetime. But he is the God of yesterday (your history), today (your life right now), and all your tomorrows and for all eternity. From your birth and through out all your eternity God wants to be your God, every day of your eternal life. So the time for awakening is now. Don't waste another day being separated from the Lord. Receive him into your life and let him help and guide you through the rest of your eternal life. I mean if God is with you, who can be against you?

Therefore when you pray you must first believe that he "is God" and that he does hear you and that he's ready to work with you or help you as needed now in your present day. Then and only then can you begin to pray with expectation that God will answer your prayer. All too often we're caught up in the teachings of both the churches and the intellectual mind of man. Some claiming there is no God, no heaven and no hell. Others say oh yes there is a heaven up there in the sky somewhere and others saying that it's after the return of the Lord, who will make heaven on earth. Then for many others it's become a chase around the block looking for miracles that are never there. Here, there and everywhere they search, chasing moonbeams and ending up disillusioned. Yet if we only understood that the Kingdom of Heaven, isn't out there in some mysterious unreachable place but it's in you, in me and in all of us. Yes, that's the mystery of the gospel, it's in each of us. Luke 17:21, Jesus says, *the Kingdom of God is not coming with things that can be observed; nor will they say, 'Look, here it is!' or 'There it is!' For in fact the Kingdom of God is in you.* All we have to do is search within ourselves to find the miracle of our Lord Jesus Christ. For when you begin to take the time out each day to meditate with yourself and pray quietly in the privacy of your room you will encounter your truth, you will discover your spirit (soul) and you will get to know the Lord Jesus Christ. As you come to know yourself and know Jesus with each new day you begin to see the light and desire to change your life, seeking a new life living in obedience to God, living in a son ship with God. And as Jesus says in John 8:31, *If you continue in my word, you are truly my disciples; and you will know the truth and the truth shall set you free.* He said further in verse 34, *Very truly, I tell you, everyone who commits sin is a slave to sin. The slave does not have a permanent place in the household; the son has a place there forever. So if the Son makes you free, you will be free indeed.* So there you have it again quoting directly from the Lord himself. Life in the flesh is a life in sin and has no permanent home in the Kingdom of God, but the Son of God who is the permanent resident does. And if he frees you (forgives you from your sins) then truly free (saved) you are indeed and because of him receive son ship with the Father and a permanent place in the kingdom of heaven. Folks it just doesn't get any better than that. That there is the grand prize we all should be seeking in life, a permanent place in the kingdom of heaven. That beats anything here on earth, for nothing in the world can promise you eternal life of eternal happiness.

We are each responsible to come to God on our own and communicate with him. We can't leave the work to the pastors and rabbis of the world. They can intercede on our behalf, offering prayers to God on our behalf, but in the end you will have to come before God yourself and pray. For we each need to deal with God directly and not always use intermediaries such as the ministry to do this work for us. As Jesus said go into your private room (your soul) and pray to God and speak to God yourself. Let God work faith into your heart for it's here with faith that one comes to believe, for God gives faith to each and everyone of us so that we can believe and know the truth. Romans 10:17, says it best, *So faith comes from what is heard, and what is heard comes through the word of Christ.*

We also know from the book of Hebrews, chapter 11: 1-3, *Now faith is being sure of what we hope for and certain of what we do not see. This is what the ancients were commended for.By faith we understand that the universe was formed at God's command, so that what is seen was not made out of what was visible.*

Also, when praying whether it be to thank God or to seek his help. Don't just pray wordless repetitious words. Talk to him with all the honesty in your heart. If there's pain in you heart, speak to him about it and ask for his help and healing to get you past this situation in your life.

If you have something against someone else, take it to God, asking him for the wisdom and the knowledge to understand your situation. Ask him to give you the love and the mercy to love and forgive this person and to forgive you in you mishandling of the problem.

This is just the beginning of a whole new life for you. From this moment on God will fill you with his Holy Spirit, who will teach you all things. You'll be a new creation as Saint Paul says in II Cor., 5:17, *So if anyone be in Christ, there is a new creation: everything old has past away; see, everything has become new.* And this is my desire for all of you, that we all be in Christ, all new creations living a full life in the spirit. A life in Christ that if we each pursue it will give to saving the world, ending all wars, ending all sufferings, all injustices and all inequalities. Where every man, woman and child can enjoy a life to the fullest, completely free to love and to worship God, Amen.

You know it's so funny that so many find the name of God an offense, yet they all expect God to be there for them when it's time to die and leave this world. How can God allow sin to enter into the kingdom of God, as Jesus tells us in the book of Matthews 12:25, *Every kingdom divided against itself is brought to desolation; and every city or house divided against itself cannot stand.* So the question then is this: if God is an embarrassment to you or an offense to you, then why should God allow you into the kingdom of heaven when you die to disrupt and divide His house? Listen the bible says in Romans 3:23, *for all have sinned and come short of the glory of God.* In the book of Romans Paul says, *If because of the one man's trespass, death exercised dominion through that one (Adam), much more surely will those who receive the abundance of grace and the free gift of righteousness exercise dominion in life through the one man, Jesus Christ."*

Therefore just as one man's trespass (Adam) led to condemnation for all, so one man's act of righteousness (Jesus Christ) leads to justification and life for all. For just as by one man's disobedience (Adam) the many were made sinners, so by the one man's obedience (Jesus Christ) the many will be made righteous. But the law came in, with the result that the trespass multiplied; but where sin increased, grace abounded all the more, so that, just as sin exercised dominion in death, so grace might also exercise dominion through justification leading to eternal life through Jesus Christ our Lord.

What then are we to say? Should we continue in sin in order that grace may abound? By no means! How can we who died to sin go on living in it? Do you not know that all of us who have been baptized into Christ Jesus were baptized buried with him by baptism into death, so that, just as Christ was raised from the dead by the glory of Father, so we too might walk in newness of life.

For if we have been united with him in a death like his, we will certainly be united with him in a resurrection like his. We know that our old self was crucified with him so that the body of sin might be destroyed, and we might no longer be enslaved to sin. For whoever is died is freed from sin. But if we have died with Christ, we believe that we will also live with him. We know that Christ, being raised from the dead, will never die again; death no longer has dominion over him. The death he died, he died to sin, once and for all; but the life he lives, he lives to God. So you also must consider yourselves dead to sin and alive to God in Christ Jesus.

Therefore, do not let sin exercise dominion in your mortal bodies, to make obey their passions. No longer present your members to sin as instruments of wickedness, but present yourselves to God as instruments of righteousness. For sin will have no dominion over you, since you are not under law but under grace.

What then, should we sin because we are not under law but under grace? By no means! Do you not know that if you present yourselves to anyone as obedient slaves, you are slave of the one whom you obey, either of sin, which leads to death, or of obedience, which leads to righteousness. But thanks be to God that you, having once been slave of sin, have become obedient from the heart to the form of teaching to which you were entrusted, and that you, having been set free from sin, have become slaves of righteousness. I am speaking in human terms because of you natural limitations. For just as you once presented your members as slaves to impurity and to greater and greater iniquity, so now present our members as slaves to righteousness for sanctification.

When you were slaves of sin, you were free in regard to righteousness. So what advantage did you then get from the things of which you now are ashamed. The end of those things is death. But now you have been freed from sin and enslaved to God, the advantage you get is sanctification. The end is eternal life. For the wages of sin is death, but the free gift of God is eternal life in Christ Jesus our Lord (Romans 5:18 to 6:12)."

We must always keep in mind that deception and pride are the key elements in causing man to fall into sin. It's what caused Adam and Eve, to fall into sin as the serpent deceived them from the truth to a lie. As we see in Genesis the serpent says to Eve, *Did God say, You shall not eat from any tree in the garden'? And Eve replied We may eat of the fruit of the trees in the garden' but God said You shall not eat of the fruit of the tree that is in the middle of the garden, nor shall you touch it, or you shall die (Genesis 3:1-3).*

Then the serpent said to the woman "You will not die, for God knows that when you eat of it your eyes will be opened, and you will be like God, knowing good and evil. And when the woman saw that the fruit was good for food, and a delight to the eyes, and that the tree was to be desired to make one wise, she took of its fruit and ate; and she also gave some to her husband, who was with her and he ate(Genesis 3:4-6).

So there we have three things causing Eve, to fall into sin along with Adam. First, she gave ear to the devil; who was too crafty and only too quick to deceive her. Sounds familiar, for that's how we all get caught into sin; we give ear to those who wish us to join them in their sin. Misery always loves company. That's how teenagers get caught so often into doing drugs, joining gangs and becoming society drop outs, by giving ear to others their age doing the same. Listen if you don't give an ear and hear them out you can't fall. But once you stop to listen and give ear you're trapped, for then comes the deception to lure you in with lies. I remember only to well when in high school how other kids my age tried so hard to get me to take drugs and booze, and I gave an ear and sure enough I was deceived and began drinking. And so it went on through my twenties until I was doing drugs and ruining my life.

You now see the first two deadly ploys to get you into sinning: listening (giving an ear to) and deception. Once you accept the deception then the third enemy lust of the eyes will to lead you into sin. You look with desire to try it out and before you know you're hooked. You become a slave to sin no matter what that sin is, it's your master, and it becomes your God. First John, Chapter 1:8 says, *If we say that we have no sin, we deceive (there's that word again) ourselves, and the truth is not in us.*

It also says in Romans, Chapter 7:11 through 8:17, Paul the Apostle writes:

For sin, seizing an opportunity in the commandments, deceived me (again there's that word again, deceived) and through it killed me. So the law is holy, and the commandment is holy and just and good."

"Did what is good, then, bring death to me? By no means! It was sin, working death in me through what is good, in order that sin might be shown to be sin, and through the commandment might become sinful beyond measure."

"For we know that the law is spiritual; but I am of the flesh, sold into slavery under sin. I do not understand my own actions. For I do not do what I want but I do the very thing I hate (isn't that the truth for so many of us whether its hate, anger, drugs, lust, etc. We're in a trap of our own doing). Now if I do what I do not want, I agree that the law is good. But in fact it no longer I that do it, but sin that dwells within me. For I know that nothing good dwells within me, that is, in my flesh. I can will what is right, but I cannot do it. For I do not do the good I want, but the evil I do not want is what I do. Now if I do what I do not want, it is no longer I that do it, but sin that dwells within me."

"So I find it to be a law that when I want to do what is good, evil lies close at hand. For I delight in the law of God in my inmost self, but I see in my members another law at war with the law of my mind, making me captive to the law of sin that dwells in my members. Wretched man that I am! Who will rescue me from this body of death? Thanks be to God through Jesus Christ our Lord!"

"So then, with my mind I am a slave to the law of God, but with my flesh I am a slave to the law of sin."

"There is therefore now no condemnation for those who are in Christ Jesus. For the law of the Spirit of life in Christ Jesus has set you free from the law of sin and of death. For God has done what the law, weakened by the flesh, could not do. By sending his own Son in the likeness of sinful flesh, and to deal with sin, he condemned sin in the flesh so that the just requirement of the law might be fulfilled in us, who walk not according to the flesh but according to the Spirit. For those who live according to the Spirit set their minds on the things of the Spirit.

To set the mind on the flesh is death, but to set the mind on the Spirit is life and peace. For this reason the mind that is set on the flesh is hostile to God; it does not submit to God's law – indeed it cannot, and those who are in the flesh cannot please God."

"But you are not in the flesh; you are in the Spirit, since the Spirit of God dwells in you. Anyone who does not have the Spirit of Christ does not belong to him. But if Christ is in you, though the body is dead because of sin, the Spirit is life because of righteousness. If the Spirit of him who raised Jesus from the dead dwells in you, he who raised Christ from the dead will give life to your mortal bodies also through his Spirit that dwells in you."

"So then, brothers and sisters, we are debtors not to the flesh – for if you live according to the flesh, you will die; but if by the Spirit you put to death the deeds of the body, you will live. For all who are led by the Spirit of God are children of God. For you did not receive a spirit of slavery to fall back into fear, but you have received a spirit of adoption. When we cry, "Abba, Father!" It is that very Spirit bearing witness with our spirit that we are children of God, and if children, the heirs, heirs of God and joint heirs with Christ – if, in fact, we suffer with him so that we may also be glorified with him.

Remember biblical prophecy of the end times is all contingent. It will happen as written if "we continue on the pathway we're living in". We don't have to have a World War III or an Armageddon, but we will if we don't start today and now to change our ways and to find our pathways to God and a spirit filled life. And God stands at the door to our hearts waiting for us to make the first move. Jesus says so in Matt 7:7, *ask and it will be given to you; seek and you will find; knock and the door will be opened to you. For everyone who asks, receives; and the one who seeks, finds; and to the one who knocks, the door will be opened.* So don't let anyone steal the truth from you, test it for yourself. Prove to yourself whether or not Jesus Christ is the Son of God. Don't let the politics of religions and their religious ways rob you of the truth and your chance to find you true self and God.

There is one God, there is one Spirit, and there is one you. You only have now to find your true self, your soul and your place with God. Don't confuse God with religion. Religions are the many different avenues man chooses to worship God, to reach out to God and how he even perceives God through their own set of rules, doctrines and disciplines of their respective religions.

Much too often religion has been used as a means of controlling people to gain control of their will and their money. Often times we find new religions popping up being led by fanatical leaders, who are false prophets leading people astray. All too often we see where too many religions box God in where God is limited to the doctrines and dogmas of their religion. Consequently God becomes a powerless God, non effectual and in doing so bounds one from the freedom of believing and receiving God into one's life in all the fullness and splendor that He is. We only get to know of God by how he's handed out to us by the church fathers, according to their religious doctrines of their perception of God. They know what's best for us and in what manner we should perceive God. Well I call that "religious tunnel-vision" and it deprives us the right to search for God and to know God on a true personal level. That's the reason most people never have miracles in their lives.

If it's God you want in your life, the Father and creator of all mankind, then call on Him. If you never had a miracle or a blessing from God in your life then you've been absent from God for too long. Take your liberty now and go inside to the closet of your soul and pray and meditate and find our about yourself and at the same time pray and talk to God. Seek his help, his guidance and his truth for your life. Remember this and remember it well for on judgment day you will be judged by you, your acts and your heart. You won't be able to use any excuses as to this being how you learned it in church. For if the blind lead the blind, the bible says both will end up in the ditch. So no excuses, you are responsible for yourself before God, and you are responsible for your own salvation not the churches. They can't save you, only God can if you are willing to repent to God, ask the Lord Jesus into your life to send you his Holy Spirit, to begin helping you to make the changes you need in life to develop into a spiritual person. Don't delay and do it now, only you can help you! Don't put it off till tomorrow, next week or for some distant future. You may not be around then. No one knows how long he or she will live or how short. Death respects no one, it comes when it comes and you're gone. So the time for getting your life right for yourself and with God is today.

Since my life was turned around some twenty-three years ago, I have been blessed with dozens of miracles and blessings in my life from God. From clearing me up from bankruptcy in six months rather than the seven years it normally takes to buying two homes within two years of the bankruptcy.

At another unfortunate time of my life I had lost my life long partner. Instead of seeking God's help for myself, I had allowed myself to become deeply depressed over the loss. Thus taking my eyes off God, I allowed myself to become weak and turned to drinking to sooth the pain. It nearly cost me my life, for in this awful state of depression I consumed two quarts of scotch and vodka leaving me totally unconscious on the floor of my home. To complicate the situation I had just moved into this house and no one yet knew where I had moved to for I hadn't time to put in a phone to contact my friends and family. So there I lay dying on the floor and no one had a clue to my situation. No one but save just one, Jesus himself knew. As I lay there unconscious for what I later came to understand was several hours, Jesus Christ went to work for me. He went to the places of business of three of my friends who each worked in different jobs. He told each one, stop working for your brother Ray is deep peril and will this day die without your help. Each one, God bless them went immediately to their bosses telling of the emergency and got the rest of the day off. They jumped into their cars not knowing where I lived and asked Jesus to guide them. As they later told me they heard the voice of the Lord clearly all the way they each drove and followed his directions. They found the town I had moved to and were lead to the very block. They parked their cars and to their amazement to encounter one another and discover that the Lord had called the three of them. When the Lord Jesus, told them which house I lived in they went and kicked in the door without knocking. They knew in their hearts if God sent them, then I was there. Sure enough they found me lying unconscious on the floor. Thank God for their faithfulness to answer God's call, for the faith they each had to believe in God and come running. I am alive today because God so loved me and three brothers so loved me to believe and come to my rescue. Folks God isn't short on miracles and blessings; it's us who are short of faith and believing in God.

Another valuable lesson to keep in mind is that we're all a part of each other. The one cannot live without the other. That's how God intended it and the sooner we all learn and accept this truth the sooner we will find the love and peace to live in harmony with one another and care for one another. Romans 12: 3-6, the Paul writes, *For by the grace given to me I say to everyone among you not to think of yourself more highly than you ought to think, but to think with sober judgment, each according to the measure of faith that God has assigned. For as in one body we have many members, and not all the members have the same function, so we, who are many, are one body in Christ, and individually we are members one of another.*

Remember the kingdom of heaven is here and not in some impossible to reach place. Everyone searches here, there and everywhere for answers that they have already but are too blind to see. The answers to life's most difficult questions and problems lie within us. The problem is we've never practiced going within ourselves to seek the truth or answers to our most mysterious questions and problems. We usually won't admit that we are the problem, but usually try to look elsewhere to put the blame. But it's not the blame that's the problem, it doesn't matter who's to blame for us being the way we are or in the fix we're in, what matters is that we are sick and in need of healing. Stop wasting your time pointing the finger at someone to put the blame on for your situation, but instead forgive and move on with yourself and look for a solution.

And you will find the answer lies within yourself. Yes within yourself, in the spiritual realm, deep in your soul. That's where you have to go within yourself, tapping into the treasures of your life, seeing yourself for who you are and for whom you are not. Seeing the good in you but also acknowledging the bad and or the ugly side of you. It is here where you will find peace, love, God, healing and a new life for here is where you will find the kingdom of heaven which lies within you. It's where you commune with yourself and with God and its here where you will discover the power of prayer and how through prayer you start coming to the realization of yourself, your needs, desires and the changes you need to make for yourself.

They will probably seem monumental and impossible for you to accomplish but keep at it and in the course of that new fellowship with yourself you will turn to God. And that my friend will be the greatest day of your life when you finally open a dialogue with the creator and you'll be amazed at how much clearer things will become. Solutions and answers will come to you readily and your heart will find ways to opening and releasing itself from the pains of those awful years. You will discover yes that you are willing and capable of turning your life around and so it begins. That's where you will connect with God, that's where you will be transformed from your old self to the new person, free from the hang-ups, bad habits that brought your life down, free from the anger that rages within you, free from the bitterness that scarred you all those years. You will find yourself open in your heart to receiving the Lord into your life, to bringing you peace as you never knew it. You will find in time as you continue to search within your spirit that through prayer and meditation you have found the strength in the Lord, and are ready to make those changes in your life. Wanting to change your mind and the way you think, to clean up your act. You will be able in time to accept yourself for who you are and not be concerned with blaming anyone for it but accepting the fact that it's who you are and you are ready to change that old man into the new man in the Lord.

Revenge and getting even will no longer concern you, for in the love that lives in you now your concern is for others, for them to set themselves free in the Lord and to live their lives in the newness that you have found. In Romans, Chapter 12, Saint Paul writes, *I appeal to you therefore, brothers and sisters, by the mercies of God, to present your bodies as a living sacrifice, holy and acceptable to God, which is you spiritual worship. Do not be conformed to this world, but be transformed by the renewing of your minds, so that you may discern what is the will of God—what is good and acceptable and perfect.*

For by the grace given to me I say to everyone among you not to think of yourself more highly than you ought to think, but to think sober judgment, each according to the measure of faith that God has assigned. For as in one body we have many members, and not all the members have the same function, so we, who are many, are one body in Christ, and individually we are members one of another. We have gifts that differ according to the grace given to us; prophecy, in proportion to faith; ministry, in ministering; the teacher, in teaching; the exhorter, in exhortation; the giver, in generosity; the leader, in diligence; the compassionate, in cheerfulness.

Let love be genuine; hate what is evil, hold fast to what is good; love one another with mutual affection; outdo one another in showing honor. Do not lag in zeal, be ardent in spirit, and serve the Lord. Rejoice in hope, be patient in suffering, persevere in prayer. Contribute to the needs of the saints; extend hospitality to strangers.

Bless those who persecute you; bless and do not curse them. Rejoice with those who rejoice, weep with those who weep. Live in harmony with one another; do not be haughty, but associate with the lowly; do not claim to be wiser than you are. Do not repay anyone evil for evil, but take thought for what is noble in the sight of all. Beloved, never avenge yourselves, but leave room for the wrath of God; for it is written, *"Vengeance is mine, I will repay, says the Lord."* No, *"if your enemies are hungry, feed them; if they are thirsty, give them something to drink; for by doing this you will heap burning coals on their heads." Do not be overcome by evil, but overcome evil with good.*

And again in I Corinthians, Chapter 12:1-26, Saint Paul writes, *Now concerning spiritual gifts, brothers and sisters, I do not want you to be uninformed. You know that when you were pagans, you were enticed and led astray to idols that could not speak. Therefore I want you to understand that no one speaking by the Spirit of God ever says "Let Jesus be cursed!" And no one can say, "Jesus is Lord" except by the Holy Spirit.*

Now there are varieties of gifts, but the same Spirit; and there are varieties of services, but the same Lord; and there are varieties of activities, but it is the same God who activates all of them in everyone. To each is given the manifestation of the Spirit for the common good. To one is given through the Spirit the utterance of wisdom, and to another the utterance of knowledge according to the same Spirit, to another faith by the same Spirit, to another gifts of healing by the one Spirit, to another the working of miracles. To another prophecy, to another the discernment of spirits, to another various kinds of tongues, to another the interpretation of tongues. All these are activated by one and the same Spirit, who allots to each one individually just as the Spirit chooses.

For just as the body is one and has many members, and all the members of the body, though many, are one body, so it I with Christ. For in the one Spirit we were all baptized into one body—Jews or Greeks, slaves or free—and we were all made to drink of one Spirit.

Indeed, the body does not consist of one member but of many. If the foot would say, "Because I am not a hand, I do not belong to the body," that would not make it any less a part of the body. And if the ear would say, "Because I am not an eye, I do not belong to the body," that would not make it any less a part of the body. If the whole body were an eye, where would the hearing be? If the whole body were hearing, where would the sense of smell be? But as it is, God arranged the members in the body, each one of them as he chose. If all were a single member, where would the body be? As it is, there are many members, yet one body. The eye cannot say to the hand, "I have no need of you," nor again the head to the feet, "I have no need of you." On the contrary, those members of the body that seem to be weaker are indispensable, and those members we think less honorable we clothe with greater honor, and our less respectable members are treated with greater respect; whereas our more respectable members do not need this. But God has so arranged the body, giving the greater honor to the inferior member, that there may be no dissension within the body, but the members may have the same care for one another. If one member suffers, all suffer together with it; if one member is honored, all rejoice together with it."

So there you are, we've seen how sin works itself into peoples lives and commences a process of self destruction which begun simply enough as an implanted thought (seed) and grew until it culminated in it's fruition of a destroyed soul. Sin takes its time working its nature in you and as the years go by one becomes more and more accustomed to living a sinful nature. This is the craftiness of the enemy not to devour you in one sitting but to pinch you a little at a time. Thus allowing you to become addicted to you sinful nature so it becomes you natural way of being, and in doing so making you the fall guy for your sinful ways not him. Sins are bad habits and addictions that after years become almost impossible to break. They all become habits and a part of one's daily life. They become a part of who you are and before long you can't tell the real you from the one accustomed to committing all those sins. So consequently you accept your sinful nature as a normal way of living and can't see the sin in it. You have allowed yourself to be deceived by the enemy, by yourself, and by the nature of the way most people live in the world today. The truth is always there whether we choose to see it and acknowledge it or to ignore it. And we can all see the truth by just looking around and looking at our history as a people on planet earth. In the history of man, have we found a way to live with one another without bigotry, hate, wars, domination, and enslavement of others (especially children in third world nations)? We steal, cheat, fight, gossip, slander others, and deny others their rights. The rich are separated from the masses and treat the masses as a contagious disease. They take the wealth of the world to themselves, getting richer by the day yet millions of children and adults die every year of starvation. It's been this way since the beginning of time and with all these thousands of years passing by, with the vast technological and scientific achievements made this century, we're no better off as a people than we were before the time of Jesus Christ. We marvel at man's genius to sent rockets to the moon and beyond. We can get oil from deep in the oceans costing hundreds of millions of dollars. We can build weapons of warfare that can wipe out the world six times over. Yet we can't feed the hungry, shelter the homeless, heal the sick or provide good and equal employment for all people. Children around the world are being abused, forced to work hard labor to manufacture clothes, footwear and carpeting at slave wages working long hours under inhuman conditions. This so that an elect few and the spoiled in society can have their "hand made" trinkets. Then we have the problem of sexual perversion, which was a problem back then going back to the beginning of time, and is still to this day a major problem in all societies. It's worse than ever bringing to the world diseases such as AIDS, that baffle the best minds in this world and kill tens of thousands, millions in fact. So the answer is yes, in our hearts we all know the truth whether we chose to admit it or not.

Repenting to God and asking God for his mercy and help is the best place to start no matter where you are in life. It cleanses the soul, and you instantly feel a giant weight fall off your shoulders. You feel renewed within and ready to search and receive all that's there for you to learn from him. Yet the question many ask is why repent? There's nothing wrong with my life. I'm as good as all others and I'm no sinner. For sin as most of us see it is what the other guy does, not us. It's the headliners who make the news, killing people, raping, robbing, etc. But it's never us.

What we all need to define is what sin to us is as we see it applied to our own life? And how do we think God sees us as we live our lives from day to day, for here is where the rubber meats the road. It's the everyday life where sin breeds and blossoms into bad habits that before long becomes our persona. For most sins are not the sins one commits against others or against God, although they are bad in themselves, but they are sins we commit against ourselves. I feel these are the hardest sins to detect and call sin, to acknowledge and recognize as sin. For whether we eat ourselves into heart attacks, become alcoholics, sexual perverts, drug addicts or maybe something more subtle like being obsessed over money or material possessions, we each have one or more things that needs to be given attention too. For none of us are perfect and if we take a look we have created or allowed to create in us bad habits that for some are even self-destructive. For others their sins are habits or obsessions forming ugly persons out of them, unloving, uncaring types who are totally self indulgent with little or no regards for others. Others it is the lying, cheating, gossiping that over the years has created an unfaithful, unreliable person of them.

Basically what I'm saying is that we all have faults that destroy or steal our health both physical and mental. We lose our love, our inner peace and evolve into people full of stress, headaches, worry-some or just plain nervous wrecks. We drive ourselves crazy with obsessions for sex, money, and power driving ourselves to limits that are inhumane and definitely detrimental to our health. Then we wonder why we suffer from so much heart disease, cancer, body disorders, strokes, diabetes, etc. This type of living is sinful because it bears bad karma and that is that we are killing of ourselves because of these drives and stressful conditions. It's not the devil doing it to us, but it's us killing us all by ourselves. The enemy just sits and laughs at our stupidity.

You see we miss the mark in life in so many numerous ways, and what's worse is that many of these missed marks in life become repetitious and go on eventually without being noticed. Eventually it becomes habit forming, and we've become conditioned into believing the missed marks, the errors we make in life are the norm of life. That's how we become deceived in our lives and sin then takes hold of us separating us from the love of God. Before long you begin to develop a personality that is in line with the bad habits you've allowed yourself to fall into. Even your manners and language will take on a new flare dependent on the bad habits you've given yourself into. Many become sassy, using fowl language a lot. They become ill tempered, argumentative and quarrelsome, and before long people will begin to keep away, long time friendships falling away, relatives distancing themselves from you. If you look at this with an honest heart and take a good look at your own life, you can easily see the wrong in you life and what needs to be CHANGED. And I know there are many out there living in denial, saying hey there is no sin in a little pot, or some casual sex. I know them all for I've been there and done that, and I've learned one most important lesson in life. If what you are doing doesn't help to build you into a better person but diminishes the person you are then its sin. For whether you know it or not you are sinning for against yourself and against the temple of God which is again you, for it is in your soul where God lives.

Most of us will insist we don't need a priest or a rabbi or even a psychiatrist or a psychoanalyst to tell us what we already know about ourselves or about good and bad. Yet in reality we do need help from someone for most of us are fooling ourselves into believing all is well with us and we need no help. That we're no different than the next guy and everyone lives alike and does all things alike so we can't all be sinners. And yet the word of God says in Romans 3:23, *All have sinned and fall short of the glory of God.* It doesn't say just some sin, or it must be some others that sin for surely I don't sin, we've all heard all that mumbo jumbo. God's word says that we are all sinners and fall short of the glory of God. And you know yourself and deep inside you know the truth of yourself and that there is a sinful nature in you. What kind of sin you find yourself guilty of is not what's important for sin is sin, but what is important is that it's your sin separating you from God. And that is what repentance is all about. You deciding to make the changes needed in your life to make you a better person and likable and pleasing to God as well as to yourself. It is a commitment from you to you and to God, to stop the sins in your life that tear you life down.

Many say I shouldn't use the terminology of sin but sugar it up by using the word faults or something like it. But the truth is the truth so let's label it as it is. For whether I speak of my sins, your sins or sins in general, they're still sins. For it's this sin or sins in your life that is destroying you and keeping you separated from God. For many, sin keeps them blinded from seeing the truth of themselves and from acknowledging God. You always will suffer the consequences for your sins and if it goes on uncorrected will bring you to your death. Look around at your friends and relatives and associates whether in business, the work place whatever. People who have a disregard to morality, do as they want, ignore the needs of their loved ones, are self indulgent, evil, nasty, love to gossip, etc., always lose in the end. The end of their lives is so much worse than their beginnings. Even the bible warns us of this in Romans, 6:20-23, *When you were slaves of sin, you were free in regard to righteousness. So what advantage did you then get from the things of which you now are ashamed. The end of those things is death. But now that you have been freed from sin and enslaved to God, the advantage you get is sanctification. The end is eternal life. For the wages of sin is death, but the free gift of God is eternal life in Christ Jesus our Lord.*

So it begins with repentance making that commitment to God and to yourself to change your ways. Asking for God's help for you know you on your own can end the sin cycle of your life without his help. Then you will need time to allow the change to become a reality for bad habits aren't always easy to break. Trusting in God and letting him help you to change is the joint task needed to get you on the road to recovery. For none of us can do it alone, and strangely enough God alone can't change you if you are unwilling to change. So it's a joint effort to bring help to you and to help you to change. God is already there for you knocking on the door to your heart asking to let him in and he will help you and save you, BUT YOU MUST OPEN THE DOOR. You must make a short 12inch journey that goes from your brain (the flesh) to your heart (the soul) and open the door to your heart and to God. You must make the commitment to yourself and to God to want his help and work with him in changing your life around. And guess what he will work with you and you will change at a pace best suited for you to handle. In Rev. 3:20, Jesus says, *I stand at the door, knocking; if you hear my voice and open the door I will come in to you and eat with you, and you with me.* I mean think of this promise of God. He stands at the door to your heart and is knocking. This is going on throughout your entire life, God is knocking at your heart hoping that you will hear him and open the door. He's always there for you ready on the spot for that day you will open the door. And then comes the best part to those who hear his voice and open the door to their hearts, his reward. He comes in and saves your soul. You become born again in the spirit through the trust and faith you have given to God to save you. To admit to him yes Lord, I was wrong; I erred with my life and need you to change me into a new person. Cleanse me from all my unrighteousness and make me whole and pleasing in your sight.

In the book of Matthew, chapter 22:37-40, the Lord Jesus, told us that there are two great commandments of God were, *You shall love the Lord you God with all your heart, and with all your soul, and with all your mind. This is the greatest and first commandment. And a second is like it: You shall love your neighbor as yourself.'* On these two commandments hang all the law and the prophets. There is no mention of color, race, religions or sexual preferences, but just to love your neighbor as you love yourself. These are the two greatest commandments of God, greater than the Ten Commandments. Why, because as Jesus said on these two commandments hang all the law and the prophets. Imagine that, all the laws of God hang on the first two great commandments of God. They are both commandments to love. First commandment is to love God with all of our hearts, minds and strength. The second is to love one another as we love ourselves.

And if we do this, then what Jesus was trying to teach us will become a reality. That by our love for God and for one another will make all the laws of God become naturally imbedded in hour hearts. Imbedded by his Holy

Spirit and through this process we will learn to live and obey all the ways of God and live by his will for our lives. This is the life of the true believer for it's the life of a truly spiritual person.

Love is the key ingredient to everything including eternal life. Without love we can't put an end to bigotry, hate, violence and wars. Without love we can't be saved of God, for we can't please God or even be near to God. For Jesus to stand in our place before God, we must believe in him and love him with all of our heart, our soul and our mind. Remember Jesus so loved us that He willingly let himself be crucified on the cross to take on all of the sins of the world. For those who refuse to change their ways and end up rejecting God completely, theirs will be the pains of loss and a total separation from God. They'll have eternity yes, but an eternity in total separation from God, because they had "no love." Love my friend is the cornerstone of all life and without it life will cease to exist for then only chaos and mayhem can be the outcome. That's where this world today is at chaos and mayhem. How much longer can we go on before the end comes upon us? The solution is so simple and yet so difficult for most to do. It's as if we can't see the forest through the trees! Our Lord is waiting patiently for each of us to make a move towards him, but time is running out. Don't waste today for you can't count on a tomorrow. There is an old saying "yesterday is like a cancelled check, it's no good today for the money has been spent. Tomorrow is like a promissory note you can't spend it for you have to wait until tomorrow to get it. So therefore all you have is the cash on hand today, spend it wisely for tomorrow may never come. Amen.

CHAPTER THREE

DOMESTIC VIOLENCE AND CHILD ABUSE

Have you ever wondered how much your actions affect other people's lives? Whether it's happened in your family or a friend most of us probably know of cases of child or spousal abuse. Many of us are witnesses to the destructive nature of this type of sin and how it has destroyed the lives of its victims. I know that many people who are caught in the vise of this sin of repeated rape in the case of the children and repeated beatings in the case of spousal abuse, its violent nature, its hate and anger were often victims themselves at some time in their life. Or you life was seriously affected by it from being raised in a dysfunctional family. It's part of what's made you that way. Some others are trapped in their inability to control themselves in moments of stress and end up erupting in acts of violence against the ones they love. Proof of this is all across our country where domestic violence is one of the leading crimes in this country.

I feel that child abuse is what I call "the closeted sin." For it's the sin no one wants to talk about for in most cases it is perpetrated by members of ones own family. I know I've been there, a victim of both being sexually abused from the age of 4 until I was thirteen years old and also spending my childhood in a dysfunctional family with warring parents. My childhood was a virtual hell both in the home and away from it. As a kid in Brooklyn, going to school and trying to have a social life with friends after school often meant having to put your life in harms way. The city streets were a violent place. Most days meant having to fight my way either to get to school or to get home from school. There were youth gangs with teenagers of all ages one had to fight through, and too often blood spilled through the streets of Brooklyn. Just the lost of one child's life is too much to bear, in Brooklyn it was a frequent occurrence. In the 1950's in Brooklyn, gang wars were the norm in a war torn city and besides the dying many others ended up in prison. I myself had to get together with all the kids on my block and we formed a gang called the Tiny Tims. The oldest among us was I think 9 years old, but there was no other way for us to survive. We knew that we could survive in numbers but not on our own. Looking back now at those days I think how frightening it was for us for yes we were scared to the bones. But we were tight, we were brave like the musketeers and together we would fight to the end to protect each other.

At home life was much like the streets. My parents fought like cats and dogs one minute and were passionate the next. Often the fights went as far as my father hitting my mom violently and me hitting on my father to try and stop him. This always resulted in our moving out to my grandmother's house until my parents found a way to reconcile their differences. Gratefully they always did, except when I was thirteen years old and they had the fight to end all fights. He hit my mom pretty bad, but I jumped in between them with a knife in my hands and grabbed my father saying to him "no mas (no more), this is the last time you hit her. If you ever touch her again, I'll kill you." I was overwhelmed with fear that day, for the fights had escalated to a level much too violent and I feared for my mom's life. We moved away and I stayed on with my grandmother while my mom moved to California, to start a new life for us. I refused to go for I loved both my parents and could not choose between them, so I stayed with my grandmother and lived with her for three years.

My parents remained separated for almost three years and in that time I discovered the wonders of love and how it can heal broken and damaged hearts. I continued to see my father on weekends and he never stopped supporting me and he would take me home every weekend to spend them with him. He never missed a weekend and his love for me grew so very deep that we were more than father and son, we were now best of friends. He could talk to me and me to him about anything. For the first time my father saw me in a new light, I was no longer a child but he saw me as his son all grown up into a man. He began to respect me and grew to love me with a father's passion I had never known. What brought us together was my openness to love him in spite of everything that had happened and to forgive him. Through this newly found love with my father we began to look like a family again, only my mom was missing from the picture. As he and I grew closer and closer, he found his way back to my mom. They had lived all their married lives in a common law marriage. When they reconciled their marriage they both agreed to honor my request that they get formally married by the church. And so it was when I was sixteen years old I walked my mother down the isle to give her away to my father. We settled down in Los Angeles after that and they lived happily ever after.

This dysfunctional life at home was complicated by the fact that I was also being sexually abused from the age of four until I was thirteen years old. One of my relatives and one street gang member were sexually abusing me. I was imprisoned in a heart of bitterness and anger between being sexually abused, seeing my parents at constant war and then having my own wars in the streets with the local gangs. The bitterness and emotional scars stayed with me in my travels until I was around 40 years old. It nearly destroyed me hadn't it been for the love and mercy given to me by Jesus Christ on his first visitation to me. He came bringing me all his love for me in spite of what I had become. I, who had lost my faith in God, fell at his feet with a heart of thanksgiving and dedicated the rest of my life to following Him.

Thank God I was one of the lucky ones who never became an abuser of children or fell into a life of crime in an attempt to revenge the pains I had suffered as a child. I found freedom from the shackles of this violent nature through the constant soul searching of my heart. Although unknown to me at the time, love was the nature of my being and I could never resort to any criminal lifestyle even if I had tried. For me it could never be an eye for an eye. The best decision I had ever made in life was to endure the suffering and to continue my soul searching in my heart through all those years for some relief, a healing that could make it all go away. Fortunately for me it brought Jesus Christ into my life. I wasn't happy with myself for I had spent the better part of my life punishing myself and blaming myself for all the mishaps in my childhood.

Another problem was that I didn't want to spend the whole of my life blaming everyone including myself for the misfortunes that was befalling me in my adult life. It used to drive my crazy for I know blaming myself or anyone else wouldn't give me the healing I was looking for. I lost too many years losing opportunities to better myself, get a good education because I was too busy punishing myself. I wanted relief yes, but more I wanted a freedom so I could start loving and enjoying my life. And I searched within for days that led to weeks to months to years to finally that wonderful day when Jesus Christ came into my house to visit me and set me free. I believe that much too many of society's problems have gone unresolved, unhealed for we spend too much time running in the wrong direction, blaming ourselves or others for our situations. Seeking the help of doctors, ministers and counselors to help us and always coming up short. Not that I find any fault with doctors and psychiatrists, absolutely not they're fabulous people doing unbelievably great works for man. But man offers a medical solution to a problem that needs spiritual healing. A little soul searching can go a long way to curing oneself especially when it brings God and new life into your heart. When one finds a spiritual path for one's life guided by the spirit of God, one then finds the cure for all that ails him no matter what it may be. After Jesus finding me and bringing a new life of salvation he then taught me the secret to my healing and that was to do a most simple act on my part. It's called "forgiveness!" Strange you may think, but yet it was the right answer, the only answer. I needed to forgive the evil doers in my life from the bottom of my heart for only in forgiveness could I then redeem my life, find peace and then find love. Without Jesus and his teachings I don't think I would have made it to today. The damage was very deep, yet now the scars are healed and I can look back without hate, without bitterness but with love.

We must start the process of finding our way back to ourselves, and to the truth that lies within us and with God. These are areas where medical science can't help us because we're the ones who must help ourselves. You can't get cured if you don't know you're sick or don't think you're sick. The bible says in Romans, 3:10-24, *No one is righteous not even one. No one is truly wise; no one is seeking God. All have turned away; all have become useless. No one does good, not a single one. Their talk is foul, like the stench from an open grave. Their tongues are filled with lies. Snake venom drips from their lips. Their mouths are full of cursing and bitterness. They rush to commit murder. Destruction and misery always follow them. They don't know where to find peace. They have no fear of God at all.*

But now a new righteousness from God, apart from the law, has been made known to which the Law and the Prophets testify. This righteousness from God comes through faith in Jesus Christ to all who believe (to all meaning all people of all races and religions around the world). There is no difference. For all have sinned and fall short of the glory of God, and are justified freely by his grace through the redemption that came by Christ Jesus.

That's where God and His truth steps in to shine the light on you and your problems and illuminate the pathways to healing for you. It took much time to heal me, much time for me to forgive others as well as myself. In the past twenty years since my first visitation with Jesus Christ much has happened. As the Lord was blessing me and teaching me the way of God, he also had to have me deal with my karma, the law of cause and effect. During those years I've had to undergo eight operations. Five were for kidney stones that required one month of hospitalization in the hospital each time and on one of them I fell into a coma that lasted three days. Beyond that an operation for a broken ankle, a heart attack which was miraculously healed while in intensive care for three days, a brain operation for a benign tumor and then prostate cancer. I was operated for the prostate cancer, but the operation turned out unsuccessful due to unforeseen complications of my having too many scars from previous operations and the fact that the doctors found too much cancer inside me. I was told to get my affairs in order for there was nothing the doctors could do for me. I was going to die from prostate cancer. Needless to say my heart nearly stopped beating, I felt like the life had been drained out of me and I was falling into a deep crevice. Yes I was scared to the bone for I didn't want to die and yet here was this reality from these doctors. Do I accept what they say and go home with my lover and just prepare myself to die. How does one prepare oneself for death? My mind was swimming in a whirlpool of confusion and despair. I didn't want to scare my lover and be strong for him, but I was failing at that. He actually became my strength, my rock and would be the one to fight on my behalf. He didn't want me to die either and was determined to talk to every doctor on Long Island if necessary to find help for me.

And my lover succeeded where all the doctors failed for they didn't know Jesus Christ and he had other plans for me. He sent us a young urologist who had read my case and said to me "if you can put your trust in me, I think I can help you." He explained the treatment of radiation beam therapy and estrogen injections. It was no guarantee, but there weren't many choices for me and he felt it would work. Well I'm no rocket scientist so my answer was yes I will trust you for I want to live. And thanks to God, they treated me with 48 radiation beam treatments and with estrogen injections and it's been 6 years and no more cancer. These were hard lessons for me, but lessons I needed to learn and to understand. God was not only there to teach me and guide me through it all but also He gave all the miracles needed each time to heal me and keep me alive.

Remember this and remember it well. Our goal in life is not to save the life we have on earth as it will always be a temporal life and we must shed this body which is designed to last a short time. Our goal is to save our eternal life which never dies and that can only be achieved through Jesus Christ. I have learned this lesson well and will never again let myself fear for my life for I am God's child and my desire is to live with Him in His eternal kingdom.

Always keep seeking and never stop looking, for God does hear you and will help you and in time you will hear God. Which I know is a law of life, which today is better known as "keep on keeping on" which in the bible can be related to the woman with the hemorrhages. In Matthew 9:20-22, the bible says, *then suddenly a woman who had been suffering from hemorrhages for twelve years came up behind him and touched the fringe of his cloak, for she said to herself, if I only touch his cloak, I will be healed. Jesus turned and seeing her he said, "take heart, daughter, your faith has made you well." And instantly the woman was made well.* Amen to that. You see the principle. She lived in misery and pain all her life, and chose to finally do something about her situation and reached out from the darkness in her life and stepped into the light in faith to Christ and by faith God restored her to complete health.

Believe me I know it works, I'm proof of it. As they say been there, done that. For I battled against all my demons from the sexual child abuse I suffered to the bigotry I had to endure as a Latino and as a gay man. I was lost in a world of sex, booze and drugs, depressed and unhappy with my life. It was all I knew to hide from my problems, to escape. Being a teenager I just couldn't deal with all the hate and the bigotry. I wasn't mad because I was gay but I was bitter and hated God for allowing all that abuse on me.

When the sexual abuse stopped after ten long years, I turned to prostitution and remained in that life for many years. So for 38 years I dwelt in the dark side of my life, growing more depressed and bitter as I went through a series of failures in every aspect of my life from jobs to relationships.

I lived in rebellion for the fact that I felt cheated in life. I was tormented by questions of my homosexuality and whether it was a natural selection in my life or was it an acquired way of life as a result of the child abuse. I was further tormented by all the hate thrown at me for being Latino coupled with the bigotry and hate spewed by the church against all gays. Too often I was denied jobs when applying for jobs or denied promotions at companies I that I was working for because of my race. I had the talent and the knowledge to do the work better than anyone else, but because I was a minority I couldn't get the promotion or the job I was applying for. To add insult to injury, many times I was asked to help train the one promoted over me for they didn't know the job well enough. I was fighting wars on all sides, which I allowed to drive me into a rebellious state where by choice I then chose to live in the dark side of life. Yes I was sinning against God and that was obvious, but what wasn't obvious to me at the time was that I was sinning against myself, against my own soul and thereby I was destroying myself. My spirit was dying because of my self-induced neglect of myself. I became an abuser of myself, whoring myself where ever and with whom ever. I soon began to hate God and the churches for excluding or better excommunicating me because I was gay and I hated society for not including me as an equal citizen but treated me like an outcast, for Latinos and gays weren't welcomed in this country. This went of for many years of me constantly seeking answers about my situation, where my happiness lied, could I be who I am and accept my homosexuality as a natural way of life. I for sure had no answers to any of it be it the child abuse or the homosexuality, but I began to constantly search within my soul for answers. I was gay and nothing would change that but I wanted to be free of this mental anguish, the question that always remained foremost in my mind. Was I gay by natural selection of genes or was it as a result of all the child abuse I suffered through? Jesus once said that only those with something to hide live in darkness, loving the sin. But those who are spiritually reborn, having the sinful nature depart from them, no longer having anything to hide then come to the light to live under the care and guidance of God and His Holy Spirit. Somewhere inside me I knew I had a little faith, however little it may have been, but I had faith to believe I would find the answers and the healing to my life.

Then on one glorious day it happened, all my questions, my doubts, my angers quenched in a moment in time. That wonderful day came when I was 38 years old, I was home alone one quiet Saturday night, eating supper and ironing clothes to go out that night to a local disco while watching the Olympic Games on television. Jesus Christ walked into my home to save my soul. I didn't see him face to face but he called out to me that night very audibly "my son, my son I love you and want you to follow me." Unfortunately I was alone and no one was there to witness this event, but my first impression was of alarm or scare. I can't remember exactly but it seemed that both fear and excitement riddled through my mind and my heart. I looked around for where that voice could have come from but all I could hear was Jim McKay, commenting on the games over the television. Then the voice called out again saying "my son, I love you and want to talk to you." I jumped ran to the television and shut it down. I stood there and listened as the house was quiet now, not a sound could be heard. I then yelled out "if anyone's there speak to me" for I thought maybe it was the ghost of my father who had passed on. Then the voice called out to me again "my son, my son, I love you and want you to follow me." I started to tremble and my mind was racing with a thousand thoughts of whom it could possibly be and then my heart leaped up in my chest and I felt my heart saying it's Jesus. Tears started swelling in my eyes when I called out "is it you Lord Jesus", and he answered me "yes my son and I came to tell you that I love you and want you to follow me from this day on." I fell to the floor crying like a baby, saying "Lord Jesus, is it really you?" He answered me saying "yes my son, it is I and I come to tell you how much I love you and want you to follow me." I then said "oh my Lord, how can you come to me a man so filled in filth and sin. I'm so dirty I'm so ashamed of myself and what I have become." The tears flowed all over the carpet like a waterfall as I was releasing years and years of torment and pain. Jesus then replied with a love beyond all my understanding "my son because I love you, and want you to follow me." I was overcome with gratitude and humbleness as I bent down to what seemed like to kiss his feet. A joy I had never known leaped up inside of me as now for the first time in my life I had an answer. I knew for sure, God was real and alive and that he loved me as I was, a gay man. He came for me to save my life from near death and brought salvation for my soul. He brought new life into my heart and soul and my spirit came alive with new and eternal life. I answered him saying "oh yes Lord, I will follow you to the ends of time, but you know me, I'm such a weak man filled with sin and filth. You know I am going to fall back over and over in this walk with you. How can I do it?" And he simply answered me saying "just follow me and I will show you the pathway for your life and I will raise you up and teach you the word of God." I said to him "yes Lord you know I will follow you for all eternity, but I'm a weak man given easily to temptations and will stumble and fall often on this journey with you. Why not pick yourself someone else more able and strong." And he replied "I will be with you all the way throughout eternity and when you fall I will lift you up, as often as needed I will lift you up and even carry you, just you follow me." And so I have ever since. It's not been a perfect journey but becoming more like my savior with each and everyday that passes by and the good news here is SO CAN YOU! By faith he healed the woman with the hemorrhages after 15 years of battling with the disease, by faith he healed me after I continually kept knocking on the door to my soul seeking and searching for answers. And so can you. Notice the one thing both that the woman and I had in common that saved us is that we never gave up and somewhere deep inside of us we believed. We both acknowledged and believed in God. Somehow the years hadn't destroyed our faith within and there was always hope. The first thing I did was to acknowledge his deity and I receive him as my God. The next thing I did was to acknowledge all my sinfulness to him and he forgave me my sins and has since led me on a world win journey of my life. Has it all been up, absolutely not, as I mentioned before being forgiven doesn't mean you don't pay for the wrongs of your life. Your karma is out of sink and can only get in sink by the law of cause and effect. So yes I did the great payback with the numerous illnesses that resulted in my having eight operations (two for cancer) and a heart attack. The good news is that as bad as it was God was there and brought me through and I recovered beautifully from them all. My family and friends think I'm like a cat with nine lives. They are all certain that I am called of God to work for him, which is where this book comes from. But whatever the reason I give all the glory to God, the author and finisher of my faith. For even all this that I endured was a minor issue compared to his mighty work in restoring my life. I came through every operation with flying colors for always through it all I had put my faith in God and He with his love and patience broke my vessel of clay and with His hands he remade me into a beautiful vessel in His image. And this is what I bring to you, this which God has done for me He will do for you no matter your faith, your religion, your nationality or your sexual preferences. The Father in heaven is interested in the salvation of every child He has on earth and folks there are six billion plus of us here on earth. Get the message?

I say this earnestly and with all the strength I possess in my being that God is alive and well and working with millions upon millions of us. Healing us, forgiving us and saving us for his eternal kingdom. What He's done for the multitude of us he is waiting to do for all. It's His free gift to all of us, to heal us, to bring us mercy and grace and save our eternal souls and to fill us with His Love. He will heal, forgive and change your life around but only if you let Him in. I am not trying to offend anyone by mentioning Jesus so frequently in this book. But I must make this point clear to all. Whenever a miracle happens in anyone's life in this world, it is Jesus giving the miracle to that person. Whether it's a healing miracle from a dreaded disease or a salvation as in my case with the visitation from Christ Jesus or a miracle that saves your life from a serious accident where one should have been killed, Jesus Christ was the one bringing the miracle. I have never heard of anyone else stepping down from heaven to give miracles, not Moses, not Abraham, not Elijah, not Mohammed but only Jesus Christ.

Another point I would like to mention here is this it wasn't my intention to give witness of my life, but that I felt it necessary for you to have my testimonial. I know the best testimonials are the one's coming from people who have suffered and endured much pain in life and through the help of God have found their way out of it. So I felt compelled to give some witness of my old life so that you can understand where I came from and to where God has delivered me. This was His gift to me and it's His gift to you, if you are ready to reach out and save yourself. The journey, the search begins from within. May you have blessed journey, amen.

CHAPTER FOUR

HOMOSEXUALITY RIGHT OR WRONG, GOD IS THE JUDGE NOT US!

I'm writing a special chapter for gay people who through the ages have been the object of scorn, ridicule, bigotry, hate and both physical and emotional abuse and to include their genocide as happened in World War II. They have been separated from the mainstream of society and by the churches, all stemming from political and religious bigotry. The message here is, don't let the politics, nor the bigotry and especially not the religious fanaticism of others steal you from your place with God. For what defines sin in a person's life is not by "who" you are, but by "what" you do? Today being no different than the past several thousand years, Gays are condemned as sinners for just being gay. Yet being gay just identifies who you are which is no different than one saying they are heterosexual. The teachings in the church and temples in this country is so contrary to the teachings of Jesus Christ. For you cannot be a sinner for being what you are no more than a Black man is a sinner for being born black, or an Asian man for being born yellow or a heterosexual person for being heterosexual.

Matthew 15:17-20 explains sin best as it's explained by Christ himself. Jesus says, *Don't you see that whatever enters the mouth goes into the stomach and then out of the body? But the things the come out of the mouth come from the heart, and these make a man 'unclean.' For out of the heart come evil thoughts, murder, adultery, sexual immorality, theft, false testimony, slander. These are what make a man unclean; but eating with unwashed hands doe not make him 'unclean.*

For what defines sin is not who you are or how you were born, but by what you do with you life for what you do in life emanates from your heart. People whether they are straight or Gay, living their lives cleanly onto God, will be judged righteously by God. On the other hand if you live you life a sham, filled with lust and sexual immorality, crime, hate or whatever else that is evil, then yes you are a sinner whether you are straight or gay. Sin has no distinction and respects no man. We're all sinners before God for none of us are perfect but one, God himself. As we see in the book of Romans 3:23-24, *All have sinned and come short of the glory of God; they are now justified by his grace as a gift, through the redemption that is in Christ Jesus.* No one except the Lord Jesus Christ was born and lived a righteous life without sin. But thanks to God who made a way out for all sinners, that through repentance and faith in Christ we all have redemption for our souls. And redemption is truly a key word both for us and for God for He is the redeemer who sets us free from our sins. We on the other hand must show true repentance of the heart when we ask His forgiveness and his salvation. I remember when I was first visited by Jesus, I felt so filthy and unclean as my sins were instantly before me and my heart was broken for what I had become and made of myself. Psalm 51:1-13 describes my sorrow before Christ Jesus and what then turned into the desire of my heart without myself knowing or realizing it, *Have mercy on me, O God, according to thy loving kindness: according unto the multitude of thy tender mercies blot out the stain of my sins. Wash me clean from my guilt. Purify me from my sin. For I recognize my rebellion; it haunts me day and night. Against you, and you alone, have I sinned; I have done what is evil in your sight. You will be proved right in what you say, and your judgment against me is just. For I was born a sinner — yes, from the moment my mother conceived me. But you desire honesty from the womb, teaching me wisdom even there. Purify me from my sins, and I will be clean; wash me, and I will be whiter than snow. Oh, give me back my joy again; you have broken me — now let me rejoice. Don't keep looking at my sins. Remove the stain of my guilt. Create in me a clean heart, O God. Renew a right spirit within me. Cast me not away from thy presence; and take not thy holy spirit from me. Restore unto me the joy of thy salvation; and uphold me with thy free spirit. Then will I teach transgressors thy ways; and sinners shall be converted unto thee."*

In Psalm 103:8 it says, *the Lord is merciful and gracious, slow to anger, and plenteous in mercy.* And in verse 12, it says, *As far as the east is from the west, so far hath he removed our transgressions from us.* I mean it just doesn't ever get better than that. No matter what you do in life, what you accomplish, nothing gets better than to know the mercy and forgiveness of God for yourself. It's your guarantee of eternal life in the Kingdom of God, and that's one guarantee you can take to the bank.

Moses is credited with the writing of the Pentateuch, the Torah. These are the first five books of the bible, which God gave to him on Mt Sinai, for the nation of Israel. Within these books were all the laws for the nation of Israel to follow if they were to serve God and be His people. The book of Leviticus contains many of the laws God gave them. One being, it is wrong for man to lie with another man as he does with a woman, or another stating that its wrong to commit adultery, and another stating that it is wrong to sleep with your relatives no matter who; parents, grand parents, uncles, sisters, brothers, etc. Incest was sinful and punishable by death be it whether you slept with your siblings, your relatives or your parents. It was also sinful to eat pig, rabbit or any animal that didn't have a split hoof and chewed the cud. Adultery was punishable by death. It was a sin to wear garments made from two different kinds of fabric. Any sort of cheating on one's spouse was punishable by death and also the sexual acts by people of the same sex. Even to curse one's parents was a dreadful sin and also punishable by death. All these don'ts and if you broke the law was punishable by death. Yet here we are thousands of years later and these laws have been put to rest. No one is killed for breaking these laws and most aren't even considered sins in the world today. So then how come gays are still being condemned? Mainly because they are different, just like black people are different. Does this mean gays are free from all sin, absolutely not? They are responsible for their own lives and must answer to God for the wrongs they do in their lives, but they will not be judged just because they are gay but will be judged by what they did in their lives.

Looking back to Adam and Eve, the first two people on earth and all of us being the descendants of them, how then one would ask, did the world get populated if not by incest? Then again if we also go back to when God destroyed the entire world by water saving only Lot and his family, again, how else did the world get populated if not by incest? They were the only ones living in the entire world. Yet incest is a forbidden law of God given to Moses. Consequently we must come to understanding that the laws of God are conditional in many cases dependent upon the need of His people. Sure God is the same yesterday, today and forever, but many of His laws are conditional. The same applies to the law man should not lie with man (Leviticus 18:22). At that time in history, Israel wasn't even a small nation but more of a tribe of people. Homosexuality although widely accepted throughout the world then would only hurt the small tiny tribe of Israel from growing into a large prosperous nation. So then the law stating that man shouldn't lie with man as with woman became a law of God for that time. However curious is the fact that the law didn't stipulate women lying with other women as they do with men. So the obvious conclusion then is that women didn't pose a threat to the growing population needs of the new nation. Also note that although considered sinful by many today, incest back then was the norm for society. For it was through incest that the world became populated from Adam and Eve, with brothers and sisters and then cousins marrying one another. Also one must take note then that homosexuality itself wasn't the sin, but the endangerment of the birth rate for this young nation. Take note also that incest, which wasn't a sin in the beginning, now was declared a sin as the world was now well on its way to becoming populated. So there was no more need for incest, which from what we can tell now was allowed conditionally to populate the world.

Then somewhere as the years went forward, none of these sins were considered punishable by death anymore. Yet no where's in the bible is there an account from God, saying the sins listed in the Torah, are put aside and yet put aside most of them were. Yes if you commit adultery, curse your parents, commit sexual immorality, you have committed sinful acts, but no longer punishable by death. Therefore the question arises that if put aside all the sins of Leviticus except the one involving men laying with men, by who's authority do you do so? And if you put all those sins aside then you must put them all aside. You can't pick and choose. This is probably why as man evolved in this world it was determined that repentance and sacrificial acts at the temple would cleanse one from one's sins. Then moving forward we come to the age of the New Testament, and the teachings of Jesus Christ. He taught us that if we believed in Him that He is the son of God, and we repented through faith with a true change of heart that we would be saved.

We also take notice in the New Testament that the laws against eating pig, rabbit or shellfish or any animal outside of those stipulated in the law of Leviticus, were rescinded. For we now live by faith and times have changed, so all meat is permitted for food. This takes place in the New Testament in Acts, chapter 15, where we find a declaration of fact to rescind the old law.

Then with one sweeping hand the apostles rescind the written laws of the Old Testament, putting forth the new law that salvation is by faith, by one's belief in Jesus Christ and the repentance of one's sinfulness. Prior to that we were given implications of such a change from the written law to the one in which we live by faith. This is shown when Jesus said that nothing consumed from outside the body causes one to sin, for it doesn't go to the heart but leaves the body as waste. But what comes forth from one's mouth originates from one's heart. This is where sin lies. And then we have the dream of Peter who while in a trance saw a sheet descending from heaven. On it was placed before him all manner of four footed beasts, wild beasts, creeping things and fowls of the air to eat which were formerly forbidden. And a voice spoke telling him to eat, that they were now declared clean by God for all to eat (Acts 10:11-12). So here again we see that laws are conditional and subject to change as God deems it so.

Looking further on into the history of man and of the bible, the law that a man shouldn't lie with another man was never again mentioned in the bible, yet all the other laws still remain to this day. Incest is still a sin, illicit sex, prostitution and fornication are all still sins and they apply to heterosexuals as well as homosexuals. The difference being that they are sins one commits against oneself as well as against God. For you are defiling the temple of God, which is in each one of us, for it is God's dwelling place. But homosexuality is a lifestyle in itself no different than heterosexuality. Lived properly according to the will of God, you are then as much a part of God as anyone else. Salvation is for you as much as for anyone else. God never intended to exclude Gays from salvation nor does he exclude Gays from salvation. God hates all sin this is true, but He hates the sin no matter who commits it, heterosexuals or homosexuals. God doesn't judge us as sinners because of who we are, but by what we do for it is by what we do that was conceived in our hearts. For who we are be it Jewish, Chinese, Hispanic, Black, Gay or White has no bearing on the heart of God, but what we do with our lives does for all our evil deeds come from our hearts where sin dwells.

When we examine ancient history one discovers that homosexuality was a common and accepted lifestyle right through the Roman Empire, including Israel. It was never mentioned by any of the apostles or by Jesus Christ, as being sinful, yet it was all around them. Only the apostle Paul mentions it in his letter to the Romans, not because homosexuality was a sin, but because to leave one's normal lifestyle to engage in sex with another lifestyle not normal to one Paul considered it sinful. Paul, only addressed this to the Romans, and never mentioned it to any of the other cities he traveled and preached too or wrote his letters too. This was because it was common for the Romans to live bisexual lifestyles and frequently maintained two homes. One home was for their heterosexual marriage where their wife and family lived. The other home was for their gay marriage where they kept their young lovers who were male servants they castrated to keep as lovers. So these men married with wives and children, were keeping lovers on the side and Paul felt the need to address this form of adultery as sin, for it was still adultery whether it was with a woman or another man.

We know this for there were gays living openly and commonly accepted all over the known world where Paul preached, but he never addressed them as sinners nor had a need other than to treat them and preach to them as he did everyone else, as equals. Paul wrote many letters to his Christian brethren as one finds in the bible with letters to the Corinthians, the Ephesians, the Galatians and the Philippians. In none of them does he mention any problems with homosexuality or singles them out for any reason. So one can only conclude that the problem in Rome was a unique situation to the people of that city.

We can also conclude from this, that it was man in his religious bigotry that declared all gays as sinners and separated them from God and the church. Consequently sin which we call sin today is not so much what God has called sin, but what man has redefined as sin through his bigotry and religions doctrines. This is why today we all find ourselves belonging to hundreds of different religions, believing in a quandary of different doctrines and religious rules and yet believing in the same one God. For the Jew its Jehovah, for the Middle Easterner it is Allah, for the Christian it is God, one God, the same for all but our religions and beliefs differ tremendously. Yet each one be it Hinduism, Buddhism, Christianity, Judaism, Islam or whatever, claim to be the right church to lead you to God. If so then we have a great problem for none of them agree with one another and only one can be right. Then if one is right then the world has been lied to for all the others are false religions leading their people astray from God. Now you know why the world is such a mess and at the verge of going into World War III. Religion has been the one catalyst to separate the people of the world from one another and cause such friction and disagreement between one another that we have been at war with one another from the very beginning of man on earth.

Therefore care must be given to whom we give ear to in the preaching of God's word. For much of what is taught in our different churches, in our different faiths often boils down to the understanding of God by the one doing the preaching or the teaching as the case may be. Religion also acts to govern and dominate groups of people with religious doctrines that they created as they decided to interpret the word of God. They take from God's word what they want and reject the rest. This creates a serious problem for it creates religious bigotry or prejudices, turning man against man. Many men of the cloth in all religions have preached their bigoted and hateful ways from the pulpit, thus causing many to fall away from the church and from God. That's why Jesus warned us not to follow the blind, for if the blind follow the blind both will fall into the ditch. Or in other words both will be lost. Religion is good, but it cannot save your soul and no religion on earth is perfect. If preached in a church, synagogue or temple spewing hate, or false doctrine from what is in the word of God then you are in danger of losing yourself by following such preaching. When what is being preached at a church or temple isn't the love for all people and the inclusion for all people, then flee from it for it has nothing to do with God. None of us have any excuse for not knowing the word of God. To place all your faith and belief system in God based on the preaching and teaching of the various religious leaders of the many faiths in the world is wrong. They are men and interpret the word no better than you can yourself and besides too many of them are politically motivated to teaching the doctrines of their religion and not of God. The bible is available to all people not only in English but in most languages throughout the world. There's no excuse for not knowing the word of God for you can buy bibles in any bookstore around the world. Ask anyone who has read and knows the word of God, and they will tell you that yes indeed it is more informative and a lot different from what's preached from the pulpits across the world. It's free of religious doctrines and religious political views. It's free for your own interpretation and God will be there with you inspiring you and teaching you His holy word. Staying in a hotel for a few days, usually you will find a Gideon's Bible in the night stand? Take it home and read it, it's there for you to have.

No one has no right to preach separation from church because of a person's lifestyle, or because of a person's sinning nature, or because of the color of you skin nor for any other reason. No one should preach to you the separation from family, friends because of their different faiths, color, sex or any other bigoted reason. That's not a church of God but more like some off the wall cult. For the church of God is open to everyone including the sinners for how else would a sinner get saved if not by God? How are we suppose to help one another in finding God, in finding healing and salvation if we separate ourselves from those we deem unequal? For there by the grace of God go all of us sinners all, even worse than those we separate ourselves from. Our memory is short to remember how merciful God was to us when we were dead in our sins. For as Jesus says in Luke 6:36-37, *be ye therefore merciful as your Father, is also merciful. Judge not, and ye shall not be judged; condemn not, and ye shall not be condemned: forgive, and ye shall be forgiven.* Jesus also said and the first shall be last and the last first, therefore in God's eyes we're all equal. Neither should they be preaching condemnation of people because they are of a different religion than your own, as I've seen so often in born again churches. Preaching that you can no longer maintain relationships with Catholic relatives and friends for they are all sinners and will cause you to lose you salvation. Boy how many times have I heard those comments made and preached in born again churches. From such as those flee, for they have become the Pharisees of today's modern churches. They are blind leaders leading you astray from the truth of God, who is all loving and all forgiving to all who repent and receive Him, into their hearts. The best advice I can offer anyone is this read your bible for yourself. Pray before reading it, asking God to give you understanding and knowledge of his holy word, whether you read the Holy Bible, the Kings James version or the more modern English translations. Please do it for yourself and for your family, then no one can ever deceive you for you know the truth of the word of God for yourself and the word will set you free!

Another issue that needs exploring is sex. Sex was meant to be part of one's expression of love toward another human being as well as the method used for procreation. Unfortunately we've allowed love to be confused and perverted through the ages with prostitution, lust, perversion and degradation turning it into a sinful thing. For thousands of years man has been indulging himself in the lustful pleasures of sex. More and more as we come forward to modern times, sex has had more and more of a strangle hold on many people throughout the world. So intense is this lust for free sex that sex has become a billion dollar industry throughout the world, bringing along with it a multitude of diseases culminating today with AIDS. Contrary to what some may think AIDS isn't a gay problem, but a people problem as heterosexuals are just as promiscuous as gays. AIDS was discovered in the African continent among the heterosexuals first before it spread its venom around the world People were long indulging themselves in the lusts of sex and had brought prostitution and sexual idolatry even into their churches and temples all the way back to the time of Moses and before then. Even in the Sinai desert many of the Jews still turned away from God and brought sex and perversion to the altar and began to worship false Gods, after having received the multitude of miracles of God to free them from the clutches of Egypt and then to receive the Torah written by the finger of God, given to Moses on Mt. Sinai. God then destroyed all the evil doers and sanctified his people once more.

Back then God had become disgusted with man's aberrations and his lust for sin, for committing perverted, degrading and immoral acts. Man had become selfish and greedy on top of it and had lost his way with God. His focus was solely on the pleasures of his flesh in those days and an end of it all was imminent. God decided to put an end to the world with the great flood saving only those he felt were righteous. In this case only Noah and his family were found to be righteous. And who determined who the righteous would be, only God and only God decides who is righteous.

Make note here that being gay wasn't the problem in the world that brought on the judgment of God and the great flood. But that all men and women were filled with so much sinfulness that it went beyond what God could put up with. When God, intervenes as he did here it's because man has reached a point of total loss. He had become totally separated from God, choosing his own god's to serve or choosing himself as god. He had given himself over to a life uncaring and of inhospitality to others and his only concern is the self—satisfaction of his physical or fleshly needs.

All through the ages people have suffered the consequences of their sinfulness and their perverted ways of living. Romans 6:23, St. Paul states that the wages of sin is death. St. Paul also says that we do reap what we sow in this world. Not may reap, but will reap what we sow in life. *Do not deceive yourselves, for God is not mocked. For whatever a man sows he will reap. For he that sows to the flesh, (worldliness) reaps corruption; but he that sows to the Spirit shall of the Spirit reap everlasting life (Gal 6:7-8).* If one chooses to live one's life based solely on worldly values. A life filled with sin, hatefulness, lusts, perversions, and greed. Then yes, you will always reap the whirlwind for the rewards of that type of lifestyle and of sin is the death of your soul, a separation from God brought on by yourself. We all deserve better than this and God made a way out for all of us through faith in his Son Jesus Christ. For through our repentance of our ways and acknowledgment of Christ as the Savior, He will send us the Holy Spirit to teach us and guide us to a new spiritual and righteous way of life. It's not impossible, for nothing is impossible for God. I know, for he saved me from the shell of my existence and raised me up as His child. Yes I am a new creation in Christ, and no longer do the things I used to do, but do that which the Holy Spirit of God has taught me and He will teach you if you give him a chance with your life. You are probably thinking will the change come instantly and the answer to that is yes and no. Your salvation is secured in Christ, but the changes you will be making in your life for some will be instant and for others like me it won't be as fast. Some of us have deep pains or wounds to heal and they take more time but healed you will be.

I think we can conclude from all this that sin in all its forms is a powerful force over man whether its sex, drugs, murder, stealing, greed, selfishness or whatever one does that becomes habitual and destructive to one's life. If you tried it once and found you were able to walk away from it, feeling this wasn't right for you then amen, you've listened to the spirit in you. You're a person who prefers life in the spirit guided by the light in you, the light of God. You've maintained your own spirituality in God as the dominant force in your life. But on the other hand, once you've indulged into the dark side of yourself and find that you enjoyed it and go back for more the vice gets a hold on your life and doesn't let go. Whether its sex, drugs, money, stealing and oftentimes its something unnoticeable like power or pride, you're hooked into main line sinning. Remember Lucifer was an arc angel of God before he became Satan. His sin wasn't something so terrible like murder but something simple as pride. It was pride that destroyed Lucifer and caused his fall from heaven. Whatever it is that gets to you and turns you on to the dark side, it gets a hold on you and you're hooked. The pleasures and highs you get can't be satisfied and you need more and more, just like a junkies hooked on drugs. Before you know it you've developed a bad habit, you're addicted to this thing that tears you life down. This has become your new god in your life who controls and destroys your life.

You see sin comes in many forms, but we choose not to see it. We've become accustomed to the many sinful things in society that we no longer see them as sin anymore. The shock value is gone out of them. You hear people saying everyday, what's the big deal? Everyone is doing it. And yes many are doing it but not everybody. We should also note that sin as well disguised as it's become in today's society that it is accepted often as the norm in society and yet it still does kill the soul. And as it says in the bible "the wages of sin is death", and we have millions of lost souls buried in cemeteries, people who died in their sins, lost and dead souls. If all these so called OK things were truly OK, then they wouldn't kill people. People never die from too much love or too much kindness, but they do die from overdoses and abuse, neglect, hate and the multitude of sins that kill one's soul. Put simply if something causes death flee from it. If you're caught in a situation where you can't get out of then pray for God to keep you from all harm and free you from that situation.

Since the middle ages or what some prefer to call the Dark Ages, gays have become more and more the scorn of societies. But it wasn't always that way. For back in the time of Ancient Rome, homosexuality was an open and very accepted lifestyle. Many men lived openly in gay relationships and gay marriages all through the ancient world from Greece, throughout the Roman Empire. Many of the leaders of the world back then from the Caesars, to the ministers and saints of the church were gay men.

Many men believed it to be the preferred life of a man, but they maintained separate homes for wives to have children with and otherwise lived with their husbands in their gay homes.

Homosexuality came into disfavor only in the middle ages, when a few prominent leaders of the world and the church had decided as homosexuality wasn't for them, then it shouldn't be for anyone else. The church controlled the laws in many countries (and still do to this day), and the contents and publication of the bible, chose to create their own doctrines of societal living and made it the law of the church and other religions followed suit until it became a common acceptance.

Well coming from man and not from God, I think we can see how man got off on the wrong foot. For as history has shown us, man with all his knowledge, science and technology has always been preoccupied with himself, with power, with money and with his own self-satisfactions. His major contributions to the world have been the advancements in science, technology and all the inventions that have brought the world to its present day and WAR, and the art of killing one another in massive numbers. And from these great minds we are to allow ourselves to be guided and ruled in life? No way, its time to realize that we do have someone who is perfect and can lead us to a righteous life and that person is God himself. Why trust in imperfect men whose primary interest is in control and domination over the masses for their own gains, when you can trust in one so great as God who gives to all freely and without obligation all that you need for a complete, healthy, happy and fulfilled life.

Man has been so fouled up in his thinking wanting to do everything his own way with no need of God. His wanting to be his own god or making fool hardy gods of political and religious leaders, or the wild imaginations of his mind knowing that they want only to control and defeat him. Look at what's happened to the world today, a complete collapse of our economy because a handful of greedy politicians and bankers and investment CEO's. Their greed betrayed them and God exposed them for what they are. Then they take the taxpayer's money to undo the errors and greed of their ways, so they can go back and continue to deceive and rob the public. And now we're expected to believe that the leaders of the world today are perfect and righteous and have our best interest at heart and will work to total equality for all including gays, blacks, latino's and other minority groups. I think not! From such as these we should all flee, vote them out of office, imprison the guilty and take back the money they stole and remove them from their thrones and ivory palaces and put the righteous, the loving to run this world.

We see how easily politicians can persuade and mislead us. During his campaign for president, Mr. Obama, promised us to be a president of change. One who would change the status quo, change the way government did business and save our country from ruin. Well he's been president close to five months now and what have we learned of our president. He's politics as usual, old time politics of big government, big spending and what else, more taxes. And according to the news he plans now to introduce a "value added Federal Sales Tax" of 25% on everything we buy from food to whatever. Well if things aren't bad enough with millions losing their jobs, now a new Federal sales tax of 25% plus the existing state sales taxes will make shopping a thing of the past. For the working class and poor will have no money except for essentials and even there will have to cut back seriously.

One needs only to look back to the Dark Ages in this country's history as I call it. From the birth of our nation which was founded on the quest for liberty, religious freedom and freedom from all oppression. Europeans fleeing their homelands to come to this new land of America the land of milk and honey only then to turn around and spew their hatred for Blacks, for the American Indian and for all people different in color. The white man would travel to Africa, to kidnap the Blacks from their homes to enslave them as prisoners to a life of slavery, brutality and death working the farms of rich white men in America. The white man also came to the New World, and killed and destroyed an entire nation of American Indians, for his own selfishness to possess the land for himself. Why couldn't we share America, with its original inhabitants, whom to this day live in concentration camps (but to save face we call them reservations) and are treated as nomads.

What's so amazing is that back then even the Catholic Church and her Pope's had huge armies, marching to wars against other nations. They were killing innocent people in the name of God? During World War II, the Catholic Church and the Pope befriended Hitler and Mussolini. Yet they would stand as judges, pillars of the church and the community deciding who is and who isn't sinning? Creating and formulating the doctrines of the church for all to follow and obey as if they were so righteous, I don't think so. I myself was born a Roman Catholic, but I fled from the church at the age of thirteen, never to trust or believe in their religion again. I found their doctrines unbearable and too strict to be coming from God. I found them to be hypocrites telling us to live one way, while they did as they wished as if they had special dispensation to sin. Considering the many visitations I have had with Jesus Christ, I know I've made the right decision. But I'm not here to condemn the Catholic Church they already do that best on their own. Just look at the scandal of their priests abusing young boys by the hundreds and probably thousands while the church covered it up for decades and probably for centuries. There is not way one could or should even put any trust in these leaders in society.

But there is an answer for all of us whether we're gay or straight and that is to keep our eyes and minds on God and trust him with all of our hearts.

God is the truth, the light and the way for all of us. Give him all your sins, and problems and bad habits. With the mouth confess what's in your heart admitting to Him, Lord I'm lost and cannot help myself and I need you to help me and to please forgive me for my sins. I'm truly sorry and do repent of my ways. Please Lord Jesus, come into my heart and become the Lord and Savior of my life. Help me and fill me with your Holy Spirit, and teach me. Help me make a whole person of myself that both you and I can be proud of. Thank you, amen. And believe me that prayer is probably the hardest thing for anyone to do, to humble oneself before God and confess one's sinfulness. To come to the cross and be broken as the Lord was broken at the cross. That whether you are gay or straight you want God to help make you the best you can be.

I know being gay myself how tough it's been to live in a society that hates gays and keeps us out of the mainstream. Where the churches teach and preach that homosexuality is a sin and use the bible as the authority in this. Well this is wrong teaching and not in the word of God. It doesn't say anywhere in the bible that being Gay is sinful. As a matter of fact the bible only speaks of Gays a few times. In the book of Isaiah, Chap. 56:4-5: where God speaks to Isaiah, *For thus says the Lord unto to eunuchs that keep my Sabbaths, and choose the things that please me, and take hold of my covenant; even unto them will I give in mine house and within my walls a place and a name better than of sons and of daughters: I will give them an everlasting name, that shall not be cut off.* The eunuchs were men who were castrated or born without testes and used as chambermaids to guard their master's harems. Others were used in the service of their masters to provide sexual pleasures for their masters who used the eunuchs as sex tools to avoid sleeping with their own wives. This was a method of birth control to avoid having too many children and for others who were bisexual and needed male companionship. The eunuchs, many of them being gay men, enjoyed the arrangement as it made them a mistress of their masters, providing for them food and shelter and all the comforts of home.

In Matthew, Chap. 19, verses 10-12, the disciples were talking to Jesus, learning about the rules for marriage. In this Jesus concludes his teaching stating in verse 9, *and I say unto you, whoever divorces his wife, except it be for fornication and shall marry another commits adultery. And whoso marries her that is divorced commits adultery with her.*

His disciples said to him, *if such is the case of a man with his wife it is better not to marry.* But he said to them, *Not everyone can accept this teaching, but only those to whom it is given. For some are eunuchs because they were born that way; others were made that way by men; and others have renounced marriage because of the kingdom of heaven. The one who can accept this, should accept this.* In other words most people will never accept this teaching of remaining unmarried even though God does. For the Lord knew man had too many prejudices to accept this teaching of the eunuchs, which they knew included homosexuals as well as heterosexuals. Consequently this teaching although right with God is for those who can understand and accept it in their hearts.

So here we have a definitive statement from the Lord Jesus Christ, himself. He states that being gay in and of itself is not a sin, as he knew that many eunuchs were gay also. We know this by his statement saying "not everyone can accept this teaching, but only to those to whom it is given." Well now, if all eunuchs had been heterosexual there wouldn't have been any problem of the churches accepting them and accepting this teaching. But the Lord says, not everyone will accept this teaching. Why do you suppose? Obviously because they wouldn't accept gays, what else? If the eunuchs had all been heterosexuals then there would have never been a need for the Lord to mention this teaching, it would have been an obvious conclusion. But many if not most eunuchs were gay men and they would not be accepted and the Lord knew this.

Whatever is man's problem in accepting gays remember this one most important fact. You aren't forgotten and are as much a part of God, as are all the people in this world who are believers in Him. You too, are a child of God. Always remember that God loves you whether or not man does. I wouldn't concern myself with whom man chooses or chooses not to love seeing where man is coming from and what he's managed to do to this world. So then the problem is for the churches to accept gays and to stop the gay bashing from within the churches. For when our churches, synagogues, temples and other holy places open their doors to gays and to all people of color and race will acceptance begin to happen in the mainstream of society bringing a final end to all types of bigotry and true freedom for everyone.

Man has always wanted to believe homosexuality is a chosen way of life and not a lifestyle born out of natural selection. But now we have the word of God saying not so, that being gay can be a part of the natural selection of life as well as it can be from a forced lifestyle through abuse. So being gay isn't a sin just because of you're being gay like heterosexuality isn't a sin for those who are heterosexual. It's what we do that determines if we sin or not.

Besides we can all use a little commonsense in how we regard or treat homosexuality. It doesn't take much to realize that no one in their right mind would chose a lifestyle like homosexuality when the results would be to live a life of ridicule, abuse, separation and denial of equal rights. It's obvious that the gay person had no choice in their lifestyle but it came as a natural way of life for them or as a result of sexual molestation as a child. Do you consider becoming a heterosexual? No of course not and that is because its not your natural way to be just as it is with homosexuals not desiring to be heterosexual as it isn't their natural way to be. It's time that man examine and search his heart for the truth and the word of God and not accept cart blanche what is preached from the various pulpits throughout the world or the bigotry that spews out of the mouth of men. Test every spirit, every doctrine and every dogma. If it doesn't line up with the truth and it doesn't line up with the word of God, don't accept it and don't obey it and don't apply it to your life no matter who is preaching it. Remember if you allow yourself to be deceived even by the ministry, you must account for it by yourself. For Jesus said if the blind lead the blind, both will fall into the ditch. Meaning even though you were duped or deceived into believing wrong dogma and you lived and acted upon it you are still responsible for yourself.

The word of God is available to all to read and learn and know the truth of God. This applies to all dogma and doctrines of the churches of which there are so many. We must ascertain that they are sound and rightful doctrines/dogma and that they are in alignment with the word of God. It's time for gays to find churches to go to and go in big numbers. You need to make your presence felt in the churches and force them to deal with you the gay brethren. If a church can't deal with gays, it has no right being a church, for gays are part of the family of God. I say to all gays, put on you Sunday best and fill the pews of all churches, synagogues and temples and show the world that you will not be excluded from the church as God has never excluded you from Him. No matter if your Jewish, Christian, Muslim, Islamic or whatever. Get back into church and be proud to be a child of God. Pray about it to the Lord and he will lead you to the churches best for you to go to.

So when one says that homosexuality is a sin because it's against the way of normal men. I would ask you what is normal in the way heterosexuals live. Does anybody have it right? Shouldn't the right way of living be judged by God, remembering that the word of God testifies that all have sinned and fall short of the glory of God? And if nothing good comes from man, then why is man being the judge of man. I think it's time for heterosexuals to get off their high horses of religiosity and stop judging what the homosexual world is or is not. There is enough sin in each and every one of us that we don't need to meddle in other people's sins as if we were their gods. Let God be God, and who alone has the power to save the soul will do so no matter who we are heterosexual or homosexual. Jesus says it best in Matthew 7:1-6, *Do not judge, so that you may not be judged. For with the judgment you make you will be judged, and the measure you give will be the measure you get. Why do you see the speck in your neighbor's eye, but do not notice the log in your own eye? Or how can you say to your neighbor, 'Let me take the speck out of your eye, while the log is in your own eye? You hypocrite, first take the log out of your own eye, and then you will see clearly to take the speck out of your neighbor's eye.*

Let's take a look at what the word of God says about sexual sin. In 1Cor, 1 . . . 16 the bible says, *Do you not know that you are God's temple and that God's Spirit dwells in you? If anyone destroys God's temple God will destroy that person, for God's temple is holy, and you are that temple.* Also in 1Cor, 6, 16-20 the bible also says, *Do you not know that whoever is united to a prostitute becomes one body with her? For it is said "The two shall be one flesh" But anyone united to the Lord becomes one spirit with him. Shun fornication! Every sin that a person commits is outside the body, but the fornicator sins against the body itself. Or do you not know that your body is a temple of the Holy Spirit within you, which you have from God, and that you are not your own? For you were bought with a price (when Christ died on the cross for all of us); therefore glorify God in your body. Consequently sins of fornication apply the same both to heterosexuals and homosexuals, do them and you sin against your own body, which is a temple of God.*

Believe me you have to be born gay to be able to endure the bigotry and abuse that goes along with it. Or you would have to have been a victim of child abuse for some years, which formed your life as a gay person. Either way you have no other choice; you cannot change yourself into something you're not. Just like people of color cannot change to be white to please the white man. We are what we are from birth. That society and the church hate it and find it sinful is their wrongful perception of things and their wrongful interpretations of the scriptures. Society says that homosexuals are whores, doing immoral acts and living perverted lives. Not like society itself. Well yes some gays may be like that but they are a small minority of the whole gay population. Most gays live normal lives, work 9 to 5, pay taxes, and make a major and prominent contribution to society. Most of all they seldom commit the crimes that are committed in this country everyday. Besides the sins of immorality, fornication and perversion are even more prevalent among heterosexuals than with homosexuals. Just take a look at this country and all the peep shows, and strip joints there are besides all the street prostitution that goes on, but I wouldn't label heterosexuals as whores and perverts for this again is but a minority of all people who do this.

Then we have the crimes committed in this country and truly they are a heterosexual problem not a gay one. For heterosexuals commit the majority of all crimes in the world today. They control the governments of the world, the corporations of the world and the armies of the world. When there is war, and there is always a war, it's a heterosexual decision and off we go to killing and maiming one another in the name of some holy or political war. That's a heterosexual male mentality that is totally foreign to gay people. Gays don't build the weapons of warfare including the atomic bombs that someday will destroy the world, heterosexuals do.

Then there is this blaming of the Aids epidemic on gays which is totally unwarranted and unfounded. The disease is believed to have originated in the African continent. The people affected worldwide are mostly heterosexual not homosexual. The Christian churches label it as God's vengeance on Gays. Yet gay woman never get the disease unless they practice unsafe sex with unclean males or do intravenous drugs with unclean needles. Therefore do we conclude then that Lesbians are the chosen of God? Well the answer to that is yes they are, but so are you, me and all of us gay or straight who do the will of God. We are all his chosen ones for the kingdom of heaven.

Then there are the infamous quotations from the scriptures, that the clergy always uses in their preaching that it is a sin to be gay. I will begin with the Old Testament, as it was written first and stands today as the bible of the Jewish people.

Leviticus 18-22, *You shall not lie with a male as with a woman; it is an abomination.* Yes I think that is straight forward, and in Lev. 19-13, it says further they both should be put to death. But so also is the sin of uncovering a woman who is pregnant and revealing her nakedness, or incest, or stealing. You shall not lie to one another, or give false witness and the list goes on and on. Taking a more careful look at the scriptures here is a sampling of what you will find as the laws of God, written in the book of Leviticus.

Leviticus, chapter one says we must sacrifice animals at the altar for the atonement of sins. Well we no longer do this today. Obviously man did away with this law even though it was God's law for man. Either the Jewish people changed the law on their own, or it was just ignored as time went on but definitely many of the Mosaic laws are not being practiced anymore. The question then is, are we in sin for not complying with the Mosaic laws, as it's shown in the bible? Later on I will show how Christianity resolved this issue by declaring that the Mosaic laws would not apply to Christians.

In Leviticus, chapter 19, the law of God says you shall not sow your fields with two kinds of seed. Nor shall you wear a garment made of two different materials for these are sin. Again, man did away with these two laws as I guess man felt what the heck, they weren't important enough to keep. Yes they were God's law back then, but aren't practiced any longer. But again aren't they sins if they're in the bible? A good question don't you think? Well if not sin anymore, when did it stop being a sin?

In this same chapter 19, it also says you shall not eat anything with its blood. Well obviously this law didn't last too long with man, for today it is common to eat beef with its blood in the meat. Many people all around the world love rare meats on the plate. Is it sinful? Think about it, for obviously this too is no longer a sin today!

This chapter also says one should not practice augury (fortune telling, parapsychology), for this is a sin punishable by death (vs. 31). Well no one today would be putting any psychics to death and further more many in the world today believe in the work performed by psychics and fortune tellers. We praise the work of Nostradamus, Jean Dixon and Edgar Cayce, and the many accurate prophecies they left us of the future. But whether we believe in them or not, we don't condemn and punish them with stoning as indicated in the bible. Here again, we no longer treat this as sin and we no longer put these people to death. So when did this stop being a sin?

Leviticus, chapter 20, says adultery is punishable by death and so is all forms of it, whether with a stranger, a neighbors wife, or with a relative. It also says that mediums and magicians are sinners and should be put to death by stoning. Do you think magicians are seen in this light today? As men worthy of death by stoning because their practice is considered sinful. Of course not and even more we find magicians invited to church fairs to entertain the congregation. So when did magic stop being a sin? It's in the bible then obviously something changed over the centuries. And that's my point, something changed to remove the sinfulness from many of these acts and consequently much of the Mosaic laws, don't apply to us today. Not even the Jews are practicing many of the Mosaic laws. Why do you suppose? I believe because these laws were contingent laws for the times that they were given when Israel was but a small tribe of people. These were laws given for the times to control and establish order for a very young, small, but growing nation. They obviously weren't meant to be laws for man to follow forever and have since been abolished. Then why are the churches holding on to only one of these laws, the one mentioning gays. If we put all the Mosaic laws to rest, then they are all at rest including the law pertaining to gays. Furthermore the Apostles put to rest all the written laws of he Old Testament, as man now would live by grace having faith in Christ Jesus, who would be the author and finisher of our faith. So let us now examine this new ruling. As history in the bible has shown, the Mosaic laws were too burdensome and no one in Israel could ever obey them all. So why then put such a burden on Christians. So the apostles decided that no such burden would be placed on Christians, who were saved by faith in Jesus Christ, and Christ now lived in their hearts. So as we see in the book of Acts, Chapter 15, the apostles including Paul, have decided that Christians, would no longer be subjected to the written laws of the Old Testament. No mention of homosexuality at all and probably because all through the ancient world homosexuality was viewed as a normal lifestyle along with heterosexuality. Both lifestyles stood side by side throughout the Roman and Grecian empires, which was the entire known world then. Therefore as we see from the New Testament, the Apostles abolished all the Mosaic laws.

Consequently the law against gays was abolished with the rest of the Mosaic laws. The question remaining is, was this the right thing to do? Must be for the bible has been written and cannot be changed or altered after that. As the bible closes, it closes with a warning to man from Jesus Christ himself. Rev. 22:18 John solemnly warns everyone who hears the prophetic words of this book, *if any add anything to them, God will add to their punishment the plagues described in this book. And if any take anything away from the prophetic words of this book; God will take away from them their share of the fruit of the tree of life and of the Holy City, which is described in this book.* So there you have the final word. What's been forgiven is completely forgiven by God and it is written and cannot be changed. So all people heterosexual and homosexual have the same rights with God the father and the salvation of God is open to all people, bar none. It's a free gift of God to all who believe in Him, be you straight or gay.

Homosexuality was never mentioned as sin in the bible but doing homosexual acts by heterosexual men, which was against their natural way was mentioned as sin as one can see in the book of Romans, chapter one, in the New Testament. To leave one's wife to sleep with one's male servants was the sin mentioned in the bible in the book of Romans, as this was a common practice in ancient times throughout the Roman world. But no where's in the bible does it say man must not love another man or woman must not love another woman and form any bonds of unity or marriage. I believe this is because God honors all relationships that are monogamous founded in love and spiritual unity, as any good marriage is whether it is a heterosexual marriage or a homosexual marriage. That's why God included the story of King David and his relationship with Jonathan. Then there's the story of Daniel and the chief eunuch all of these beautiful gay relationships of people God loved and never condemned. With one exception and that is King David whose life was filled with sinful acts especially with his coveting Uriah's wife Bathsheba, which ended in David committing murder and adultery. But what was the most important issue in David's life, the murder, the covering of his neighbor's wife, the lying and cheating or the fact that he was probably bi-sexual. No, none of these! The most important issue in his life was the God knew David's heart and he had a heart that was sold out to God. So God knew David in his heart and although he had committed some very serious sins he was still a man sold out to God, and he repented of his wicked ways and God forgave him all his sins just like he will forgive all of us who repent of our wicked or sinful ways.

In Romans 1: 21-27 the bible says, *for though they knew God, they did not honor him as God or give thanks to him, but they became futile in their thinking and their senseless minds were darkened. Claiming to be wise they became fools; and they exchanged the glory of the immortal God for images resembling a mortal human being or birds or four-footed animals or reptiles.*

Therefore God gave them up in the lusts of their hearts to impurity, to the degrading of their bodies among themselves, because they exchanged the truth about God for a lie and worshipped and served the creature rather than the Creator, who is blessed forever! Amen.

For this reason God gave them up to degrading passions. Their women exchanged natural intercourse for unnatural, and in the same way also the men, giving up natural intercourse for women, were consumed with passion for one another.

It sounds heavy and is, but it wasn't written to gays. Note in this verse it speaks of heterosexuals who are already sinning out of control with no care or concern for God. It's then that God gives them up to their perversions and they then are given to a degrading life. But they were first in their natural way, heterosexuals. If Paul had been speaking about gays, he would have then addressed it simply by stating that homosexuality between men or between women was sinful, but it doesn't say that at all. It speaks of heterosexuals who are throwing their lives away in sin as adulterers. And having no concern for God, were exchanging their natural way for what was unnatural for their life style. It wasn't written saying homosexuality is a sin, if so it would just say so. St Paul wasn't one to mince around with words. But in fact he wrote this letter to the Christians at Rome and to them only. Why, because it was a problem already existing among the Romans, but no where else in the world. We take note of this for although there was homosexuality all over the world including Israel, Corinth, Galatia and Ephesia among the many cities he preached in, Paul was only addressing the Romans, because it was a custom in Rome for the men (especially those who owned slaves and eunuchs) to have male sexual companions outside of their relationships with their wives. Many had both living under the same roof or others maintained separate homes for their wives and their gay lover. These were heterosexual men who leaving their normal way with the wives took to sleeping with their male slaves which was not the normal thing for them to do. It was adultery, which often resulted in men abandoning their families and their family responsibilities, families that they started themselves and soon thereafter abandoned. This was the sin being addressed here by Paul.

Does that mean gays aren't sinners? Absolutely not, they sin just like anyone else and need salvation, as does all of humanity. But they aren't sinners just by the fact of their being homosexual. The word of God says in Romans, Chapter 3:23, *all have sinned and fall short of the glory of God.* So you can see repentance and salvation is for all, the straight and the gay.

Another biblical story needing to be addressed is the story of Sodom and Gomorrah. All through our lives we've been told they were destroyed because of homosexuality. But homosexuals weren't the only citizens of these cities. There were heterosexual men and women such as Lot and his family as well as other families with children, grand parents, etc. How do we know this? The bible tells us in the accounting of the story. Lot's daughters were engaged to be married to young men of Sodom. These men were heterosexual, sons of heterosexual families who all died in the destruction of Sodom. Men, women and children all died in this destruction. Why, because they weren't righteous in the eyes of God, only the righteous was saved and that was Lot and his family. They were all destroyed both heterosexuals and homosexuals. If surely God hated just the homosexuals and was destroying these cities because of that, then He would have removed all the heterosexuals from the city as he did Lot. But He didn't, he removed only Lot and his family for only they were found to be righteous. Yet the Lord said to Abraham, before sending the angels to Sodom, that if they were as few as ten righteous he would spare the city. But there weren't even ten righteous and all both heterosexual and homosexuals were destroyed in Sodom. So right there it kills the theory that God condemned and destroyed the cities because of homosexuality. All through the centuries the churches have preached that Sodom and Gomorrah were destroyed because of homosexuality. When in fact we know that the truth was the complete opposite. Lot's family is proof of that, for the young men betrothed to his daughters surely had families there and they too were destroyed.

There is an answer about this also that we get from Jesus Christ, in the book of Matthew. Jesus tells us the problem wasn't homosexuality but "in-hospitality" by all its citizens. They were people of means, well being with wealth and luxury, but who had a total indifference to the blight and sufferings of the unfortunate. They were inhospitable to strangers and cared only for self-indulgence, merriment and good times. Now we can see the truth and it makes more sense.

Another point also needs to be made here. Back in the days of Sodom it was common in many towns and villages for the men of the towns to attack, sexually abuse and beat strangers coming into town. This was done to make sure that all strangers respected the citizenry of the town especially the town woman. Here is the point that Jesus Christ was making of these people about their in-hospitality to strangers. So in view of this revelation, who were the men that wanted to sexually abuse the angels of God visiting with Lot? They were all the men of the city consisting of both heterosexual and homosexual men, both young and old. We see this in Genesis, Chapter 19: vs. 4, which states, *but before they lay down, the men of the city both young and old, all the people to the last man, surrounded the house.* Right here you see that it was all the people of the city, men, women and senior citizens who came to know and abuse the angels. This isn't homosexuality, this is mob rule, vigilantism, and as Jesus Christ labeled it in-hospitality. Again, this was a common practice of the citizenry of these cities to attack, sexually abuse all male strangers entering their towns to teach them to respect the women in their cities. Could this have been what they were intending to do?

From this knowledge alone one can see how dangerous it is to accept the careless preaching from the many altars that preach hate, separation and discrimination of any of its people, heterosexual or homosexual. Surely this type of preaching isn't from God, and is unacceptable to God and has gone on for too many centuries leading their people astray. Don't be foolish allowing false prophets and false teachings to blind you from the truth or to lead you astray into false teachings. Go and get yourself a bible and pray and study it for yourself. It's printed in modern everyday English for those who don't understand the King James Version. Don't let yourself to be blinded by others but keep in mind what Jesus said, *It's the blind leading the blind and both will fall into the ditch.* So check the word of God out for yourself and don't lose your salvation because you followed the wrong teachings of a priest, pastor, a rabbi, an evangelist or whatever or whomever. Test everything that they teach you and make sure for yourself it lines up with the word of God. Just don't accept teachings or doctrines for granted. If it doesn't line up with the word of God, ignore it, don't accept it, don't do it and if you must then leave that church and go to one that does preach the truth according to God's word, then do it.

For when the day comes for you to stand before God on that judgment day, you won't be able to use that excuse that this is what was taught you. You'll be judged for you and how you treated and loved all your fellow men. If you allowed yourself to be misled and blinded by others, you'll not be able to use that as an excuse. You're still going to be held responsible for yourself. A word to the wise is sufficient.

Another point I would like to bring forth in this study of homosexuality. We turn to the book of Ezekiel, Chapter 16, vs. 49, *This was the guilt of your sister Sodom: she and her daughters had pride, excess of food, and prosperous ease, but did not aid the poor and needy. They were haughty, and did abominable things before me; therefore I removed them when I saw it.*

Again no mention of homosexuality, but the first mention was the sin of pride (the sin that caused of fall of Lucifer from heaven and then becoming Satan). Then it goes on to show their complete selfishness and disregard for their fellow man. Again a very inhospitable people who also committed sexual sins which I would believe were the abominable things they did before God. And I believe these sins were committed by both the heterosexual and homosexual people of those cities. If one goes back to the book of Exodus, which gives account of the story of Moses and the Jews leaving Egypt and wandering in the desert for forty years. You will find in chapter 32, that while Moses was visiting with God on the mountain top of Sinai, the people began to lose their faith in God and decided to create their own god made of Gold in the shape of a calf. They danced, drank unto drunkenness and did all kinds of lewd and sexual acts, so much so that God had them all destroyed and only the righteous went on to the promised land. So just like in Sodom and Gomorrah, God destroyed all those people because of their sinfulness and their complete rejection of God.

Furthermore, the bible does speak about gays very favorably in the Old Testament. It shows the love affair between David and Prince Jonathan son of King Saul. The love here truly shows that Jonathan was gay and completely in love with David and visa versa. For David so completely loved Jonathan more than even the woman he married, Jonathan's sister. For David says in 2 Sam 1:26, *Jonathan lies slain upon your high places, I am distressed for you, my brother Jonathan; greatly beloved were you to me; your love to me was wonderful, passing the love of women.* It seems that both men were gay living dual lives of being both gay and straight or as it's called today bisexuality.

So there you have it, the word of God concerning homosexuality. To all of you who are Gay, go for the brass ring and accept nothing less. Jesus is here today as he was always from the beginning to receive you into the kingdom of God. Don't let anyone, any church, any synagogue, any temple, and group religious or lay or political rob you of your place God. Test it for yourself. Don't take my word for it. Call on God for your own salvation meet with him in the closet of your heart. He'll be there for you as he has been there for millions of us. The Lord is no respecter of persons he loves us all.

And that's just the first step to your healing, to your freedom. This book is written from my personal experiences and from my walk with God today. My life was a really tough one and much too many people with their politics and religions tried to destroy all that I am. But I had a friend always in Jesus, who when the going got really tough for me, he came to save me and tell me how much he loved me. I'm completely devoted to the Lord and have surrendered my will and spirit to him. He lives in me and guides me through all of my life. My life has been so completely changed and I live a life filled with happiness and joy. My spirit soaring from glory to glory as the Lord leads me to my eternal destiny.

So much of this book is a witnessing and testimony of my life and experiences and from my walk with God. It is very hard for me to write about the hard times of my life, but necessary. For if I can help anyone out there it can only be with the truth as I experienced it. It's not the final truth, for only God has the final truth. It won't be the truth for some and yet the truth for others. Not all will apply to your life yet many parts will be very important to you. It's the truth as I experienced life both as a sinner and as a child of God. Digest it and take for yourself what helps you, but take hold of yourself and your spirit and make a commitment to do something good for yourself. To search within yourself to find the truths that lie in you. To find out the pains that still lurk there in the dark corners of your heart, pains, open wounds remaining unhealed. Call upon the Lord and ask him for help. There is so much we all suffer from both obvious to us and not so obvious. But the Lord can help us and deliver us from all of it. From the many other problems we face in life that tears us down and drives us apart. God provides the strength and power to endure, and the love to change all that's needed to be changed.

I know most of us find this concept hard to believe. Yet on the other hand most of us profess to believe in God. Well hello, if you profess to believe in God, then what God do you believe in? A god that's worshipped in churches and synagogues and temples alone, where we go once a week to pray and then leave and return to the sins, miseries and confusions of life. What help, what good is that doing any of us? If that is all that God is, then no one would have a need for God. Man has always been a quick fix person interested only in satisfying the flesh for that moment and then before long is hungry once again, and what good has that been? What we all really need to realize is that our souls require more satisfaction in life than quick fixes. Our souls need to grow. It's a process of learning, understanding and obtaining wisdom, which is continual and never ending. It's the most vital part of our life here on earth, but we're too busy feeding the flesh, with visual desires for money, fame, lust, sex, and material possessions.

We're hurting but won't admit it. We're unhappy and again won't admit it. We're afraid, always afraid of being ridiculed, laughed at. The world looks at those who follow and serve the Lord as sissy like, weak, unstable people. So as to save face we then do nothing, give in to peer pressures and follow the pact. It's the blind leading blind. You know what? Who cares what others think as long as you know you've made a commitment to finally help yourself making a commitment that will not only save your life and soul but will guarantee your place in eternity in God's kingdom of heaven. So if others want to laugh and ridicule me for my faith and love of God go ahead and ridicule me for I count it a joy to suffer for the glory of God. But one thing I know and I know for sure and that is that I have the promises of God for my life. God has granted me eternity with him, how about you? Can you claim the same? Don't let yourself be fooled or duped by the world, for it's you who comes out a loser in the end.

If you are gay, then become a spirit filled gay person. Allow God his place in your life, in your heart and in your soul. You'll never regret it and will live life to the fullness of your spirit in harmony with God. This doesn't mean an end to living, to having fun and enjoyment in your life. But you will when you learn to live your life in the spirit to enjoy your work, your career, your family and friends to the complete fullness of your heart. You will begin to find a peace and contentment in your life and able to ward off more stresses from coming your way. You'll find a new wisdom entering your mind and heart and find that you're able to help out others through this. It's a gift from God to you, for God gives us wisdom. Love will become a very real thing to you and become the most important part of your existence. It will unite you to your maker and to your very soul enabling you to truly see the world through new eyes that are filled with love for everyone.

Have you looked back at your life and taken note of the painful times and the affects it had on you and how you evolved as a person as a result of it? Or the affect it had on others around you, probably not? And like most people don't even want to go there and revisit the pain and sufferings anymore. Yet I think before we go on and put the cart before the horse it is necessary to explore these areas of our lives, for it's here were healing starts, forgiveness and mercy begin.

This is the purpose of the book, for us to look at pain, at sin, at misery, at hurt, at suffering, at abuse and see through our own eyes how we've been affected by these things in our own lives and how we affect others. Maybe you're the recipient of these things that caused ever-lasting damage to your heart and soul or maybe you're the one who did things to others causing these things to them. Open your hearts to the truth in your lives and face the pains and sins and hurts. Many of you may find you still hurt and I'm not surprised. I was sexually abuse from the age of 4 to 13, yet at the age of 38, when I first started to examine my life through the love that Jesus Christ, had given to me. I found to my surprise the immense pain I was in and the hatred that had been built up in me through all those years. But living as a worldly person, I could never see this in me and you know why? For I did as the majority in this world do, I masked it, hid it away in the depths of my heart where it could not bother me. I chose to escape into a world of drinking, drugs and sex, where I didn't have to face the truth, but run from it. I became revengeful and I turned myself into a tough guy who wouldn't be hurt anymore but would be the one to do the hurting. I would play my best cards knowing that I was quit the handsome young man and would take advantage of that. I lived hard and played hard and in the end almost lost my life because of the fool I made of myself. But God in His mercy came to me and saved me from myself making a new life for me completed in Christ Jesus.

I say put on the brakes on your life and stop right now, take a deep breath and a deep look at yourself, your heart and your soul. Don't be satisfied with what the world has dished out to you but demand the best, the things that last forever, not the quick fixes in life. Seek the riches of glory that God has promised all his kids. The fullness of the Holy Spirit to live in you and through you for all that you are and all that you do in life and that you want to know the truth and have the fullness of love in your heart and in your life. That you want to walk it, talk it and live it everyday as the natural way of your life. Say to yourself that I want to know that I know that I know that God has my place reserved in the kingdom of heaven for eternity.

And why do we all want this in the end? Because in all of our hearts whether we're students of the bible, or have no relationship at all with God we know that life is "eternal" and we will have to spend it living somewhere. There's heaven and there's hell, which is your choice? Some say there is no hell as spoken of in the bible. Yet the same people believe there is a heaven as spoken of in the bible. I say if you believe in God, then believe all that's written in the bible, for its God's legacy to us. It's the only source given to man in the history of the world that connects us to his word, his truth, and his love. No matter what your faith, what you walk is like or how much or little you believe all of us have only His book, His holy word to connect us to God. Maybe hell isn't fire and brimstone, but I do believe there is a death to one's soul as Jesus tells us. It could just mean eternal separation from God. Think about it and think about yourself. Do something good today for yourself and talk to God and say hello. I choose to call him God; you can address him in the best manner your heart can determine truthful to you. In either case I'm sure he'll understand and is more concerned with your communications with him than no communications at all, happy hunting for the truth, the whole truth and nothing but the truth so help you God.

CHAPTER FIVE

THE CREATION VS EVOLUTION—CAN BOTH BE RIGHT?

This is the age old topic that science and the church have argued over for almost a century. Ever since Darwin said that man had descended from the animal kingdom and later on science declared that the universe was some fifteen billion years old and started with a Big Bang. On the other hand the church says no way, God created the universe in seven days, actually it was six and He rested on the seventh day. And that too is another problem man should look into. Which is the seventh day of the week? Man says it is Sunday because man chose Sunday as the day of rest. Some rest, most businesses are open on Sundays with work as usual and money the primary reason for being open. Yet God gave us Saturday as the seventh day. Seems to me God knows best after all he created the whole universe and set the days of the week.

But getting back to the creation you can see the dilemma man has. Who to believe? Science sells its theory of evolution so well that most people accept it as fact and many have turned away from the church doubting in God and becoming disillusioned. Is this another one of those deceptions of man by the elite or is it fact indeed. Then Darwin tells us that in the process of evolution man descended from the animal kingdom, truth or fiction?

Then finally and foremost is the word of God and it should be the final word on the creation and yet it is not. Too many doubt its accuracy or truth. In my humble opinion I offer this that maybe they are all right or mostly right with a few exceptions, could that be a possibility? So where does one go to find the truth? I believe we must first explore their theories and test them against the word of God. So let's begin with the Big Bang Theory, it states:

About 15 billion years ago a tremendous explosion started the expansion of the universe. This explosion is known as the Big Bang. At the point of this event all of the matter and energy of space was contained at one point. What existed prior to this event is completely unknown and is a matter of pure speculation. This occurrence was not a conventional explosion but rather an event filling all of space with all of the particles of the embryonic universe rushing away from each other. The Big Bang actually consisted of an explosion of space within itself unlike an explosion of a bomb where fragments are thrown outward. The galaxies were not all clumped together, but rather the Big Bang lay the foundations for the universe.

Since the Big Bang, the universe has been continuously expanding and, thus, there has been more and more distance between clusters of galaxies. This phenomenon of galaxies moving farther away from each other is known as the red shift. As light from distant galaxies approach earth there is an increase of space between earth and the galaxy, which leads to wavelengths being stretched.

In addition to the understanding of the velocity of galaxies emanating from a single point, there is further evidence for the Big Bang. In 1964, two astronomers, Arno Penzias and Robert Wilson, in an attempt to detect microwaves from outer space, inadvertently discovered a noise of extraterrestrial origin. The noise did not seem to emanate from one location but instead, it came from all directions at once. It became obvious that what they heard was radiation from the farthest reaches of the universe which had been left over from the Big Bang. This discovery of the radioactive aftermath of the initial explosion lent much credence to the Big Bang theory. This information researched from the Internet.

Now for Darwin's Theory which implies but never comes out and says definitively that man descended from animals. To try to simplify this, evolution refers to changes in the genes of a species from one generation to another. This is caused by processes known as variation, reproduction and selection. Genes passed onto an offspring produce the inherited traits however offspring may also develop altered traits caused by either mutations in the genes or the transfer of genes between populations and between species.

Natural selection is one of the major processes which cause heritable traits to survive and reproduce and become common in a population or species and for unfavorable or harmful traits to become less common.

The other major process known as genetic drift meaning that probability plays a part in whether a given trait will be passed on as individuals survive and reproduce. The changes are subtle and small between generations but over a series of generations can cause significant changes in a population and eventually end up with a new species.

So we can conclude that evolution is a cumulative process of changes that occur in a population over a long period of time. These are genetic changes where genes mutate or recombine in different or new ways during the reproduction cycle and are passed down to later generations that will follow. Sometimes these new genetic changes will become predominant in an individual and become a frequent occurrence in other individuals while other individuals in the population show no inheritance of the new genes. Over a period of time those with the new inherited gene become the dominant group in a population and those without the new gene become less dominant and this process of evolution and change is known as natural selection.

Now science tells us this process of the genes going through new variations may occur randomly, but that the process of natural selection is not random at all. Sounds a little confusing I agree and that is because science has yet to be absolute in their theories. They are pretty sure this is how it works, but can't say absolutely yes. After all they aren't God, who is the only one who truly has the answer to all this.

Now the question arises does evolution negate the existence of God? Absolutely no, but it tries to explain how God may have done the creation for those who choose to believe in God. Science neither confirms nor denies the existence of God, but when it comes to evolution they deal only with subjects, their history and the major events science feels significant in genetic changes and the processes in this world.

So how does the word of God compare to all of this Big Bang and Evolution theories of man? Well that's where the differences between church and science gets really hot and has remained that way for over 100 years, when Darwin introduced his theory. But let me be one individual to offer his personal opinion on all of this and that I believe both the church and science are right with a few minor exceptions. I offer the following as comparison from the word of God, found in Genesis 1:1-2:23:

In the beginning God created the heaven and the earth. 2And the earth was without form, and void and darkness was on the face of the deep. And the Spirit of God moved on the face of the waters. 3And God said, let there be light: and there was light. 4And God saw the light, that it was good; and God divided the light from the darkness. 5And God called the light day, and the darkness he called night. And the evening and the morning were the first day. 6And God said, Let there be a firmament in the middle of the waters, and let it divided the waters from the waters. 7And God made the firmament, and divided the waters which were under the firmament from the waters which were above the firmament: and it was so. 8And God called the firmament Heaven. And the evening and the morning were the second day. 9And God said, Let the waters under the heaven be gathered together to one place, and let the dry land appear; and it was so. 10And God called the dry land Earth and the gathering together of the waters called he Seas; and God saw that it was good. 11And God said, Let the earth bring forth grass, the herb yielding seed, and the fruit tree yielding fruit after his kind, whose seed is in itself, on the earth; and it was so. 12And the earth brought forth grass, and herb yielding seed after his kind, and the tree yielding fruit, whose seed was in itself, after his kind and God saw that it was good. 13And the evening and the morning were the third day. 14And God said, Let there be lights in the firmament of the heaven to divide the day from the night; and let them be for signs, and for seasons, and for days, and years: 15And let them be for lights in the firmament of the heaven to give light on the earth it was so. 16And God made two great lights: the greatest light to rule the day, and the lesser light to rule the night: he made the stars also. 17And God set them in the firmament of the heaven to give light on the earth. 18And to rule over the day and over the night, and to divide the light from the darkness: and God saw that it was good. 19And the evening and the morning were the fourth day. 20And God said, Let the waters bring forth abundantly the moving creature that has life, and fowl that may fly above the arth in the open firmament of heaven. 21And God created great whales, every living creature that moves, which the waters brought forth abundantly, after their king, and every winged fowl after his find; and God saw that it was good. 22And God blessed them, saying, Be fruitful, and multiply, and fill the waters in the seas, and let fowl multiply in the earth. 23And the evening and the morning were the fifth day. 24And God said, Let the earth bring forth the living creature after his kind, cattle, and creeping thing, and beast of the earth after his kind; and it was so. 25And God made the beast of the earth after his kind, and cattle after their kind, and every—thing that creeps on the earth after his kind; and God saw that it was good. 26And God said, Let us make man in our image, after our likeness; and let them have dominion over the fish of the sea, over the fowl of the air, and over the cattle, and over all the earth, and over every creeping thing that creeps on the earth. 27So God created man in his own image, in the image of God created he him; male and female created he them. 28And God blessed, them and God said to them, Be fruitful, and multiply, and replenish the earth, and subdue it: and have dominion over the fish of the sea, and over the fowl of the air, and over every living thing that moves on the earth. 29And God said, Behold, I have given you every herb bearing seed, which is on the face of all the earth, and every tree, in the which is the fruit of a tree yielding seed; to you it shall be for meat. 30And to every beast of the earth, and to every fowl of the air, and to everything that creeps on the earth, wherein there is life, I have given every green herb for meat: and it was so. 31And God saw everything that he had made, and, behold it was very good. And the evening and the morning were the sixth day.

2-1Thus the heavens and the earth were finished, and all the host of them. 2And on the seventh day God ended his work which he had made; and he rested on the seventh day from all his work which he had made. 3And God blessed the seventh day, and sanctified it: because that in it he had rested from all his work which God created and made. 4These are the generations of the heavens and of the earth when they were created, in the day that the Lord God made the earth and the heavens. 5And every plant of the field before it was in the earth, and every herb of the field before it grew: for the Lord God had not caused it to rain on the earth, and there was not a man to till the ground. 6But there went up a mist from the earth, and watered the whole face of the ground. 7And the Lord God formed man of the dust of the ground, and breathed into his nostrils the breath of life; and man became a living soul. 8And the Lord God planted a garden eastward in Eden, and there he put the man whom he had formed. 9And out of the ground made the Lord God to grow every tree that is pleasant to the sight, and good for food; the tree of life also in the middle of the garden, and the tree of knowledge of good and evil. 10And a river went out of Eden to water the garden; and from there it was parted, and became into four heads. 13The name of the first is Pison: that is it *which compasses the whole land of Havilah, where there is gold; 12And the gold of that land is good: there is bdellium and the onyx stone. 13And the name of the second river is Gihon: the same is it that compasses the whole land of Ethiopia. 14And the name of the third river is Hiddekel: that is it which goes toward the east of Assyria. And the fourth river is Euphrates. 15And the Lord God took the man, and put him into the garden of Eden to dress it and to keep it. 16And the Lord God commanded the man, saying, Of every tree of the garden you may freely eat: 17But of the tree of the knowledge of good and evil, you shall not eat of it: for in the day that you eat thereof you shall surely die. 18And the Lord God said, It is not god that the man should be alone: I will make him an help meet for him. 19And out of the ground the Lord God formed every beast of the field, and every fowl of the air; and brought them to Adam to see what he would call them: and whatever Adam called every living creature, that was the name thereof. 20And Adam gave names to all cattle, and to the fowl of the air, and to every beast of the field; but for Adam there was not found an help meet for him. 21And the Lord God caused a deep sleep to fall on Adam, and he slept: and he took one of his ribs, and closed up the flesh instead thereof: 22Anmd the rib, which the Lord God had taken from man, made he a woman, and brought her to the man. 23And Adam said, This is now bone of my bones, and flesh of my flesh: she shall be called woman, because she was taken out of man.*

Now it's obvious that there are many differences between the creation given to us from God compared to The Big Bang Theory and Darwin's Theory of Evolution. Yet even in checking here there seems to be some similarities, we see from the very beginning in Genesis that the earth was formless and empty and darkness covered the deep waters. I believe that means there was nothing in the beginning and then God said let there be light and the process of creation began. This could have been and most probably is the Big Bang Theory which God himself started? Why not after all science has not a clue as to how the Big Bang started or what existed before there was a Big Bang, for there was a void, nothing, nada and science cannot figure out how it got going or who started the Big Bang. That's because science doesn't deal in faith or in the belief in God. Yet God filled in his absolute love decided to create man so he could have himself a people to love and worship him. To do this God first had to create a world for man to live in and thus God made the earth for man and the universe to serve man and the earth, but I'm getting ahead of myself. I will explain all this as we go on.

Science tells us the process of the universe took billions of years to form. From anywhere's of seven to fifteen billion years to be exact. And scientists tell us earth came into being ten billion years ago. Science insisting that it couldn't have been six days, but billions of years. Now in the bible codes it goes even further, giving more clarity to the creation, where God says in the codes that a day in the Lord was equal to about one billion years or more. That makes the earth a little over four billion years old, and the universe close to that which agrees with science and the Big

Bang Theory give or take a few billion years. I say give or take for scientist can only estimate the age of the universe claiming it to be between seven and fifteen billion years old, which agrees to God's statement that it took place over seven billion years ago

But one thing must always be kept in mind and that was that the creation wasn't by chance it was intended by God with the purpose of making himself a people to worship him and therefore everything was planned by God and everything and every one of us has a purpose designed by God.

In the word of God, there is an agreement to some of what science says. The earth is very old, but it was not a accidental creation of gases and rocks cooling in space and forming the suns, the planets and the moons. For if we accept science's theory then there should be many planets like earth throughout the universe with intelligent life very similar to what we have here on earth, but the word of God tells us science in this area is incorrect. For the earth was God's first creation, not the universe and we find this in chapter 1 verse 9, God tells us how he made the earth and called for the earth to sprout with vegetation of all sorts and trees and fruits and so on. That was the completion of the third day of creation. On the fourth day of creation God created the Sun to give light in the day and the Moon to give light in the night and also the stars and that was the fourth day of creation. So here there is an agreement that both the earth and the universe are old but earth came first then the universe. And why did the earth come first? Because God was planning a world for man to live in, and man remember was created in the image of God, which we can now conclude was the most important thing to God. And we can state with assuredness that there are no other intelligent life forces out there in the universe for man was created by God and the earth and the universe created for man. Otherwise we would just be one of many civilizations in existence.

I believe what has scientist stumped is the method of creation used by God. For science keeps telling us that there is no God because science can prove that evolution and the natural selection process was how everything including all life evolved both in the universes and on this planet. Now when we compare this to God's word; it's obvious to see that the whole creation process of God was done scientifically perfect. God used evolution for the creation for an orderly process plus one that was perfect in every way. So we start at a void, then came the light (the Big Bang), then the separation of the waters creating a sky and a planet earth, then the creation of the sun, the moon and then stars in the heavens all created to serve the earth, God's footstool.

God finally has his universe and his very next step isn't the creation of man, but its creating all the supportive life forms needed to support man. God begins first creating the sea animals to fill the oceans, and next he creates the birds to fill and fly through the sky. After that God creates all the animals that will live on the earth, and then comes the last two creations he makes which is man and woman. So we can conclude from all this is that God in all his majestic being, in all his majestic wisdom, knowledge and understanding that He would have to create a universe for man to live in that was created perfect. Created in a sequence of events that would lead one event onto the next creating a universe and a world where man felt he had a purpose, a belonging, a world he had control over and a free will to choose his destiny. It would have to be a world made perfect so that it could support man for his food but also a world perfect for man to live in, to grow and develop and to evolve in. Anything else would have made us all robots just being yes men to God and neither God nor man would have been happy with that result. Faith, hope and charity (love) would have never come into the world.

With that said we must now note that God created all creatures including man from the earth.

So there is a link there somewhere between man and the animals all being created from the earth, and from dust we came and to dust we return be it animals or humans. Therefore, with an open mind instead of all the feuding between science and the churches, we should be embracing one another knowing that there is a commonality to our beliefs with minor differences. That we are on the right tract and need just to know that the missing link in science isn't some strange little creature that existed fifty or one hundred million ago, but that the missing link is GOD! This is just like some of the differences we face in life today between one another or the differences we have between religions, all meaningless differences which divide man against man. We need to see the similarities and embrace one another in the spirit of God, of love and pray constantly for God to unite us in one belief, in one spirit as one people under God. Just think of the possibilities this could bring to the world: peace, end to hunger, freedom and equality for everyone, and cure for all diseases and an end to all suffering. There is no end to what we could accomplish in a world united under God. Can we get there one day, saving ourselves, our planet for today, tomorrow and forever. My answer is yes we can, but each one of us must be willing to start now, today to change our lives for the better. To begin a life in the spirit, under God and sure enough everyone throughout the world can one day have life, liberty and the pursuit of happiness.

Now for a more updated version of the creation of the universe shown on television on the History channel and I must admit this one left me speechless. A group of renowned and reputable astronomers, now state that our universe is finite and that beyond its wall exist another parallel universe exactly the same as ours. That this parallel universe contains the same galaxies and stars and planets as our universe and with a planet earth exactly like ours, in other words clone universes. That we each are duplicated or cloned exactly the same in that universe as we exist here, but probably living different type of lives. To go even further they claim there to be many universes all the same and all duplicates of one another. Consequently, according to these scientists we exist countless of times in all these universes. Well if scientists are now believing this new creation theory of theirs, then you can throw out The Big Band Theory, for in the beginning the big event exploding to create a universe would have had to create two, ten, twenty or hundreds of universes. Finally if we could even stretch our imaginations to conceive of the possibility of this, would mean one thing and that is that God is the creator of it all. For it would take an intelligent being to create numerous universes as they suggest and all clones of one another down to the intelligent life forms on all those planet earths. For then the random creation of a universe by their Big Bang theory becomes nonexistent for in random creation does not clones make. For such a thing to be guarantees there is a God beyond anything that science knows or will ever know who formulates and creates all these universes the same. Well I think we can best leave this theory of science as just that conjecture. This only compounds the problem of science vs. God, makes a mockery of science with so many theories and conjectures and little proof of any. The one thing we do know is Jesus Christ lived and died on the cross for each and every one of us. We know the history of man from Adam and Eve to man today and it can all be verified. That's enough for me and hopefully it is enough for you. Amen to that.

CHAPTER SIX

REINCARNATION AND KARMA

I've mentioned karma a lot and with it I should also answer the question of reincarnation. Is it real? I know that Christianity today doesn't believe in reincarnation although at one time they did. Not to get too deeply into it, but karma and reincarnation were the belief of the early Christian church. This until the coming of Saint Augustine, who brought us a new doctrine of his own which simply stated that God created our souls out of nothing and that we never were a part of God, and that each soul had only one life to live. Justinian, emperor of Rome liking what Augustine had to say (for it fell in line with Roman beliefs with their gods), changed the church doctrine to that which is accepted today in the Christian world, based solely on the personal beliefs of one man. All of the writings and teachings of reincarnation were removed when making the first holy bible. The same applied to all of the writings of Jesus. They too were destroyed not to be included in the holy bible. Consequently the actual teachings of Jesus are few to be mentioned in the New Testament. Yes we have the four gospels of Matthew, Luke, Mark and John. But the four say little more then to validate the life of Christ, giving us a biography of his life. Outside of the few teachings shown in the four gospels, not much more is known. Yet we know he preached to man for three years, yet all those teachings were destroyed and not included in the holy bible.

However now with the discovery of the bible codes in the Torah (as well as in the Vedas and the Koran) we know the truth from God himself. Karma is definitely a law of God to right the wrongs we do in life and we do have to pay back the wrongs no matter what. Also God shows in the bible codes that reincarnation is a true fact of life. We do come back as often as necessary to make right our lives until our karma is in sink and in balance with god, hence the ying and the yang. How often depends on us, and how long it takes us to get it right. You see God is our Father, and as a father his desire is to lose none of his children from Adam and Eve to you and me. He knows how bad some of his children have been down through history, but they are his children never the less. So God will bring them back over and over to live new lives, getting their karma back in sink by repaying the wrongs they've done until they get it right with God and learn to live a true spiritual life. Some may not make it in the end, but at least God gave them every possible chance. I know this for I believe I am living in my final reincarnation here on earth as my life was totally turned midstream by a visitation from Christ Jesus. I went from a hard line sinner to a man of God. Does that mean I didn't have to right the wrongs I did, absolutely not for since the day my life was turned around all forms of disease and illness fell upon me. Over the next twenty years of my life I've had to suffer much in getting my karma back in balance. It began with a heart attack, then diabetes, high blood pressure, underwent five kidney stone operations (being comatose in the last one for three days), surgery to remove a brain tumor and my last battle with prostate cancer. That one being as serious as it can get. My doctor operated me and found too much cancer inside and too much damage from previous operations that they closed me up. I was told to make arrangements for dying as they couldn't do anything for me. But they didn't know Jesus. Sure I went through hell some would say, but I rejoiced through it all for the glory of God. And God led me to a young doctor who asked me to trust him, that he felt he could save my life and 48 radiation treatments later all the cancer was gone. It's been over five years and I remain clean and healthy thanks to God. I never complained, for in my heart I knew this was payback for my nasty and sinful life. God was righting the wrongs with me and bringing my karma back in balance. God saved me through the heart attack, the numerous operations and the cancer. Today I live a healthy life filled with the glory of God because of His love for me. What's important to me is that I have cleaned my slate with God, and have accepted my punishment as just. That's how this book came into being. It was another visitation with Jesus Christ, who summoned me to write the book with the guidance of the Holy Spirit, as I was now ready to bring his message to the world having become a repented and changed child of God.

Even Jesus confirms reincarnation in the New Testament in Matthew 11:13 saying, *And if you are willing to accept what I say, he is Elijah, the one the* prophets said would come (speaking of John the Baptist). Where is the karma here you may ask? Remember the story of Elijah in I Kings, 18:21-40 where Elijah had challenged the prophets of Baal as to who was to be worshipped. Elijah comes to the people asking them in verse 21, How much longer will you waver hobbling between two opinions? If the Lord is God, follow him! But if Baal is God, then follow him! But the people were completely silent. The story goes on where Elijah challenges the prophets of Baal, to prove to the people Baal is God, and Elijah will prove to the people that the Lord is God. The challenge is to bring a bull to the altar for a burnt offering to God. The prophets (900 in all) bring their bull and slay it and put in on the altar for a burnt offering. They are not to set fire to it but pray to Baal to consume it. They do and nothing happens. Then Elijah, the only prophet of God challenging the 900 of Baal, brings his bull and places in on another altar. Elijah first drowns the bull with water and then prays to God and God consumes his bull with fire. Now all of Israel believes in God because of Elijah.

Elijah now orders the 900 prophets of Baal be taken down to Kishon Valley, where Elijah has them all killed by the sword. Now Elijah was one of the most important prophets of God, in his day. So righteous and holy that he never experienced death. Instead we see in II Kings 2, where the Lord takes Elijah to heaven in a whirl wind. However one must note that Elijah left earth with a debt unsettled. Even though God took him to heaven, he still had to do right of the 900 prophets he killed. And that's where we find him reincarnated as John the Baptist a very holy man of God, a prophet preparing the way for Jesus Christ. It is also here in this life as John the Baptist, that the karma had to be made right and John the Baptist, pays with his life as he is beheaded at the request of Salome to King Herod. So even a man as holy as Elijah had to repay his sin and because he was in heaven he could not escape his debt. God sends him back as John the Baptist, and the debt is settled. The final word on karma is from Jesus himself when he says, Put away the sword. Those who use the sword will die by the sword (Matthew 26:52).

Another account of karma in the bible is in the life of Moses, the greatest of all prophets of God. He was picked of God to lead the Jews from bondage in Egypt after four hundred years of captivity. He was a prince in Egypt, adopted son of the Pharaoh's daughter and was raised up in the court of the Pharaoh. In time Moses discovers his true identity of that being a Jew, and that his mother is his adopted mother and he begins to take compassion for the captive Jews. One day he witnesses an Egyptian beating one of his fellow Hebrews. Moses, after checking to make sure the area was clear killed the Egyptian and buried his body in the sand.

The word gets out of what he had done and the word gets back to Pharaoh, who then tries to have Moses killed. Moses out of fear for his life flees Egypt and settles in the land of Midian, where he eventually meets the woman he marries. Years have passed as Moses lived a life of a shepherd tending the flock of his father-in-law, when the Lord appeared to him in a burning bush. He commanded Moses to go back into Egypt to Pharaoh, and tell Pharaoh to release all the Jews and lead them to freedom. After much tests and trials with Pharaoh, the Jews are allowed their freedom. They escape into the wilderness after Pharaoh recants his promise and sends his soldiers to kill all the Jews. But God was there and made a way out and the Jews entered the wilderness safely led by Moses. After forty years in the wilderness they finally reach the promised land of God, Israel. And here is where karma steps in. God shows all the land of Israel to Moses from a mountain top, but tells Moses his people can go in and possess the land but he cannot. Because of his sin of murdering a man, his karma is that God denies him entrance into the Promised Land. Moses ends up dying in the land of Moab and God buries him in place that is secret to this day.

There is speculation that the two witnesses of the Book of Revelation will be the reincarnation of Moses and Elijah. This speculation is based on the account in the Book of Revelations of the miracles they are able to perform. One witness with the power to cause droughts, stop the rain and in turn water to blood. This is in line with the type of power of that of Elijah given to him by God. The other witness has the power to bring all types of plagues on the world and this is in line with the power given to Moses by God.

With all this in mind there is a choice to be made and you alone can make it. Should you continue in your darkened state or choose God and step into the light. Now for the first time you know and should consider the consequences of a godless life. Consequences, yes I said consequences, for there is nothing in life that we do that doesn't have an effect somewhere or elsewhere in our lives or to those we know. For the principle law of God shown to us over and over in the bible is the law of "Cause and Effect" or karma. What you and I do good or bad always has consequences, good or bad depending on which one we did. Jesus said it best we all reap what we sow, better known as karma. It can't be escaped for it's the law of God and proves in itself the existence of God for we cannot shake it from us. Karma goes with us every day and is the payback for out deeds good or bad. Adam and Eve ate the fruit and paid the consequence for their disobedience and that was their karma. It wasn't that the fruit was the sin, it wasn't. It was their hearts, for in their hearts they yielded their will to the world and chose to eat the fruit. The consequence of their actions was the penalty of death. They were given lives to live eternally and exchanged them for pain and suffering and death, which they brought upon themselves. Second was their banishment from the Garden of Eden.

Another point that I would like to make is that we should never confuse spirituality with religiosity. For religion is there for us to choose to follow according to our faith or as in most cases is chosen for us by the families we're born and reared in. Whatever the religion one's family follows, it usually becomes the religion we stay with. However spirituality goes much deeper than religion for it's the opening of our hearts to God, asking him into our lives and acknowledging our belief in him and our willingness to live according to his perfect will and in doing so thus creating for ourselves a daily walk with God to last us through all of eternity. For no matter the religion you belong too, again God should be at the center of your faith and of your heart. This no matter what you faith or religion is be it be Judaism, Christianity, Hinduism, Buddhism or Islam, God/Allah should be at the helm of our faith and our hearts. For this is where spirituality begins in one's life. Without God there can be no spirituality, without spirituality we can not know love and the love of God. Without love and having the oneness of God in our hearts, there can never be peace, wars' will never end and man will one day, cease to exist. Without God there can be no enlightenment for enlightenment is of God.

Folks we don't need anymore wars but what we need is a new life of spirituality within each and every one of us. Wherever you go today people are searching for answers, frightened by the constant threat of wars and acts of terrorism. People are losing jobs by the millions, the housing market is in chaos and the stock market has taken a beating and is in deep decline from the fear and panic setting in the hearts of many in fear of the future. Businesses are failing all over the country and the auto industry is amok.

We are headed into a great depression that will make the one back in 1929 seem like a mild recession. We have millions of men, women and children starving every year throughout the world and wars breaking out all over the place. Too many or most just throw the hands up in the air and say what can we do? Why is that? Could it be that man no matter what is only concerned for his position in the world, with power, the greed in his heart for money and material treasures, than the dire consequences of war or the eventual end of the world as we know it is of no consequences to him? Is the loss of some money or luxuries more important to man than millions of starving and dying children all over the world? Shouldn't we be our brother's keeper? But instead greed has taken hold of our society not only here but around the world. Indifference and selfishness is the way of life today and because of this karma will strike and is striking us hard. If we don't change soon then it's going to be too late and everything will fall apart and the dollar bill won't be worth the paper it's printed on.

Here in the Western Hemisphere, people have no clue what it's like to have wars fought in their own homeland. To see your neighborhoods destroyed, your families and friends killed by the bombings or even worse by the atrocities of mad men. The last war on American soil was the Civil War and none of have any idea or any concept of how that was. Here in America, we see the world from our safe enclaves, witnessing everything from our safety net, the television set. This is our view of the world, like an MGM motion picture it's awful, it's sad but those things can never happen here to us. Well I think maybe September 11, 2001, changed all that. Today there's a new reality, a new truth and that is that war has no boundaries like in former wars. It can and will reach all over the globe for the first time in the history of man.

We hear from the multitudes a profession to love God and a show of religiosity as they attend churches and temples all over the world. The poor giving what they have, reaching out in hopeless despair for a miracle, while others are pouring handsome checks in the church offerings not because they are giving it onto God to help the church and the needy, but because it gives them status, influence and recognition in the church and in the community. In other words, it's a power tool and not an act of love and kindness. Who are they fooling? Surely they are not fooling God, for God cannot be mocked! We can't go on fighting, killing and destroying one another and expect the blessings of God upon us while we live such rebellious lives. Nothing has changed for man in all of his history. The few possess it all and the masses suffer at their beck and call. Don't think so then take a look at corporate America and corporate Europe and Japan. CEO's making thirty, forty and even hundreds of millions of dollars a year in salary while they lay off ten of thousands because business is supposedly bad, yet not bad enough for them to take a pay cut or better yet work without pay for a period of time. Well if you lay off three thousand workers because business is slow and yet your CEO is being paid fifty million dollars a year plus stock options then guess who is fooling who? The problem with the rich is that they can't get rich enough. The more they have they more they want no matter at whose expense. No wonder Jesus said, *I tell you the truth, it is hard for a rich man to enter the kingdom of heaven. Again I tell you, it is easier for a camel to go through the eye of a needle than for a rich man to enter the kingdom of God (Matthew 19:24).* Paul the Apostle says, *For the love of money is a root of all kinds of evil. Some people, eager for money, have wandered from the faith and pierced themselves with many sorrows (I Timothy 6:10).* Jesus also said, *No one can serve two masters. Either he will hate the one and love the other, or he will be devoted to the one and despise the other. You cannot serve both God and Money (Matthew 6:24).* We are no different than the world was two, three thousand years ago. A world controlled by those with the wealth and power. Food for thought, I definitely think so.

Surely man needs only to take stock of the world and see how God has blessed the nations of the world since the beginning of time. For whenever man has turned away from God choosing to live a materialistic life over a spiritual one, God in turn has removed his blessings from those nations and those nations fell into destruction. We see this all throughout the bible, from the Great Flood that destroyed the entire known world at that time to Sodom and Gomorrah. Both were destroyed for God could no longer stand the site of all their sinfulness. Primarily the sin was materialism, selfishness, in-hospitality, greed, pride, arrogance and of course their sins of immorality and lust. It was no different for the Jews, as God over and over had to depart from them and their sins leaving them vulnerable and at the mercy of their enemies. They were the slaves of Egypt for 400 years until God sent them Moses, to fetch them out of their captivity. Later they were the slaves of Babylon and then finally the Roman Empire, who in turn destroyed Jerusalem and dispersed the Jews throughout the world without a country and remained so until 1948. The lesson to be learned here was never addressed by man in all of history. As often as Israel turned away from God to live by worldly standards their enemies would defeat them and enslave them. It never occurred to them that God couldn't bless a mess, but wanted a spiritual people to worship him. That living a spiritual life is when God draws near to you and blesses you life with all that you need. Unfortunately that message never sank into the hearts of Israel and is not sinking into the hearts of man today. Consequently God turns away from you and you're left at the mercy of your fellow man, and we all know what the results of that has been through all the thousands of years of man on earth, war, death and destruction.

So what is this deception of man? By now it's becoming apparent that it is when man turns away from his true inner self, his spirit and from God and turns to a life lived carnally, materialistically by worldly standards. He allows himself to become victim to the lures of the world thus forsaking God in pursuit of these worldly ideals and pleasures. It is apparent today that in the United States, we've reached a level in society where God is not welcomed anymore. He's become the forbidden fruit. Just like Adam and Eve in the garden, we've come about face one hundred and eighty degrees and have made God the forbidden fruit, no longer welcomed in schools, in government, or to be mentioned in public. Why just the mention of the name of God in public and people turn ballistic against you. It won't be long and who knows, the use of his name will be a crime punishable by imprisonment. Sounds crazy and yet the bible says that the mention of his name or the belief in God will one day in the end times be punishable by death to the believer.

And yet here is the double standard of man. For when trouble comes your way, or war breaks out or disaster strikes your country, the first one you turn to is God, pleading for his help. Ever notice in an accident, especially really violent ones like car crashes almost everyone calls out to God or Jesus. And that's the point, when trouble strikes each of us in life, we all call on God, on Jesus or Allah, but we call and call quickly. Yet why do so if he isn't welcomed in your land, or in your home or in your heart? Why bother if he's not allowed in your life, in your schools, place of business. Folks he isn't an errand boy running at your beck and call. You can't pass laws making God illegal in public then expect his help when in times of peril. You are either for him or against him. It's hypocritical and blasphemous to abuse God in this way, and surely as the nations of old paid for their godlessness, so will those of us today who continue in this godless way.

One of the teachings Jesus gave us in his ministry on earth was that there was one sin, which is unpardonable. We find it in Matthew 12:31 and it is the blasphemy and or the rejection of the Holy Spirit. This means to reject God from your life and God will reject you from his. Where do you fit in? If you're not in, it's not too late to start right know and change everything around. Turn to God, open your heart to him and ask him into your life. Begin for yourself a prayer life this day an everyday. Just a few minutes each day and talk to him, bear your heart out to him, praise him and thank him for whatever is good in your life. Seek his perfect will for your life.

People claim that to mention the name of God is to be choosing or forcing religion down people's throats. Is it really? Has anyone demanded we all become Catholics or Jews, or born again Christians? Has anyone demanded we all should become Muslims, Hindus or Buddhists? Absolutely not and that's because God is God of everyone. God isn't religion, he's God our Creator. He's God of everyone no matter what religion you want to belong too. So why are we so crazy about using the name of God, of loving God publicly, of acknowledging him and honoring him with our hearts? Today's world is a world in turmoil, filled with hatred, bigotry, wars, killings, diseases wiping out large segments of the populations, starvation killing millions all around the globe and weather conditions that are baffling the greatest scientific minds of our time. All you hear where ever you go is "Oh God, please help us through all of this." This coming from the same mouths that want nothing to do with God be it in public, in their everyday lives or in the lives of their children. Well you know something, think about it. You can't have your cake and eat it too. If God is unwelcome in your heart, in your mind, in your home, in your job or in the schools of your children. If he is unwanted by your town officials, state officials and by the government as a whole, then why should he bother helping us? Here in the United States we're suffering through the destructive forces of hurricanes and tornadoes, from a stock market that crashes baffling the greatest minds in Wall Street, people losing their homes in foreclosures and bankruptcy soaring to unfathomable heights and the country's economy on a verge of collapsing. And this is just to mention a few of the misfortunes happening to us in the USA. Ever stop to think it's not by chance but karma. That the law of karma, of justice has come to the United States and it's a warning that we all need to change and come to the light of God. The people of the United States need to repent with no exception, and return to God or the calamities that has befallen us will just be a prelude of much worse to come and come soon. We're a great nation but yet our fathers have done many wrongs that need to be righted. In recent history of this country we failed in Cuba and let it turn Communist, we failed in Vietnam and it ended also as a Communist nations. We made a mockery of Iraq chasing the so called weapons of mass destruction or was it really oil interests that we were concerned with. We also failed the people of Africa allowing all the genocide to occur and did nothing to stop it and at times blocked any means to stop it. Millions of Africans massacred over the years. History verifies all that the bible tells us over and over again. When nations turned their hearts away from God, God in turn then turned his blessings away from those nations and their people. So will the same happen here in America, as it happened to Persia, Egypt, Rome, Greece, Babylon, Great Britain, and the Soviet Union? All the great empires of the past gone, defeated, reduced to minor powers their influence all but gone in the world. While others have vanished from the face of the earth all together and why one would ask? Ever since the dawn of man, mighty nations have risen to world power and all of them bar none have fallen from power, all of them bar none have fallen from grace. Again when we look at their histories they were nations without God at the helm to their hearts and consequently lost the blessings of God. Great and mighty many of them were just as America is today, yet they all fell in their time. The funny thing about history is that it is always repeating itself. You would think that in one generation of man, we would awaken to our mistakes of the past and not repeat them over and over again. It's too costly to keep repeating these mistakes for today the weapons aren't bows and arrows or swords. They're atomic bombs, guided missiles, chemical and biological warfare. It wouldn't take much to do the world in.

So what then, can it happen here in the United States? Remember none of the great empires in all of history has ever remained in power permanently. They all died out after several hundred years, all bar none. What does that say for us that probably the same will hold true for us also? That's because again we're no different than the empires of the past and we're repeating the mistakes of the past all over again. We are a great nation, best democracy that ever was on earth, yet we're becoming over indulgent in the material world, becoming an arrogant, lazy, immoral and worst of all we're becoming a godless nation. We boss around other smaller nations all over the world yet can't fix the problems within our own borders. Problems such as bigotry, hatred, murder, violence, hunger and poverty, drug abuse, health insurance for the poor and the aging, equal housing, schooling and jobs for all people regardless of race, color or creed. Every chance we get we vote God out of our daily lives saying we can't mix religion with government. We can't pray in school, pledge allegiance to the flag as one nation under God, or sing God bless America in public for God is offensive to the minds of Americans. Don't you think we are beginning to look just like those empires of the past and are repeating the patterns of history? Then when will God pull the plug on us and remove his blessings from us? You say it doesn't happen anymore like that. Look again there was Great Britain, France and the Soviet Union to name a few. It is still happening for as I said before God is the same yesterday, today and forever. His blessings and his judgments are always the same, never changing.

Today we have our own version of the forbidden fruit. The fruit is called "humanism, worldliness, materialism, etc." and we don't just eat it up we devour it daily in our daily lives. The humanist's doctrine says we can't mix church and state. Well yes that's understandable when in the context of religions and the state, but why God? Acknowledging God openly is not the same as mixing church and state. God is not a religion nor can you politicize God, He's God. He is the creator of everything that is and far greater than anything any mere mortal can conjure up in his political brain. He's Christian true, but he's also Jewish, again true. But what else is God? He is Muslim, Hindu, Buddhist, Hare Krishna, he is all, he is in all and he is to all. That's why wherever you go in the world we hear that great expression thank God. Thank God, is one of the most often used phrases in the world and why? Because we all believe it and in our hearts he is the creator, he is God. We didn't try to qualify God as Christian, Jew, Muslim or whatever, just that he's our God. But as long as he remains the forbidden fruit and we embrace humanism, materialism as our way of life then the blessings of God will be absent from us. You choose humanism, materialism as your way of life, but you won't find happiness nor can it give you eternal life. You may have wealth beyond imagination but you can't buy eternity, you can't buy heaven nor can you buy happiness. As a matter of fact you can't even buy health, for we all get sick, we all get diseases and we all have to die and shed ourselves of our physical bodies. God only designed our bodies to last a few years not an eternity. We have to first earn eternity through him who created us and it's a free gift to those who choose to believe in him. Don't believe a word I'm saying, fine that's your choice but you are the one being deceived. Look around and see if anyone claims to have found eternal life? See any millionaires, billionaires denying death? Man when you got to go, you just got to go and all the money in the world won't buy you one second more of life.

Another example of the consequence of our actions is shown to us in Romans, chapter 1:18-25, *The wrath of God is revealed against all ungodliness of men who by their wickedness suppress the truth. For what can be known about God is plain to them, because God has shown it to them. Ever since the creation of the world his invisible nature, namely, his eternal power and deity, has been clearly perceived in the things that have been made. So they are without excuse; for although they knew God they did not honor him as God, or give thanks to him, but they became futile in their thinking and their senseless minds were darkened. Claiming to be wise they became fools, and exchanged the glory of the immortal God for images resembling mortal man or birds or animals or reptiles.*

Therefore God gave them up in the lusts of their hearts to impurity, to the dishonoring of their bodies among themselves, because they exchanged the truth about God for a lie and worshipped and served the creature rather than the Creator, who is blessed for ever! Amen.

Further in verses 1:28-2:11 it says, *Since they did not see fit to acknowledge God, God gave them up to a debased mind and to things that should not be done. Full of envy, murder, strife, deceit, malignity, they are gossips, slanderers, haters of God, insolent, haughty, boastful, inventors of evil, disobedient to parents, foolish, faithless, heartless, and ruthless. Though they know God's decree that those who do such things deserve to die, they not only do them but approve those who practice them.*

Therefore you have no excuse, O man, whoever you are, when you judge another; for in passing judgment upon him you condemn yourself, because you, the judge, are doing the very same things. Do you suppose, O man, you will escape the judgment of God? Or do you presume upon the riches of his forbearance and patience? But by your impenitent heart you are storing up wrath for yourself on the day when God's judgment will be revealed. For he will render to every man according to his works: to those who by patience in well doing seek for glory and honor and immortality he will give eternal life; but for those who do not obey the truth, there will be wrath and fury. There will be anguish and distress for everyone who does evil, the Jew first and also the Greek (all gentiles), but the glory and honor and peace for everyone who does good, the Jew first and also the Greek. For God shows no partiality. This is the consequence of all our actions here on earth. What we choose to do with our lives does have consequences, whether we choose to live our lives in the spirit or in a lie. All choices have consequences and once again I repeat God is the same yesterday, today and forever. He doesn't change, his love is ever constant. We're the deceivers who turn our hearts one way then another. Remember the accounting of Elijah being reincarnated as John the Baptist, karma was satisfied. As holy as Elijah was, a truly great prophet of God he could not escape justice and God wouldn't let him. If you brought justice to Elijah and set karma straight, don't you think he intends the same for all of us? That's the battle man has on earth, his humanistic ideas vs. believing and putting his trust in God. That's the deception of man, his refusal to acknowledge God becomes his refusal to acknowledge his own spiritual self. For without God, our true self, our spirit within is dead for we live in the lie of the world. This is why it is so important to begin this very day to developing a new life, a spiritual life from within us. For it's our spirit who is the true person within us and the only one who can direct our lives in all truth and lead us to the acknowledgment of God and the honoring of God into our lives.

You know what's really hard to understand is this exchange of a spiritual life which we all had from birth for a secular lifestyle filled with momentary happiness, empty promises, unfulfilled dreams and only short lived successes and pleasures. Don't get me wrong, I'm guilty too, for as soon as we're able to discern, understand, and get knowledge the world crept into our lives and raped us of our spiritual selves. Materiality, humanism, selfishness and greed set in and the successes, the wealth and all the material possessions one accumulates in life becomes one's signature, the emblem of one's success. Yet there never seems to be enough and the satisfaction of it is always short lived. You find that no matter how much you have you still hunger and crave for more and more. It obviously is the problem some or many of our super rich in the world suffer from. They are never satisfied and many willingly will step over others to get ahead no matter who gets hurt or how many are left unemployed over their greed. It's at the point where just too many people don't care the price they will pay in order to satisfy this lust, this craving of theirs. We beg, borrow, cheat and steal for the gods of our lives, far too many people living surrealistically, completely out of touch with reality. For them the quality of life is based on the monetary value of their trinkets, their homes and cars or the power they've obtained. Their home addresses become power bases and status symbols, as they lord it over the masses that have not or are less fortunate. Sounds ridiculous yes, but look around and take a good hard look. Whether it is money, power or the pursuit of material possessions or the lust of the flesh, we have an insatiable appetite to grab, take and to consume all there is and usually sharing none of it with others who are less fortunate. Greed knows no satisfaction, for it is driven by the eyes, by materialistic values and not by the spirit. Just like the corporate thieves I mentioned before, robbing their corporations blind, as we witnessed with Enron and World Com. Their greed knew no limits having lost all morality and their minds had become debased. Hoping that their wealth will secure them a place in the world, a place in history for other men to admire, or even worse to gain powerful positions of influence in the political arena or in the world. What folly, what ignorance for what does it matter what other men think of you if God rejects you? What good is all the wealth in the world if you've lost your soul and have separated yourself from God? Now today we have the great fall of Wall Street and the housing market. The Federal Government stepping in with hundreds of millions of dollars in bail outs for the banks and for Wall Street, yet has anyone in the government insisted that the CEO's and all the big executives of these firms take a huge salary cut? Of course not and why should they? We have the American tax payer to flip the bill.

Today people complain, complain and complain how unlucky they are, the good jobs always go to the other guy. They are always on the bottom of the heap, never on top. Constantly complaining and always looking to blame someone else for their downfall and short comings in life. Well like President Truman, once put it quite boldly the buck stops here. No truer words have ever been spoken. Whatever the problem is keep this one thing in mind and remember it well, you put yourself there. Whatever happened to you happened by your choice and selections in life. Even if you were born into the worse situations or conditions in life, you as you grew up and had the opportunity to do so, made choices that kept you stuck in your position or condition in life. I know it sounds a little hard to put it that way, but take a serious look at yourself first before you point the finger everywhere else. What did you do to get yourself out of your predicament? Yes it's hard sometimes, I know for I am a minority American-Puerto Rican and I am gay which I guess makes me a double minority. Yes life was tough for me right from childhood, having to fight in street gangs to keep myself alive and this complicated by the fact that I was being sexually abused by a relative which lasted for 10 years of my childhood. I quickly discovered that as a Puerto Rican, I was unwanted and unwelcomed in America. No one wanted Puerto Ricans, in their neighborhood and we were denied jobs, promotions and housing just like Blacks were being denied of the same. Heck no, it wasn't easy, it was tough and I lost out more times than I want to remember.

Am I complaining? I used to, but no more for when I look back at those years I realized that I still had choices to make that would shape my future. Unfortunately I made a lot of wrong choices that kept me stuck in my predicament. I failed miserably for I took the role of a victim and didn't fight back. I accepted my role in life as a minority Puerto Rican, and consequently was treated as such. Yes I was a minority both Gay and Latino, but I forgot that I was a man and had lost my self respect. Everything changed for me when I changed and made "new choices" in life. When I said to myself "no mas", no more am I a minority in this country. I started searching inside of myself and realized that my problems only persisted, because I allowed them to persist. I had no faith in myself, I didn't believe in myself. How could I, for I didn't even believe in God. When I looked inside of me I found fear, I found a weak, defeated person who depended on the crumbs of others for his survival. What happened in life that brought me down to such lowliness? I found a shell of a man who was quickly becoming addicted to drinking and doing drugs. Using them as an escape from my own reality and the world I made for myself. These circumstances of my life, this horror of a man that I had become, was the result of the poor choices I made in life. Tough life yes but we all are handed tough lives to live, but we don't have to make the choices of self-destruction.

What I didn't know then which I know now is the act of forgiveness. Sure life is tough, but we can't go on hating life because of our tough luck in it. Neither can we go on hating ourselves and hating everyone else because of it. What you need to do is get yourself past the pain, past the hurt and to move on with your life. Life was meant for us to move on and to grow in life. Not to be stuck in one spot filled with anger and hate till it does what it can only do best and that is to destroy us. Everything in life involves growth from a blade of grass to every living creature in the world. Without growth all life fails and dies away and so must we move on and grow and to do so we must learn to forgive. God is source of help in this inner battle and will show you the way to love and to forgive and to move on and grow. Forgive those who hurt us so badly and to forgive ourselves. Hurt, yes it hurts to humble oneself in the beginning, to face one's demon(s) and make a commitment to bring it to an end by saying from the depth on one's heart I forgive you and all that you did to me. And I forgive myself for putting myself through so many years of this pain in my heart and in my mind. Trust me as I say this with tears in my heart, it's the beginning of your healing, a beginning to putting to an end all the hatred in your heart. You will heal, you will find a new life in you and you will begin to take those first new steps to a new life both within and without yourself, amen.

I know, trust me I've been there and lived in hell for over forty years of my life. I was living in total darkness, deceived by not only the world but by my humanistic mind, my humanistic thinking. The years of sexual child abuse I had to endure left a mark of death and hate in my heart. The bigotry I faced only made life that more unbearable for me. I was living outside of my spiritual self, and I was in a self-destructive mode living for the numerous fleshly pleasures of life where I didn't have to deal with myself and with my pain. I drowned myself constantly in the darkened world of sex, alcohol and drugs where there was no reality and the mind could not function. Not function for me meant freedom from pain. I was what one could consider dead or close to it, but there was a small war raging within me. My spirit was fighting for life even though I was giving up on life. Whether by accident, self induced drunkenness or by reckless living, I walked away from death many times and each time the hand of God was involved in saving my life. He saved me from fates of death in what were termed fatal incidents. He saved me from two very serious auto accidents where I should have died yet walked away unscathed. Twice again in a drunken state I would have fallen to certain death falling out of buildings from very high floors. Each time it was a miracle from God that kept me alive. Soon a faint reality started setting in me that as much as I didn't believe in God at that time in my life it was apparent that somehow God believed in me enough to save my life those many times. The proof of it came on my twenty fifth birthday, I celebrated the day with friends at a beach party thrown for me at Jones Beach, N.Y. We brought food, drinks, booze, beer and wine and had ourselves a merry ole time. Later that day about five o'clock in the afternoon I walked down to the water and sat down to cool me feet off in the water. As I sat there a voice spoke to me from heaven and God said to me "at the appointed time I will return to speak to you." Again years later on my thirty second birth day, again God spoke to me saying again "at the appointed time I will return to talk to you." Then six years later when I was thirty eight years old commenced the most incredible and the most sensational days of my life. Jesus Christ the son of God made his first visitation to me and continued to make another dozen visits over a period of about twenty years. This culminated on his last visit which was His request for me to write this book. I've been working on the book now for over 5 years.

The good news here is that you don't have to go down that same road that I went down or any other road that takes you away from yourself, your spirit and from God. For everything you are looking for will be found within yourself, in your spirit and with God. All the truth, all the lies, all the good and all the bad about yourself will come to light from within yourself when you begin to search with God for your answers. What's great about this also is that this is where you will get to know God, your creator and find the truth, love, freedom and forgiveness for yourself and from God. You will find the light and you will be set free never having to live in the darkness again. You will find that living in life in the spirit is the best place you could ever be, for the spirit doesn't lie but leads you in all truth. For the spirit guides you in life as it is guided by the spirit of god. Jesus said it best, *when the Spirit of truth comes, he will guide you in all truth, for he will not speak on his own, but speak whatever he hears, and he will declare it to you the things that are to come. He will glorify me, because he will take what is mine and declare it to you (John 16:13-14)*. Then again in the book of John Jesus says *God is spirit, and those that worship him must worship in spirit and truth (John 4:21)*. It can't be said any plainer or better than that.

So if life's got you down, a drag, too overwhelming to handle and everything is just a terrible mess, make a new choice in your life and turn within yourself and begin a new way of living through God. If you don't change your way of life you'll always remain stuck in first gear. Life will always be an uphill battle at best always nearing the breaking points of despair. Make a change now and start meditating with yourself, quietly away somewhere alone with yourself and God. No matter what your life is like here on earth if you're not living in the spirit, your living a lie and without God. Even if you're successful in life, have all the riches in the world, if you're not living in the spirit, your living a lie without God. God isn't against your success in life. He wants only to fulfill your life to it's fullest along with all the success you have acquired so that you can have fulfillment and happiness with yourself and with God. If your life is in a mess or in ruins, fear not God will show you the way out with His Holy Spirit guiding you in your spirit to all truth. You will at last begin the greatest journey of your life, a life of enlightenment with God. This is what salvation is all about, enlightenment with God. We return back to our former selves when we were born in innocence and a part of God. For our souls are eternal and always existed and will always exist beyond our physical bodies. You see we were a part of God from the beginning and must return to God through enlightenment. Why, because God's plan is to save all of us bar none and will do whatever is necessary to win each one of us back. If that means you must live a new life a few times over suffering in each life to bring you to enlightenment, then so it will be. It isn't God's plan to punish you, but the law of karma works in all of us and can't be changed. Consequently if you don't get the message and you are living in sin and you pass away unrepented then expect to come back reincarnated in another life to pay for the sins of your former life. It's the law of karma at work in your soul.

Surely if we each begin to do our part to saving ourselves from our carnal selves, divorcing ourselves from a destructive worldly system we can save not only ourselves, but our planet also. We won't have to face a World War III or an Armageddon, for they won't happen. That's what end time prophecy is all about in the bible they are contingent upon our actions. If we don't change our ways, these dreadful things will happen to end the world as we know it. The consummate word here is "if" for it shows right away that we have choices to make. The consequences of what we do will determine if our world survives or will all of us dye in cataclysmic destruction. It always comes down to karma and the choices we make in life. If we continue to live humanistic lives outside of the spirit, continuing to live in the lies of the past and perpetuating them into the future, what outcome do you expect we will have? We must begin a new direction in life, each one of us and do it now, today while there is still time and there is still a today. We each must make a new choice in life by changing the course we've been on of worldly and humanistic living to a life in the spirit, lived in all truth with God. For whether we want to accept it or not we are each other's brother's keeper.

We were created by the creator, the one God of us all. He created everything by himself and his spoken word. He formed man from the earth and consequently we are one with mother earth, the home of father God. We can never escape the oneness, from the first Adam to you and me; we are all connected in one giant family of man. Whether your black or white, brown, yellow or red we are all connected. Every Jew, Christian, Muslim, Hindu, Buddhist, all connected. Heterosexuals, homosexuals we are all connected. We need to understand that and receive it in our spirit, for we all stem from the hands of God. When we can begin to accept and understand this, then bigotry and hatred start coming to an end and we will be able to embrace each other in brotherhood. This will surely come to pass when we all begin to live a new life in the spirit guided by the Holy Spirit of God. Amen.

In Matthew 7:15, Jesus reminds us to beware of these wolves in sheep's clothing, looking for whom they can deceive and devour. How do we recognize them? By the fruits they bare. How will you be able to discern this truth? By your spirit if you are living your life in the spirit in union with God. Otherwise you will be duped and become once more a victim of the deceiver and what did the Lord say about that, *if the blind follow the blind, both will fall into the ditch, Matt 15:14.*

Who are these blind guides? These are the men and women who are the ministers of the churches all over the world who speak out with great authority and eloquence constantly reminding us of how much they love God and how wrong this all is. Yet when we take a deeper look at them, all too many are really busy lining their pockets with money and filling themselves with power and positions of prominence. Or as we have seen in the past and even recently are guilty of sexual promiscuity and sexual abuse of children. For unfortunately today too many who are in the church, live as spiritless a life as those who are outside the church. For all too many in the church feel that their dedication to their church or to their religion is enough to get them into heaven and they need do no more. What it really shows is their ignorance and their religiosity and not their spirituality and oneness with God. Pious bunch they are preaching God, and dictating how people must live while they themselves live in ivory towers, themselves committing the same sins as in the world, thus bringing the world into the church. Fools themselves who then make fools of us leading us in blindness as we become deceived. Today too many of our churches have become a carbon copy of the churches in the time of Jesus Christ. They were run then by the sects known as Pharisees and Sadducees of ancient Israel. A bunch of pious, self righteous, blind guides of the churches whose only interest was their political prominence among the people and the power they held over the people. Blinded by their lack of faith, men who trusted only in their religion and the doctrines they created as their interpretation of God. Making God conform to the image they presented to the people, thus being able to control the masses, for political gains, power and financial fortunes. For them God wasn't alive and couldn't possibly be this man called Jesus, preaching peace, love and salvation, but the Messiah could only be one who answered the call of Israel's politics and was prepared to lead an army against Rome for Israel's sake. He was to be a warring king leading his army into battle against Rome, not a peasant preaching love, peace and the kingdom of god.

What Israel couldn't understand then is what most people don't seem to understand today, and that is that God is the father of all of the people in the world and not of a select few. How can God come down to destroy one set of his children to defend another if they're all his children? He can't, for he is complete in His love for all his children and can only put forward the plan he gave the world. That was why he would not interfere anymore with man on earth as he did in the great flood or in the destruction of Sodom and Gomorrah, but he would offer all men on earth a plan for salvation so that none would perish. He sent us Christ that through him we would find salvation. Not by religion or contrived holiness, but by faith. Opening our hearts to him and receiving a spiritual awakening and leaving our worldliness behind. Salvation is for all, for the Jew and for the gentiles. God offered us His son and no more that whoever believed in him would be saved. Saved be you Muslim, Hindu, Buddhist, Catholic or one of the many Christian faiths and religions around the world with the eternal promise of your place in the kingdom of God for all eternity. That is the promise of God, as told to us by none other than Jesus himself and it's His promise to "whoever" believes in Him shall be saved. No more demands are made on us but that simple one, and why? Because God had already tried his patience with man and man could not conform to the laws of God. Consequently God had to punish man repeatedly as he did in the great flood that destroyed the world. Now God would refrain from such actions and let man sort it out for himself, that now we shall live by faith and not just in one another, but faith in God himself. No more hundreds of laws to memorize and then forget. No more excuses of any kind for now it's by pure and simple faith. Yet still man continues in the darkness of his ways. This time when the world does come to an end it won't be at the hands of God, but by the hands of man himself.

No worse sin can man commit then to deny God entirely and instead worships in himself (sin of pride), or the things of the world (sin of idolatry and flesh) as the only thing he needs in life. This was the mistake of Lucifer, who fell from grace and became Satan, because of his pride (Isaiah, 14:12-16). This is where unfortunately many are today exchanging the truth of God for the promises of an empty world of money, power and materialism. Cheating themselves of an eternity of happiness and eternal life for a lifetime (which lasts a mere second in comparison to eternity) of worldly wealth and possessions which decay and rust and fade away. Hello, you know you can't take it with you when you die. You can accumulate all the wealth in the world but when you die it stays all here and goes to whoever is next in line. You my friend will be as poor when you die as you were when you were born. For from dust we came and to dust we return and someone else will enjoy the wealth and possessions you put together in you life.

The world governed by men will always fall short on us and disappoint us. It goes great for a short while then the bottom falls out. War breaks out, or the stock market goes into a big dive and people begin panicking all over the world, losing millions upon millions of dollars in investments. That's why we're always starving for more and more and we just can't get enough, because life has no guarantees for man. Everything is here today and gone tomorrow and this because we chase life by the flesh, governed by materiality and not by spirit. We've been duped by our own intellectuality, again the deception of man. It has us chasing moonbeams when we forget that the sun is always shining. God never gives up working while it's the world that leaves you high and dry. But it doesn't have to be that way. You can have success and happiness on earth and also eternal life in the Kingdom of God. God isn't short on blessings; it's us who are short on faith and belief in the one God.

Just imagine what life could be like if we adopted God into our daily lives, asking God for his Holy Spirit to guide us each and everyday. Imagine God and His Holy Spirit teaching us the way that we should go and to how to do his will in our lives each day. Movies, television or money (considering all the evil it can bring) are not the culprits in and of themselves. It's how we take to them and then apply them to our lives. Jesus said, *Do you not see that whatever goes into the mouth enters the stomach, and goes out into the sewer? But what comes out of the mouth proceeds from the heart, and this is what defiles.*

For out of the heart come evil intentions, murder, adultery, fornication, theft, false witness, slander. These are what defile a person, but to eat with unwashed hands does not defile.(Matthew 15:17-20). Also let me make it clear that I'm not advocating an end to watching them, but we should treat them for what they are, and that is entertainment. We should monitor that which our children watch and not allow them to watch all that filth and violence on television. I've heard so many say that it's impossible to stop. I say then lock up the TV, until the family is home together to enjoy it together. But instead too many treat them as an altar of worship, a God where so many spend hours and hours everyday being brainwashed by the useless barrage of violence and greed shown on these venues. Imagine if each one of us gave God some of the time we give TV and movies everyday to Him. What a wonderful world we could create.

Just imagine how developing a private prayer time each day of 15 or 20 minutes would alone change your life. Your spirit would be seeking out truth, increasing your capacity to love, unraveling and curing the pains and wounds that exist inside you and shinning a pathway for you towards the light, the place where God is. As you grow in your prayer life you'll be making startling discoveries about yourself and the light side as opposed to the dark side in which you have always lived. Best of all as you discover the light of God a joy begins to swell up inside you as your life begins changing and taking on a new you. You begin to hear the voice of God and develop a true relationship with Him. For the first time in your life you've learned that he isn't just a name in the Bible or a name echoed out by the ministries in all the churches throughout the world. But He is real, He is alive and is someone you can talk to and have a conversation with and one whose voice you can hear. Jesus tells us in Revelations 3:20, *I am standing at the door (your heart) knocking; if you hear my voice and open the door, I will come "in to you" and eat with you and you with me.* You say you can't hear him, but of course you can't. You're still living in the flesh and to hear God we need to be in the spirit. Why? Because your spirit is the true you, it's you and who you really are. Jesus said, *God is Spirit; they that worship him must worship him in spirit and in truth (John 4:24).*

It's as simple as that. At first you'll begin to think it's all in your mind, that it's not God you hear but your own thoughts. Don't stop, go on and be persistent with your prayer life. Soon you'll discover that it's really the Lord talking to you. As a matter of fact you will probably know the voice the first time you hear it and know that it is Jesus. In John 10:4-5 the Jesus says, *After he has gathered his own flock, he walks ahead of them, and they follow him because they know his voice. They won't follow a stranger; they will run from him because they don't know his voice.* He'll begin blessing your life and teaching you of his word and revolutionizing your life like you never thought possible. A joy will enter your heart and a peace like you never known and you'll know that you've met with Jesus. Don't just take my word for it alone, go do prove it for yourself. Go now and begin a prayer life and try to make it the same time each day to be with the Lord instead of all the TV, or other daily distractions of life and open your heart to him and let him in. Another point that is important to note is that one shouldn't just pray repetitive prayers sounding like a babbling brook. But speak to him about whatever is on your heart or in your mind, holding nothing back. Remember this, you can't shock God, he knows all about you already. What He desires of you now is the truth from your lips which is the truth pouring out of your heart. Good, bad or indifferent pour it all out, for if God is going to help you, you must speak out in all truth. As Saint Paul, so aptly put it in Romans 10:10, *For one believes with the heart and so is justified, and confesses with the mouth, and so is saved.*

Let the Lord feed and guide you in all His truth and in all His love. Believe me, in time you will grow and change and become a new creation through Him. That's what salvation is all about, opening one's heart to the Lord Jesus, and asking him in to be a part of you. This is where you will willingly from your heart want to repent of whatever wrongs you have done and of what you have become, and ask Him for His mercy and forgiveness and for the help to teach you to live a new life as a child of God. This is done in the privacy of your heart and soul known only to you and the Lord. It's not a religious act, but one that we all must do no matter what religion on earth we follow. This is an action from you to God on a one to one; that will change the rest of your life. Let God then lead you to the church or temple best suited for you, whether he calls you to be a Jew, a Hindu, a Buddhist, a Christian, a Muslim or whatever other religion God may chose for you. However and whoever you are, come as you are to God. Don't hesitate, for the hour is late. Better to get to God, poor and in rags then to miss the mark and never have another chance again. Death can come at any moment catching you unprepared and you never have repented with God and now your soul is lost. Jesus tells this best in Matthew 25:1-13 where he says, *Then the Kingdom of Heaven will be like ten bridesmaids who took their lamps and went to meet the bridegroom. Five of them were foolish, and five were wise. he five who were foolish didn't take enough olive oil for their lamps, but the other five were wise enough to take along extra oil. When the bridegroom was delayed they all became drowsy and fell asleep. At midnight they were roused by the shout, 'Look, the bridegroom is coming! Come out and meet him! All the bridesmaids got up and prepared their lamps. Then the five foolish ones asked the others, Please give us some of you oil because our lamps are going out. But the others replied, We don't have enough for all of us. Go to a shop and buy some for yourselves. But while they were gone to buy oil, the bridegroom came. Then those who were ready went with him to the marriage feast and the door was locked. Later when the other five bridesmaids returned, they stood outside, calling, 'Lord! Lord! Open the door for us! But he called back, Believe me, I don't know you!' So you, too, must keep watch! For you do not know the day or hour of my return.*

Ouch that hurts and worse than that they missed out on the Kingdom of Heaven. Where are you in the scheme of things? Are you lamps filled with oil and do you have extra oil to make sure you don't miss the bridegroom when he comes for you? I hope so for all our sakes that we all be ready with our lamps trimmed for that is the true church of Jesus Christ.

Filling the pews of all the churches and temples throughout the world alone won't do it and never has and never will. People don't change by being religious or by their acts of religiosity, but do change when submitting themselves directly to God from the heart and doing the will of God. Opening their hearts and letting Him in to live within them everyday for the rest of their lives, teaching them of the ways of God. This, my friend is what being truly "born again" is all about. It's about you and God, and the two becoming like one. It's your ultimate commitment in life when you turn within yourself to your soul and admit you need help, a change of heart, a new way for life and you turn to God surrendering to Him for his help and mercy. For your life as it has been just doesn't work out right for you and just like we all turned to our parents for daily guidance as we're growing up all the more we should turn to God, for the same and more. Think about it, when we were young we turned to our parents because they were our world and we depended on them for everything, for love, for caring, for our daily food, for clothing, for teaching and guidance and for everything that a child needed to grow up. Then how much more help can we get from the one who actually created us and gave us life and created all life? Wouldn't He know even more than our parents, and yet we chose not to tap that resource which is free for the asking? That's right "free for the asking." Jesus said in Matthew 7:7-11, *Ask and it will be given you; search, and you will find; knock, and the door will be opened for you. For everyone who searches finds, and for everyone who knocks, the door will be opened. Is there anyone among you who, if your child asks for bread, will give a stone? Or if the child asks for a fish, will give a snake? If you then, who are evil, know how to give good gifts to your children, how much more will your Father in heaven give good things to those who ask him?* Folks, it just doesn't get any better than that, you simply just have to believe it. God won't impose himself on you, but will knock politely everyday on the door to your heart in hope that one day you will finally awaken and hear the knock and say yes Lord, come into my life. Unfortunately too many never change their carnal lifestyle to a life lived in the spirit in union with the Holy Spirit of God.

Consider it this way if it will help you out. Saving yourself from the worldly life that continues to drag you down and uniting yourself to a life lived in union with God is like getting married. When you were single, life was fast, a frenzy with too many let downs, too much loneliness and longing for a permanent happiness. Sure there were good times, but they were fleeting and didn't last. Then came the love of your life and you married and ended all that misery and so it is with you, your spirit and God. It's a marriage made in heaven to righting the wrongs in your life and bringing happiness and fulfillment to your life. Jesus called it being born again of the spirit. You're bonding your soul with God and in turn his Holy Spirit begins to teach you, guide you through life and bless you all the days of your life. Does this mean you'll never suffer an illness or have an accident again? No, for we live here on earth in the physical world and are subject to the environment around us. So just like everyone else, you'll still catch colds, get headaches, and suffer all types of illnesses and diseases, for life in the physical world is temporal. Your goal must be for eternal life, beyond the life of your physical body and only God can achieve that for you.

Today we are living in the new religion of worldly worships and enslavement they call it the new age or humanism. We've become enslaved by the things we most worship in life and many among us have had the foresight to escape this and remain grounded in our souls. To develop a spiritual walk with our inner man and with God today is more important now than ever in the history of man. For never in the history of the world has there been so much to temp man and lead him astray and never before in the history of the world has man been so close to the end of all times. Never has there been any generation of man in all of history until now, that can fulfill all the end time prophecies of the bible bringing the world as we know it to an end. History tells us that many generations before us thought they were the end time generation that would see the coming of the messiah and an end to the world as we know it, but they were all wrong. Why must it be us and not them? One very important factor was missing from all the former generations of man in order to fulfill the end time prophecies. That was the prophecy of the rebirth of the nation of Israel. Simply stated it said that the Jews after having been dispersed throughout the world for close to 2,000 years without a country, following the destruction of Israel by Rome, would once again reclaim their homeland and become a nation once more. That prophecy was fulfilled in 1948. We are the only generation of man in all of history that fulfills the end time prophecies of the bible and Israel became a nation once more in our generation of time. What does this mean for you, for me, for all of us? It means we're running out of time and that being the last generation of man on earth leaves us only about 70 years from 1948, before the end the final conflict, Armageddon. So yes, the time for a new spirit filled life and an end to our worldliness and sinfulness is now, today. We may not have tomorrow and surely no one can guarantee they'll be here to see and live tomorrow. Death respects no one and comes for us at any given moment.

Living a spiritual life with God enables us to take back control of our lives and put our life back into its proper reality, founded in truth and in love. What is that reality? It is your body living in harmony with your soul and your soul living in harmony with your body and both living in harmony with the Holy Spirit of God.

Another thing you will discover is your purpose in life. That there is a question that has troubled man through the ages, why am I here? What's my purpose in this Life? Well to begin with you're here because God willed for you to be here. He planned for you before you were even conceived. He planned your birth, the color of your skin, and who your parents would be. The life you would live good or bad, but it would be a learning process for you to grow and eventually come to know and love God as He loves you. Love Him freely from your heart while learning from Him your purpose here on earth and all the hidden talents He's given you to accomplish your tasks. In Jeremiah 1:5 God tells Jeremiah, *I knew you before I formed you in your mother's womb.* In Isaiah 49:1, the bible says *The Lord called me before my birth; from within the womb he called me by name.* So you can see you are here because God planned for you to be here. You are no accident no matter how you were born, God planned for your birth. In Psalm 139:13-16, it says *You made all the delicate, inner parts of my body and knit me together in my mother's womb. Thank you for making me so wonderfully complex! Your workmanship is marvelous – how well I know it. You watched me as I was being formed in utter seclusion as I was woven together in the dark of the womb. You saw me before I was born. Every day of my life was recorded in your book. Every moment was laid out before a single day had passed.* So my friend you are here with a purpose that is from God. He planned you and me and we are each here with a purpose and that is to serve God. We need to get out of the 'me syndrome', and begin asking God for His purpose for our lives. We need to stop the selfish attitude of me, me, give me, get me and I want. It's not about you or me but about what God needs to fulfill in us. He knew the day of our birth and knows the day of our death and everything that takes place in our lives in between. He knew this before you were born and it just makes common sense to then trust him who has all knowledge of you, who created you and all that is in the universe.

Now knowing this about God and his creation of you and his plans for you doesn't that just make you curious to know more about God and his plan for you? Imagine at last a chance to find out your purpose in life. How much more you can accomplish knowing this. You can eliminate doubts, eliminate wasted efforts in you day to day living focusing on things to accomplish your newly discovered purpose. This discovery will energize you in a way you never knew to accomplish that which God prepared you for. Failure will be a thing of the past. You will be able to push aside the things that drove you life before in exchange for the drive you have now found through God. Sure you may be successful in life, wealthy with a solid career, but they don't bring peace and happiness to your soul! If they did you wouldn't be searching for your purpose in life. Then others need to push aside the drives in their lives that have served to defeat them and keep them unsuccessful and lost. It could be that you are living by doubts and fears or other things driving your life that keep you lost, defeated. Well hello, here's your chance to change all that. Only God can open the door to your truth and to His truth which has been hidden from you, because your focus was only on your situation. When you focus on just you and your situation in life, it becomes a "poor, poor me" situation. Well now you can shake loss of that monkey on your back and come to God and find the answers to your life. John 8:31-32 Jesus says to the people who believe in him *You are truly my disciples if you remain faithful to my teachings. And you will know the truth and the truth will set you free!* Amen and amen.

Remember the one most important issue in life is the salvation of your eternal soul. Life is eternal, for our souls are eternal and a part of the living God. It has always been that way from the very beginning of time we each have all been a part of God. Only our mortal life on earth has a limited engagement, but God created us to live eternally and the most important question for us is where do we want to spend it? Think seriously about it for we live on earth only a mere 70 to 80 years for most, and then what? You're buried and it ends there. I know one thing for sure my life won't end in the grave but I will live on eternally with my God, How about You?

BOOK TWO

DELIVER US FROM EVIL,

CHAPTER SEVEN

THE LAST CALL AND FINAL TESTAMENT FOR MAN

The question that should come to one's mind is why the urgency for this book, or for such a strongly worded first half of this book being focused on the many ills of mankind. Well as the title of this chapter suggests, this is the last call from God to man for we have entered the End of Times. What is the End of Times? It is the last years of man before the return of the Messiah. Years that the bible tells us will bring worldwide economic collapse (which has already begun), much famine and tragedy, World War III, and the death of tens of millions caused both by the war and by the devastations from natural disasters. Man will have finally reached his greatest achievement since he first stepped foot on earth and that is being able to bring about the total annihilation of mankind and our world as we know it and if it weren't for the return of our Messiah, none of us will survive and the earth would fail to exist forever more.

If this sounds like a fairy tale or the hallucinations of a religious quack, then I urge you to read on and do keep an open mind and an open heart and let the truth speak to you. For this is for you the reader, I already have the truth and God has already changed my life 180 degrees around. You only need to look around you and take stock at the world and the events of each day and the truth speaks out to you. We can't possibly go on much longer before World War III or something like it breaks out because of our failure to get along with one another and because of greed and lust for power and control. Right now the economy is in ruins and leaders from all over the world have gathered to find an answer to this great loss of wealth. I can only say that nothing these great leaders and their economic experts can come up with will solve the economic chaos in the world. If anything, any corrections in the economy made by man will be temporary and eventually fail. This economic collapse we are presently going through is no mistake, man in all his wisdom has failed and the world is now in chaos over the economy. Man could never understand that his greed for money and power would one day backfire. With CEO's of corporations earning salaries of tens of millions of dollars a year, housing prices that are ten to twenty times greater than what the average person makes in a year, many cars costing a year's salary to buy, could it have been of any wonder why the system is collapsing? The average man worldwide was put outside of the world markets unable to afford the housing, products and food essential to modern day living. Yet man still feels he can solve this economic problem for he is greater than God. It's amazing, but we never seem to learn.

As God has revealed to us in his prophetic word in the book of Ezekiel, chapter 38, vs. 2-6, *Son of man, turn and face Gog of the land of Magog, the prince who rules over the nations of Mesech and Tubal and prophesy against him. Give him this message from the Sovereign Lord: Gog, I am your enemy. I will turn you around and put hooks in your jaws to lead you out with your whole army-your horses and charioteers in full armor and a great horde armed with shields and swords. Persia, Ethiopia and Libya will join you, too, with all their weapons. Gomer and all its armies will also join you, along with the armies of Beth-togarmah from the distant north, and many others.* It goes on to say in vs. 7-9, that God will cause this huge army to come south and invade the nation of Israel to destroy and plunder the nation of Israel. It is here were God will intervene with all his mighty splendor and show the world who God really is by destroying the huge army killing every one of its soldiers. That it will take the Israeli people seven months to bury the dead.

So who are Gog, Mesech, Togarmar, Gomer, Ethiopia and Persia, whom God will use for this invasion of Israel and the other question is how and why? To begin with Gog is the ancient nation of Russia and Mesech is the ancient city of Moscow. Togamar is believed to be Afghanistan, Gomer represents Germany and Persia is the ancient name for Iran and Ethopia for the Middle Eastern nations. How will God do this, cause all these nations to unite and invade Israel? The hooks in their jaws that will eventually cause them to unite is an economic world collapse of the world economy leaving these nations as well as the world in financial ruins. This economic devastation will force this group of nations to invade the land of Israel, which is living at the time in peace and prosperity. We can now see the beginning of the fulfillment of this prophecy now in the year 2009, when the economy of both the United States and the rest of the world is in financial chaos. This economic devastation will be greater than the Great Depression of 1929 and could culminate in the greatest world war the world has ever known. Hundreds of millions will die all over the work but in the end the world will find peace on earth and finally know and revere God as the one true God, and Jesus will return to earth as Lord of all.

Our greatest achievements in this world to date are the fabrications of atomic and hydrogen bombs, chemical and biological weapons of mass destruction, and ingenious ways for the rich to get richer at the expense of everyone else. Little or nothing has been done to eliminate poverty, hunger, starvation and disease from this world. Nothing is being done to eliminate hate, bigotry, murder, crime and the multitude of bad ills that like a cancer are eating up the bodies and souls of all mankind. The signs are all around us and in this chapter I will endeavor to bring this truth to you using the only source proven to be 100% accurate in its prophetic warnings for man, the holy bible.

One of the most important prophecies that will signal the start of the end times has already occurred and that is the "rebirth of the nation of Israel" in 1948. Destroyed by the Romans almost two thousand years ago, the Jews were disbursed all over the world to live without a country. It was to last almost two thousand years and then in the last generation of man the Jews will return to their homeland and be given their nation back to them, and so it was in 1948. Further that they would live in safety although surrounded by their enemies and eventually find peace with their enemies. We find this in Ezekiel 38:8, *in the latter years you shall go against a land restored from war, a land where people were gathered from many nations on the mountains of Israel. Which had long laid waste; its people were brought out of the nations and are now living in safety, all of them.* The bible here goes on to give the accounts of what will happen to the people of Israel, shortly thereafter when Russia with her allies will invade Israel. This will come about after Israel finally finds true peace in the land, and her people no longer live in fear. Today we are working hard with all the Middle Eastern nations to bring about a true lasting peace to the Middle East for all and from what one sees written in the bible we will succeed in finding this true peace which as the bible shows us will be a false peace and last only a short time. It's after this than the danger of the end time exists, for it will come when least expected bringing on World War III.

We are now witnessing the end of the evil empire in Iraq. The country is being converted to a democracy so we hope with the United States along with her allies finally finding success after many years of struggling with the war. Now we have some kind of promise from the powers in office of an end to the war In Iraq and finally bringing home the troops. This could be the beginning of a new era for the Middle East, the era of peace with Israel as written in the book of Ezekiel. But caution is given here, for the bible predicts that when peace comes to the Middle East and Israel, then will the Russians and their five allies invade the south (the Middle East) and World War III will erupt.

We also know from the bible codes recently discovered in the Torah, by Eliyahu Rips of the Hebrew University in Israel, the sequence of prophetic events that will occur from here on out. Among them again is the most important one being the rebirth of the nation of Israel in 1948, for that is the date that starts the countdown for the last generation of man on earth before the return of the Messiah. A generation as explained in the bible as seventy years. Thus we can expect an end of all things and the war of Armageddon around 2018. But according to much more recent discovery of the bible codes much more will happen before that great war of Armageddon. For one is the attack on the World's Trade Center in New York City on September 11, 2001. This as written in the bible code is the most important prophecy in the history of the world for it begins the count down to the End Times. As given in the prophecy we have about ten years before the start of World War III. Another much more devastating attack on the United States of America will occur between the years of 2008 and 2011. It will be more severe than the attack of September 11, 2001, on the World Trade Center, in New York City. We will suffer a complete collapse of our economic system around the year of 2008 and culminating in 2009. This economic collapse will have started around the year 2005. As we all know this one is already being fulfilled as I write we are experiencing the worst economic collapse since the great depression of 1929, and this one as I mentioned in the prior chapter will be even worse as this one is world wide affecting all nations around the world. A series of devastating hurricanes will destroy the east coast of the United States in 2009 and 2010 and a great earthquake will destroy the west coast of the United States in and around 2010 and 2011. World War III will break out around the year of 2012, bringing much death and destruction and this probably caused by the economic collapse of 2008, still being felt and experienced by countries around the world. The appearance of the Anti Christ will occur around this time bringing great deception to the world. Huge natural upheavals will destroy the countries of Japan, the Philippines, and the state of California between the years of 2011 and 2012. The United States alone will suffer the loss of two thirds of its population and included in this will be another attack on New York City with a nuclear device exploded in midtown Manhattan.

Sounds like a Nostradamus prophecy or something predicted by Edgar Cayce, too incredible to believe. Yet it is coming from the Torah, the first five books of the Old Testament and from the bible codes. They are the only books of the bible not written by man, but given to man by God himself. How credible are the codes in the Torah. None have erred and all have come to pass. As I stated before Israel becoming a nation has come to pass. John F. Kennedy, Robert Kennedy and Martin Luther King have been assassinated as foretold on the exact dates given. Princess Diana did die in a car crash on the foretold date with the same people in the car. Saddam Hussein has been defeated and executed. The World Trade Center was destroyed on the very date given in the bible codes. Further the code states the Osama Bin Laden ordered the attack and that Mohamed Atta, led the attack. All these predictions occurring exactly as they happened, on the date they were predicted and by the perpetrators and assassins as shown in the predictions. The bible codes go even further and now predictions of our future are being discovered.

Does that mean that the future is hopeless? No, absolutely not, for prophecy is always contingent upon the man's free will. We can change things, but to do so we must change as a people. We must exercise the two greatest commandments of God as part of our daily lives, as part of how and what we are. They are first and foremost that we love God the father, with all of our hearts, with all of our strength and all of our minds. The second one as important, that we love one another as we love ourselves. On these two hang all the laws of the prophets. If we all could change and do this from our hearts, the world wouldn't have to come to an end. Four billion people need not perish in wars, earthquakes and by diseases. We can usher in the Messiah into a world of peace and love rather than a world in the midst of war and death. We must make the choices. The big question is can we make the big changes? I fear for us all for I don't believe that we can change from our selfish worldly ways to a spiritual life with God. But if enough of us do change, if enough of us do come to God and repent of our ways and accept his Son as our savior we can at least lessen the blow. But we must be submitting our lives to God, praying daily for world peace and making a difference where ever we go. Then maybe we won't have these devastating hurricanes or the earthquake in California. Once again I must remind you that all prophecies in the bible and in the bible codes are contingent upon what we as a people do. We have the free will to change everything and these prophetic warnings remain just that, warnings.

We must take note that our generation is at the same place the people of Israel were at crossing the Sinai desert out of Egypt or the people of Sodom and Gomorrah were at before God destroyed them. We can make decisions of the heart to change out ways and avoid the wrath of God upon us or just do nothing and live as we are and see the End of Days comes upon us wrecking all sorts of death and devastation as the world has never seen. Through the past hundreds of years man has been forecasting the end of the world coming upon us and it never does. Man has over the years has learned to ignore these warnings as they never come to pass. Well again one must remember that prophecies of God are contingent upon the people changing their ways. All through history it has been this way, when men changed God blessed. When man persisted in being stubborn, God punished. So it was with Israel, being held captive as slaves in Egypt and in Babylon and so it was with the profit Jonah stuck inside of a whale. God never changes and He uses this rule always. So folks it is up to us, we can forestall the End of Days and another generation in the distant future or we can do nothing and it will happen to us.

One thing that must be puzzling you at this point is how do we know these things will happen and how reliable are the bible codes? Well for one no other book in the world has produced secret codes especially in the amounts that you find in the bible. You may find by chance a group of words and names that are related, but that is about all you will find is one or two related topics. In the bible codes you find not one or two related codes, but hundreds and eventually thousands of codes all specific about a future event. Science and mathematicians are just now beginning to understand the codes and decipher them as rapidly as humanly possible. It is now believed that the codes contain the entire future of the world and even further it is now believed that every human being that has ever lived or will live is written in the bible codes from their birth to the date of their death and all that they accomplish in life.

How accurate have the codes been to date? As I stated before they have forecasted the crucifixion of Jesus Christ, the destruction of Jerusalem by Rome shortly thereafter and the dispersion of the Jews around the world to be without a country for two thousand years. The codes predicted the coming of Jesus Christ and that he is the Son of God, Savior of the world, the rise of Napoleon, World Wars I and II, the rise of Hitler, the assassinations of John F. Kennedy and Robert F. Kennedy, both on the dates of their assassinations, the locations where they take place and the names of the assassins. There are predictions of Nostradamus, Edgar Cayce, Princess Diana, and Sadam Hussein, the September 11th destruction of the World's Trade Center and the Pentagon in Washington D.C. The list of predictions goes on and on and all of them accurate to the dates and events involved. The Torah was written three thousand years ago, given to Moses by God. Consequently only God could have hidden these codes in the Torah, for only he authored the first five books of the bible and only he could have the intelligence required to create and hide such a code in the bible. No technology of this magnitude existed in the world during the time of Moses and none exists even today to create such a code in the bible. Man was barely beyond the invention of the wheel, hand tools and weapons let alone the creation of a mathematical code that has taken three thousand years and the invention of the computer to break. Since the discovery of the bible codes it has been discovered that God placed hidden codes through out the bible. In the book of Isaiah are the codes that refer to Jesus Christ, his life, that he is the Messiah who suffered for all of us and will return to save us in the end. You can do your own research of the bible codes in the Internet. Do a search in Yahoo or Google's, for the bible codes and you will be amazed of all the predictions that have been discovered and how all of them have come to pass.

Why did it take so long to find and break the code? Well for one it wasn't for not trying. Hebrew sages had been searching for thousands of years to find the codes. They knew they were there in the bible, but could not break the codes. Sir Isaac Newton was obsessed in trying to find and break the bible codes and died never having succeeded. We read in the book of Daniel of the Old Testament, that God tells Daniel to seal the book as it's not for the people to know until the last generation of earth. For it is to them that the need for understanding and the revelation of the bible codes is important for it pertains to them and what is to befall them if they do not repent. It is to the last generation who need to know the future of their world and to know that their continued worldly ways void of spirit and faith in God, will lead man to his own final destruction through wars that threaten to exterminate all life on the entire planet. It is to them God intended the bible codes for, so they could understand that it isn't God who is destroying this world but its we ourselves, man in all his selfishness, spiritless, faithless ways that is bringing all this upon himself.

Some of the critics of the bible codes say that it's a fabrication that the codes are the results of one's own interpretation and manipulation of the letters and words as they come up. And that the codes don't say the things that they have been credited for. This is also the same age-old argument that the bible itself doesn't say what it says, for its left open for interpretation. Thus the hundreds and thousands of different points of view we get from reading the bible. As well as the many different points of view creating the many different religions in this world. This made worse by the intellectual minds that refuse to believe in God who are some of the more prominent people in the world and thus have an influential affect on how the public perceive and believe in all things.

To all critics I say not so, for the codes were written three thousand years ago, and what was written doesn't need interpretation for it speaks for itself. No one could have known the future then or that they'd be a United States of America on the opposite side of the world. Remember man never knew until Columbus, that the world was round and that there were other continents and worlds on the other side of the world.

For further proof there has been discovery of prophecies in the bible codes of events before the events took place. They include for one the assassination of Prime Minister Rabin of Israel. One year before his assassination the bible code regarding his assassination was discovered, naming the place, the assassin and the date of the assassination a year later. He was given the prediction of his assassination but chose to ignore it for he wasn't going to allow a prediction stop him from his work. A year later to the date, time and by the name given in the prediction Prime Minister Rabin was assassinated. Lucky guess, manipulation of words found the bible? I think not. The prediction was right on the money.

The day of the terrorist attack on the World's Trade Center in New York City, the bible code for the attack was discovered within the hour. It had the time and date of the attack of the twin towers in New York City. Furthermore the accuracy of the prediction was such that it named the terrorist leading the attack on board the two planes, Muhammad Atta. The bible code goes on to mention the attack on the Pentagon in Washington D.C., also that same day. Still think this is a manipulation of the bible codes? I think not, it's just too accurate. Never before have there been so many predictions of future events this accurate. Folks, the bible codes don't miss. As great as Nostradamus, Edgar Casey and Jean Dixon may have been they were not 100% accurate. They were maybe 50% accurate.

The bible code foretold the election of President Clinton, and the code discovered six months before his election. The bible codes also foretold of the trouble in his presidency with Monica Lewinsky, and his survival from impeachment again predicted before their occurrence.

The narrow victory of President Bush defeating Al Gore, prediction found before the election. That he would win by a very narrow margin of votes. One thousand mysterious votes as it states in the bible code from the state of Florida. Also that at the start of his presidency Arafat will be the head of the Palestinians, and Sharon will be the Prime Minister of Israel. All predicted before George Bush won the election.

In 2000, they discovered the prediction concerning the collapse of the stock market and of the economy for this country as well as that of the entire world. By chance, no way it's too accurate and the events all come to pass as it was written. Only the hand of God could have accomplished all this.

Lucky guesses by some lucky mathematicians? I don't believe so, do you? Luck happens once and possibly twice, but never with the frequency like the bible codes. The prophecies from the bible codes are like nothing ever discovered previously in the world. They are likely the most important discoveries in the history of the world. For its God's message to us, the last generation of man on earth before the return of the Messiah. Telling us where we've come from and where we're at, this very moment in time and to where we're headed if we all (and I mean all) don't make some quick changes in our lives. Again I must remind all that prophecies are not carved in stone. They are subject to our free will as God intended. We have the power to save the world with all the six billion plus people in it or will we witness the fulfillment of the bible prophecies.

Been there, heard all that before? Not like this you haven't, because these are not like the prophecies we've heard over and over from Nostradamus, Edgar Cayce or Jean Dixon or the hundreds like them. Great seers of their times and some prophets of God as we've come to learn from the bible codes, but human never the less and subject to making errors, which accounts for the large percentage of predictions they each made that never came to pass. Every prophecy found in the bible code has come to pass. The bible codes have been absolutely accurate and nothing, not even science has been able to provide us with that degree of accuracy.

Now we're running out of time. We can't afford to be stiff necked much longer for the buck stops here with us. We are the last generations of man on earth, and we will either change our ways and save the world or we will continue on our path as we have been and destroy all that there is. We can't afford another nor do we even consider another World War. We are the atomic age generation and the next World War, will definitely unleash nuclear holocaust upon the entire world killing tens if not hundreds of millions of people.

Whether you're a student of the bible or you have never read the bible ever, the signs of the times are now obvious to all men. Whether you're very religious or an atheist, again the signs of the times are now obvious to all men. We can't afford to be intellectually stupid anymore. We must cast all politics aside. We must end all bigotry and hate on earth and enter in the age of brotherly love to last us for times to come, for God is not the enemy and judge of man, man is the enemy and judge of man. We've been fighting and judging one another or six thousand years and it must stop or we all will die. We see all around us the words virtual reality and how to experience it via computers and video games. Well folks, here is the real reality we're a dying race if we don't get with the real program, the program that offers life, liberty and the pursuit of happiness.

I offer this prayer to God, for all of us in the world. Please, feel free to pray this and ask God to show you the way to this new peaceful life, amen:

Heavenly Father, I come before you humbling myself to repent of my sinful ways. I have lived in the darkness all of my years, with sins beyond number and its pain too much to bear. I turn to you this day Father bearing all my sins to you and all the sins of my ignorance, please Father forgive me for I truly repent of my sinfulness and want to change my life with you. I do believe in your son Jesus and ask Him into my life to be my savior and guide this day and forever more.

Heavenly Father, you are the creator of all men, please help us all in this world and cleanse us from all unrighteousness and remove us from the darkness that threatens to destroy us all. Give to each of us your truth, bathe us in your love and sooth us with your grace, lifting us up with your right hand and wiping away our disgrace. Guide us with your Holy Spirit, and let your light shine the pathway in which we must follow. Forsake us not oh God, bring new life into our dried old bones. Breathe new life into us, filling us with your Holy Spirit and leading us not into temptation but delivering us from all evil, amen.

In Luke 12:34-38, Jesus tells us, *Be dressed for action and have your lamps lit; be like those who are waiting for their master to return from the wedding banquet, so that they may open the door for him as soon as he comes and knocks. Blessed are those slaves whom the master finds alert when he comes; truly I tell you, he will fasten his belt and have them sit down to eat, and he will come and serve them. If he comes during the middle of the night, or next dawn, and finds them so, blessed are those slaves.*

Just think about it for a moment. Before the discovery of the bible codes, you believed life just went on and on and you had nothing to worry about. We relied on what was preached to us by men of the cloth of the many religions around the world and by those in power and leaders of government. We accepted what they espoused as the truth and never questioned them. We followed whoever was leading for as Jesus once said the leaders are few, the sheep are many. We have been following the different leaders for thousand of years because we've been too lazy to ask questions, to ignorant to care as long as our daily material needs were being met and finally others just didn't care because they didn't believe.

But just as science and technology marches on with new discoveries being made everyday, now the most important discovery in over two thousand years since Jesus Christ walked on earth has come. That discovery is the bible codes. It brings new life into the word of God. It brings new understanding of God and of Christ. It brings God's truth to the forefront of our minds with a new reality of the end times. Yet many and better most still push it aside because they do not want to know the truth. They want to believe life will go on as it is and their only concern is the own materialistic world and family.

For centuries man has ignored the word of God and played a religious game with God. That his going to church or synagogue would be sufficient as one doesn't need to bother with God in the everyday of one's life. Only weaklings do that. Well let me say here and now that kind of thinking and belief is wrong and in error. There is no excuse for you not reading the bible and learning the word of God. You can't learn of God just from preachers and ministers and rabbis. Now with the discovery of the bible codes this should create a curiosity in every man to find out more about God, his messages and his word in the bible. The end is coming and coming soon. Don't let your ignorance cause you to lose your chance into the kingdom of heaven. There is a new world coming and in a very short time, maybe in another 10 or 15 years. Are you ready for the coming of the Messiah? Are you ready for the ending of this world and the beginning of His new world, the new millennium where life is everlasting? Will you be among the two thirds of the world's population that will perish by the end of this world or will you be apart of the one third of the world's population that will enter the everlasting life in the new world with the Messiah? Whether you believe me or refuse to believe me makes no difference, for the truth is the truth and the end is very near, don't get short living a Godless life.

Take a moment now, today while you still have a today and just pray asking God for his mercy to forgive you for everything wrong and sinful in your life. It's just that easy and in your prayer ask the Lord Jesus into your heart to be with you forever more and teach you and help you to change into a child of God. You may be thinking I am Jewish, Hindu, Muslim, Buddhist and don't believe in Jesus. Well then search out your heart and ask the one question you need to ask yourself; has my faith my belief served me any better? The answer will be probably not. Then be a Jew, a Muslim, a Hindu or a Buddhist or whatever but be it to the fullness of God and accept no less. Don't let your faith be a stumbling stone blocking you from the truth. For when the Messiah comes, there will no excuses and no time for repentance. You can't say to him you were deceived and followed the wrong guides. For if you are blind and follow the blind then both of you are doomed and both will fail. So therefore no matter what faith or religion you belong to, let the spirit of God fill you heart and receive the truth of God in your heart. He will reveal Christ to you, the Messiah of the world. It will be then up to you to choose with your heart the path you will live, and the one God whom you will serve.

The bible goes to tell us in 1st Thessalonians, Chapter 5, vs. 2-11, an epistle written by Saint Paul, *for you yourselves know very well that the day of the Lord will come like a thief in the night. When they say, "There is peace and security," then sudden destruction will come upon them, as labor pains come upon a pregnant woman, and there will be no escape! But you, beloved, are not in darkness, for that day to surprise you like a thief; for you are all children of light and children of the day; we are not of the night or of darkness. So then let us not fall asleep as others do, but let us keep awake and be sober; for those who sleep at night and those who are drunk get drunk at night. But since we belong to the day, let us be sober, and put on the breastplate of faith and love, and for a helmet the hope of salvation. For God has destined us not for wrath but for obtaining salvation through our Lord Jesus Christ, who died for us, so that whether we are awake or asleep we may live with him. Therefore encourage one another and build up each other, as indeed you are doing.*

The greatest of all end times prophecies come from Jesus himself in Matthew, chapter 24:4-14, the apostles ask Jesus what will be the sign of his coming and of the end of the age? Jesus answered them, *Beware that no one leads you astray. For many will come in my name, saying, 'I am the Messiah' and they will lead many astray. And you will hear of wars and rumors of wars, see that you are not alarmed, for this must take place, but the end is not yet. For nation will rise against nation, and kingdom against kingdom, and there will be famines, pestilence and earthquakes in various places: all this is but the beginning of the birth pangs.*

Then they will hand you over to be tortured and will put you to death, and you will be hated by all nations because of my name. Then many will fall away, and they will betray one another and hate one another. And many false prophets will arise and lead many astray. And because of the increase of lawlessness, the love of many will grow cold. But the one who endures to the end will be saved. And this good news of the kingdom will be proclaimed to all the nations; and then the end will come.

So when you see the desolating sacrilege standing in the holy place, as was spoken of by the prophet Daniel (let the reader understand). Then those in Judea must flee to the mountains, the one on the housetop must not go down to take what is in the house; the one in the field must not turn back to get a coat. Wow to those who are pregnant and to those who are nursing infants in those days! Pray that your flight may not be in winter or on a Sabbath. For at that time there will be great suffering, such as has not been from the beginning of the world until now, no, and never will be. And if those days had not been cut short, no one would be saved; but for the sake of the elect those days will be cut short. Then if anyone says to you, 'Look! Here is the Messiah!' Or 'There he is!' –do not believe it. For false messiahs and false prophets will appear and produce great signs and omens, to lead astray, if possible, even the elect. Take note, I have told you beforehand. So, if they say to you, 'Look! He is in the wilderness,' do not go out. If they say, 'Look! He is in the inner rooms,' do not believe it. For as the lightning comes from the east and flashes as far as the west, so will be the coming of the Son of Man. Wherever the corpse is, there the vulture will gather.

Immediately after the suffering of those days the sun will be darkened, and the moon will not give its light; the stars will fall from heaven, and the powers of heaven will be shaken. Then the sign of the Son of Man will appear in heaven, and then all the tribes of the earth will mourn, and they will see the Son of Man coming on the clouds of heaven with power and great glory. And he will send out his angels with a loud trumpet call, and they will gather his elect from the four winds, from one end of heaven to the other.

Now the obvious question is does this apply to us today? Are we this end times generation who will see the end to this world as we know it? I think yes and let me explain to you the reader why. First off we have one of the key prophecies in the bible from Ezekiel, in chapter 38:8, where Ezekiel is speaking about the nation of Israel being restored after a long period of desolation, her people brought back out of all nations through out the world. Well that prophecy was fulfilled in 1948, when the world gave the Jews back their homeland of Israel, a fulfillment of that prophecy and a true sign of the end times.

Then let us take a look at the prophecies given to us in Matthew, chapter 24, by Jesus Christ. He begins by saying that many will come saying I am the Messiah, false prophets who lead many astray from God. Well this has been happening over and over for the past century. We had Jim Jones, Timothy Leary, Hitler (a forerunner of the Anti Christ), and hundreds of the Jim Bakers and other false prophets and ministers playing havoc with peoples' lives.

Jesus goes on to say that we will hear of wars and rumors of wars. Nation shall rise against nation, and kingdom shall rise against kingdom. Well never in the history of the world has as many wars been fought as was fought in the twentieth century. For the first time in history we also fought two global wars, World War I and II, where over 100 million people were killed in those wars. No generation in the past has ever come near those figures. We are the first generation in all of history to fulfill this prophecy. Think still we're not in the end times?

He goes on to say that they'll be famines, pestilence and earthquakes in various places. Well the famine is here and very real and has grown worse with every passing year. Never before have so many gone hungry and died of starvation as it is with our generation. Over two million children die every year of starvation and millions more adults from the same two thirds of the world's population is under fed and half of them are starving and dying and yet the one third that has it all has disregarded the blight of the other two thirds. For here in America, as well as in Europe, brokers lend money out to third world nations, then jack up the interest rates to unbearable and UN-repayable levels that cause countries into bankruptcy and the poor end up even poorer and even more hungry. Or money is loaned out to ruthless leaders of third world nations whose intentions was never to help the poor and hungry, but to fill their coffers with the wealth coming from American tax payers. Farmers are paid to burn their crops to force unreal and manufactured high prices on food, denying the poor any chance to buy food. It is this inhumanity to man by man that has brought starvation into the world. Sure we have droughts and natural disasters, but they alone would not contribute to the levels of starvation known today. Again, never in the history of the world have we seen this level of hunger and starvation and poverty coupled with wars and natural disasters happening at the same time. End times? You bet it is. Just like earthquakes and natural disasters. Never in the recorded history of the world have we witnessed so many disasters as the world has seen in the twentieth century alone. As a matter of fact the earthquakes that occurred in the world from 1990 to the year 2000 have outnumbered all the recorded earthquakes in the history of the world combined!

Then we come to pestilence or as we call it today disease and just like it was back in the dark ages it is today. Today the scourges of man are cancer, AIDS, heart disease, diabetes, and a host of diseases through out the third world nations like malaria, small pox, influenza and the plague that are ravaging its people. AIDS in itself is promising to soon become the worst plague that man has ever known. More and more we are fulfilling the prophecies of Christ for the end times.

Another prophecy we find is in the book of Revelations, chap 13, 15-18, *He was given power to give breath to the image of the first beast, so that it could speak and cause all who refused to worship the image to be killed. He also forced everyone, small and great, rich and poor, free and slave, to receive a mark on his right hand or on his forehead, so that no one could buy or sell unless he had the mark, which is the name of the beast or the number of his name. This calls for wisdom. If anyone has insight, let him calculate the number of the beast, for it is man's number. His number is 666.*

Almost sounds like a Stephen King, novel, but upon taking a closer look at this mysterious prophecy, the very same thing is happening today and being prepared for all of us in the not so distant future. We are the fulfillment of the 666 prophecy. It's a revelation of man and who he becomes and where his heart lies. For it is a spiritual marking on the fallen man, the godless man. For those who are the children of God are known of God and are spiritually marked as the children of God.

So we have entered the age of the 666, but how about the marking on the forehead or hand? Well, that's being worked on today. We are all presently using the forerunner, the debit card. We can buy so many goods, go to the theater, and buy gas at the gas station, food at the supermarket with no cash today. We just present our bank debit cards, and its run through the credit machines and the money is paid instantly from our checking accounts to the merchant. They call them ATM cards or bank debit cards and they are quickly replacing the use of cash all over the world.

Planned for the near future is to remove all cash from society and give us one main bank debit card with a computer chip in it that contains all the information about us from birth to present day including our social security number, bank account numbers, passport, etc. This will be the card we use to buy and sell everything in the near future. To avoid losing the card, the U.S. Government, is working on a small microcomputer chip that can be injected into your forehand containing all the same information. Thus you hand becomes you bank debit card. By passing you hand across a scanner they can instantly obtain payment from your bank account. These programs have already been shown on television on The Learning Channel, and the Discovery Channel. So it's no crazy and wild interpretation on my part but a fact and a reality of what's happening today with our technology.

The debit card is already here being widely used all over the United States and Europe. The program was first started back with the bar codes being printed on all packages of food and goods we buy at the various stores we shop in like super markets, drug stores, etc. All packages, bottles, have bar codes which the cashier uses at the cash register to scan the items being bought. The computer then adds up the tab, and takes inventory at the same time of the items purchased. Every bar code is keyed with three double bars, one at the start on the left, two more in the middle of the bar code and the last two at the end of the bar code. These double bars represent the number 6, thus the three double bars, the number 666. This is the number that must be there for the computer to understand the rest of the bar code. As the prophecy in Revelations says, it is the number of man. For man invented the computer, it's his designation, his identification of the world system of man and the eventual downfall of man.

The programs that were presented on television about these debit cards said that several cities in the United States are now in the process of testing this cash-less system out, one of them being Washington, D.C. and the other Portland, Oregon. So from this you can see we are not far from the end times, as we know the world to be. We are the first generation in the history of the world to see this 666 manifestation come to a reality and the emergence of the cash-less society and the markings on our foreheads. Food for thought you think? You bet! It's time to stop and do some self re-evaluations of our lives and our relationships with one another and with God. It's time we do some deep soul searching and find a truth that works for each and every one of us. A truth that will indeed set you free, that will draw you to the light and away from the dark side and that can only be from God, for he is truth.

The Mayans before disappearing off the face of the earth left us their sacred writings and prophecies of the world's future. Strangely enough they prophesied that the end of the world would come in the year 2011-12. The sages of Israel in their ancient writings from thousand of years ago also prophesied that the world would end in the year 2011-12, coincidence you think? Further ancient sacred writings from China, were discovered and they prophesied that the world would come to an end in the year 2011. Now we have the newly discovered bible codes of the Old Testament, telling us that indeed somewhere around the year 2011/2012, will be the end for man in this present world, for these are indeed the end times.

Whether we choose to believe the prophecies of the bible even though they have been proven to be 100% accurate or choose to ignore them. One thing we all can't ignore is the truth and the world won't go much further as it is without a global war coming upon us all. And one thing is for certain and that the next world war will involve massive weapons of mass destruction like the world has never known. Too many nations in the world today are very unstable and fighting breaks out with them too frequently for one not to be concerned. Israel and the Palestinians finding it impossible to make peace with one another as they continue to operate from outside the spiritual realm. Iraq's war is being won, but will it remain a free democracy once the United States pulls its troops out. Iran, Syria, Afghanistan and Pakistan, all havens for terrorists and a pressure cooker ready to explode at any moment. Then there is Russia, China and North Korea and what we have is a very volatile situation. One day if peace is not found war will erupt like an atomic bomb and I fear to imagine what the results of that will be. The bible is explicit that in the end times two thirds of the world's population will be destroyed in the wars and natural disasters.

The only way to peace is through a life of spirituality. The only way to stop hunger, death from starvation, is through a life of spirituality. Bigotry, hatred, murder and violence all will stop with a world filled with spiritual people living life in the spirit. For when life is lived in the spirit, then all evil must come to an end. For evil cannot exist in the same house with holiness, for if you have cleaned out your house and turned your life over to God then all evil has been removed. You are out of the darkness and have entered a life in the light of God. Living life in the spirit is to live your life filled in love that pours out of you to every one you reach out to. It is a life where you are reconnected to the soul of God, your soul to His soul as it was in the beginning and should be forever more.

For it was from the soul of God that we each were created and we all came from, but in the world we got distracted by the things of the world and became disconnected from God. We are eternal souls that came from the Father and to Him we belong, and it's to Him that we return and are given the kingdom of heaven and everlasting life. Remember the soul controls the mind and the mind controls the body. In the world too many become fascinated with the things and ways of the world, then taking on to themselves the ways of the world for their lives. The consequences being a separation of their soul's from the Father, thus entering into a world of darkness, a world of sin, hardship and grief. But when we find our way back into a spiritually filled life our soul becomes reconnected to our heavenly Father, and once again we are filled with his love and his truth. Imagine a world where we all live in the absolute truth of ourselves, living life in the spirit and not by our carnal minds. Living by a love so great and powerful that it brings an end to evil and sinfulness that exists in the world today. We have the power to stop World War III, before it comes. We have the power to stop Armageddon, before it comes. We have the power to end all the evil in the world and save all the people of the world. Feed them, clothe them and see to it that no one is ever again denied their equal rights, equal housing, schooling, food and shelter or the pursuit of happiness. If when the death of one child from starvation brings guilt upon us all, then how much more guilt do we share when millions die every year of starvation? We each can answer that question for ourselves, however how do we justify ourselves to God when the judgment day comes?

So the question remains for all of us, are we ready then for the return of the Messiah, for God, for our Creator? Are you ready if he came today, tonight or maybe tomorrow or next month? We don't know the date and time of his arrival but we do know he's coming and his arrival will be a swift one. Don't do like the foolish maidens and wait for tomorrow and then another tomorrow. Tomorrow is not yours to count on, all you have is today. There is an old saying that goes like this: "yesterday is like a cancelled check, it is gone forever. Tomorrow is like a promissory note, it's not yours yet until you get there. All you have is today and you must live it as if it was all that you have." No one can count on a tomorrow, today could be your last day on earth, are you ready to stand before God? Only those like the wise maidens will enter the kingdom of heaven. Those wise ones are the ones who took the journey within their hearts and souls daily, communicating with God daily and living lives in the spirit, subduing their flesh and giving their spirits the control over their daily lives. They are the ones that kept the faith not just in God but also in themselves, being honest and truthful in all that they did and examining themselves, their burdens, their sins and their faults and bringing them to the cross to crucify them in order that they may live the spiritual life daily and not just for a season. They are the ones who upon searching for the truth found it in Jesus Christ, and repented and asked him into their lives. He is the oil in their lamps that gave the light to shine on the footprints that led them home. He is the one that leads us out of the darkness and into the light.

Are you ready to drop what you're doing and take a hard deep look inside yourself? Are you ready to examine yourself and most of all are you ready to truly love yourself and to forgive yourself, giving yourself the warm embrace you've so longed for all of your life? Are you ready to truly search deep within yourself and come to face with who and what you are and be ready to commit to making the necessary changes that your spirit has so longed for. So often we hear people saying how lonely, hard and cold the world is. How lonely and lost they feel in the world, when all too often what is really wrong is the lifestyle they chose to live. They've been living trapped in the world of materialism, money, power, sex, lust where everything is temporal always leaving one empty and starving for more. Thus your spirit grows hungry and feeling empty and incomplete because you can never have enough and just be content and satisfied. It's always a competition with you against the world and yourself to do more, show that you're bigger and better than everyone else. You find yourself battling against life everyday as the world has you chasing moonbeams. Soon you find that your tired of the chase, confused, not succeeding as others do, not achieving the big house and big cars because you lack being of the right color, religion, sex, etc. Then maybe it could be because you're an underachiever, lazy or just plain a non doer. Then on the opposite side are those with the big fancy cars and big homes who are just as unsatisfied, miserable and always searching for more, their appetites knowing no limits. Many have found themselves worn out with disease and mental illnesses from the ongoing stress this brings. You will sense this feeling of emptiness change into bitterness as it continues to grow and it begins to consume you daily thoughts. You wonder why you're feeling such emptiness, defeat, loneliness, boredom, dissatisfaction without realizing that the problem is not in the world but the problem is with you. It's your spirit that is crying out for help, for love, for acknowledgment and friendship with no one other than with yourself. You've been absent for too long and your spirit wants to get in touch with you, help you to redirect your life and to grow with you so that you can enjoy the true fruits of life in the spirit. We're always chasing after the brass ring, for that one lucky break that will change our lives forever, but fail to see that we are that brass ring and that what we're really after can only come from within. Our minds are brainwashed and controlled by the merchants of television, the advertising industry, our lust for money, greed, the Dow Jones average and by our insanity over material possessions. Harry Truman, once said the buck stops here. Well my friends, the same applies to you and to me. The buck stops with us. We must make an effort to recognize who we are, what we are and bring it to God. We need to self examine ourselves and ask God to change our ways. We can't wait for the next guy to change, or for the government to change, we must change. Each one of us must change for the bucks stops at us.

You see the basis of life isn't money, power or material possessions, but a spirit filled life lived under the guidance of God, and filled with all his love operating within us. With a well-balanced life centered in God and love, not only will you have a happy fulfilled life which God will bless with all the success and relationships you need. For in God, all things are made possible. Now you have God working with you, guiding you and you will make better and wiser choices bringing about much more solid results. With God on your side more doors will be opened and more opportunities will arise for you to choose from. God how I know this for I went through this very same situation in my life. But God was there for me as He'll be there for you. Jesus told me on one of his visits to me, that I would buy a house that was under construction and be completed in twelve months. Twelve months to the day the woman he had shown me in a vision sold me her house that had been totally renovated new for only $37,500, and a waterfront home on the bay no less. This was a steal in any book, but God did it for me. Later in my life he told me I would leave my job by end of 2002 for a much better paying job. In December of that year, six months after he had spoken to me I received two new job offers. On December 9th, I started the new job making a lot more than I had been earning previously, almost double. Folks

God isn't short on miracles it's us who are short on faith. Give God a chance with your life and you'll see miracles, believe you will not only see miracles, but you will live and experience miracles in your life. For the Father loves you and wants to give you his very, very best. It's up to you!

You can now see the importance of getting your life back on track with your spirit and with God. And if you've never had a conversation with God, then my friends I absolutely recommend turning to your spirit and honestly and vigorously getting into the practice of self-meditation, self-examination, self-explorations and self-discovery. Develop for yourself a daily prayer life. Take all the time you need and if no time is available then make the time for your life depends upon it. Remember you're doing this for you, and it's the most important thing you'll ever do in life for yourself and for those you love. And that is to get to know yourself, to find the love inside of you and turn that into true love for yourself and for God and for your loved ones. Then this love will grow and you'll find yourself loving everyone, and what an absolute joy that will be. This will give the recipients of your love a new appreciation in life and begin to grow in them. You see love is contagious and it does spread. Doctors agree that if you are always smiling then people around you begin to smile, again its contagious. Imagine if all of us around the world started spreading the love of God around, wars would end, starvation would end, homelessness would end and bigotry and hate would cease, and that's just the beginning of a new life in the light of God. You'll become one with your maker and know him when he speaks to you in your spirit. You'll find ways to heal yourself through his guidance of all the problems that bring you down and defeat you in life. You'll find him directing you and helping you to change you ways to his ways, gently, and not by force. Before you know it you'll invite Christ Jesus, into your life and be one with him, and from that moment on you'll never be the same. You'll be the happiest person you've ever been, filled with a complete knowledge and understanding that you know God and you are His child and one with Him. That assurance will never leave you and you'll never doubt your place in the world, in life, in God ever again. You'll know that you've finally found the truth and it was hidden inside you all along. You found the real you, the one you always wanted to be and hoped to become. And God showed you the way from within and into the Kingdom of Heaven. For where your heart is at, that is where you stand in life, amen. Remember the words of Jesus Christ the Kingdom of Heaven isn't in the world but in each of us.

And now you've turned your life around because you discovered a love from inside you that you never thought existed. It was like a fairy tale, love you read about but no one ever really lives or experiences. It's your Camelot coming into reality and now you know different, for God met you where it counts, in your heart. But you needed to make the journey on your own. It's the longest yet shortest journey you or anyone will ever make. It goes from your brain to your heart, from the worldly side of you to your spiritual side. As I said the soul controls the mind and the mind the body. We all originated from God the creator from His soul but got disconnected by the distractions of the world. We need to get back to the Father. The way back for man to God is by the way of his soul with Jesus Christ. By turning back within yourself and taking time to self examine yourself, meditate with yourself seeking the truth from God for yourself you will find a reconnection to God. This will bring you one day to the day of commitment, when you know that you know it is time to open your heart and commit yourself and all that you are to God and asking him into your life to be with you and guide you forever more. And the Lord will say yes and from this day on you are mine, amen.

So the final question remaining is, are you ready to make the big change in your life? To go back to the innocent child you once was, and begin to take on your daily journey from where your mind is to where your heart is. Jesus says in Matthew 18:3, when asked by his disciples, who is the greatest in the kingdom of heaven? He called a child over to them and said *truly I tell you, unless you change and become like children you will never enter the kingdom of heaven.* In other words, we must all change back to the innocence of our youth, when we were truly spiritual beings not controlled by our flesh, not given to bigotry, hate, selfishness and all the dark sides of life. That's why Jesus said you must be born again, for this is the way of salvation. It means acknowledgement of your sinfulness, repenting of your sins to God and telling Christ Jesus, that you do believe in him and want him into your life. This act is then your second birth, the first being your water birth from the womb of your mother.

I would pray that all who read this will find a need to make a change in their lives, to turn their lives over to the Lord, believing in Him, to follow Him, and in doing so freeing themselves from the clutches of death. The flesh is the fragment of ourselves, showing forth only the shallowness that we are when in the flesh, but the spirit reveals the truth in us, the depth in us, the huge capacity to love that exists in us, and it is by this that we are known. How are you known? How would you like to be known? It's up to you, to me and to all of us. We can change the world, but it starts from within. And we must want it more than anything else. We must want to know ourselves and most important of all desire a walk with God. We must above all things in life love God with all love, belief and strength we possess. For without God and without his complete love we cannot change the smallest problem on earth. For without God being the first love of our lives we cannot even begin to love one another and get along. For as it has been proven over the past 6,000 years of man, without God wars won't cease, greed and hatred will live on until that fateful day when man can no longer control the events in the world and through his own ignorance does away with man and all life on earth.

CHAPTER EIGHT

THE POWER OF PRAYER AND FAITH

Prayer is the most vital link between God and man. It's the blood flowing in our veins; it's the phone line to Him, without which there could be no communication with Him. Yet as vital a link as it is, it's the one thing in life most people do the least of. I know many are now saying oh yes but I do pray when I'm at church or temple. Others pray more often, but usually most pray the same old prayers of wanting something. Consequently most prayers are of need and supplication. We pray for remedying a crisis in our lives, or an emergency, for the lack of money, lack of health, in need of a job or a better paying one, in need of a nice home but always praying that they have a lack of something God failed to provide them with. In essence we usually pray the type of prayers informing God that He isn't a good provider. For most people pray prayers of pleading, confessing through their prayers that they aren't satisfied with the life God has given them or with their lot in life or its outcome. That we would like God to give us better blessings in life such as wealth and happiness. We're all guilty of this its human nature. Yet rather than asking God for give me, get me and I want we should be confessing to God how we wrong in life and ended up the way we did. Or better yet we seldom if ever pray for the perfect will of God for our lives. We don't ask Him for wisdom and understanding to teach us how to provide, to work for and achieve the things in life we want for ourselves and for our families. We instead ask Him only for miracles, as if miracles were the only answer to prayer and to a better life. It's the same old problem down through the ages and it's the same problem going back to Adam and Eve. They weren't satisfied with their lives and they ate the forbidden fruit and we're in the same place pleading with God and begging him to change their lives and shower them with gifts and wealth beyond measure. They are prayers of selfishness, self centeredness and void of any real love for God. For what you are doing with this type of prayer is saying to God I will only love you if you do something for me or give me this what I ask for, otherwise what? And if God granted your wish, how long would your love for God last until the next disaster in your life? You see when you operate from the flesh nothing is satisfying but only temporal. Even your professed love of God is temporal for you pray from the flesh and not from your heart and soul. Also remember this God is not an errand boy filling out every beck and call you have.

So then the next point should be how should we pray? First we must remember when asking for a miracle that miracles are only a temporary solution to whatever our problem is. Unless we're willing to learn and to change our ways, the problem comes back to haunt us again and again until we get it right or it destroys us in our efforts to succeed. Miracles are much like diets, unless you change your whole way of thinking and living, you gain back the weight you lost plus pounds more on top of it.

To start I think we should first examine what life is to all of us. Life as we all live it is a prayer life from the earliest of our childhood until our last dying breath. For we spend our entire life praying, seeking things, wanting something, desiring something and wishing for something. It could be money, love, friendship, peace, a job, and a better relationship with people we work with or for more friends or for the healing of others. It could be anything, but it's always for something you don't have and wished you did. We have all grown up as a complaining society, never satisfied but always looking for more and more. This is all a form of praying for what is prayer, but a communion with God bringing petitions before Him of what we feel we're in need of. Note the consummate word here is "we", what we want, what we feel we need.Never do we pray asking God for his best for us, for his perfect will for us or for Him to guide us in whatever situation we are going through in life.

Everything we do in our daily lives is a prayer. Be it that we're interacting with one another or we're asking or seeking something from one another. Or the flip side we're thanking one another for something. Be it work or play we're constantly trying to better ourselves, to acquire more knowledge, new skills, to getting help and assistance from one another and all this is known as prayers of supplication.

Consequently prayer is an eternal act we do from birth and will always be doing past our physical lives on earth on into eternity. Thus making prayer more vital to our lives than the blood in our veins, for only in prayer can we find salvation for our souls for only in prayer can God receive our repentance, it's the open line to God, our only way to communicate with Him. He listens to us in prayer there just is no other way. So why exclude yourself from Him and all his help by not taking the time out each day to pray. Especially when God does answer our needs through prayer, for in prayer we show our true hearts to Him and our belief in Him. There can be no fakery in your heart or unbelief for God sees you heart and the truth in you. So when you come before Him be sure that you believe He is God and that you believe in Him and that you need is genuine. Remember I have said this over and over again in this book, God cannot be mocked!

Just like we tune up a car, prayer is how we give service to our hearts. For true prayer is true love for it's in prayer that we learn to love. For in prayer we learn to examine our souls and offer our sins and mistakes up to God. For prayer makes us humble before God and fills us with humility as we pour ourselves out to the God. And we can only pour ourselves out through the love that is within us for to pray is to love and true prayer can only operate from the love within us.

We pray so that we can get to know God, to obtain wisdom and knowledge and even more to learning how to truly love God. For in prayer is our love made complete as we get to know to love God. We then get to love ourselves with a true fullness and when we're full we can share the abundance of that love with others. How do I know this, for the bible tells us so in Psalm 23:5, you prepare a table before me in the presence of my enemies; you anointed my head with oil, my cup over flowing. You see God never gives enough or just the right amount. He gives more than you'll ever need, he gives abundantly so that you can share the abundance with others in need.

We pray for the salvation of our souls, for only in prayer, can the Lord Jesus Christ hear us and petition to the Father on our behalf. In prayer we learn to love and know God. We learn to become obedient to God, and to develop holy and righteous lives. It's in prayer that we learn to go to the light and live in it thus removing ourselves from the darkness, the world and its sinful ways. We stop sinning and doing evil acts as we continue to learn to live in the light of God. In prayer as we grow we present ourselves worthy to God in his plan of salvation and its here in prayer that we finally come forth with repentance and the Lord brings to us his salvation.

For only through prayer can God fill us with his Holy Spirit, so that we can have his presence with us at all times in our lives. Jesus said in John 3:03, *Very truly, I tell you, unless you are born again, you cannot see the Kingdom of God.* He then goes on to explain we are born once of water from the womb, but now need to be born from above which is our spiritual birth. That is to put to death our old man the flesh having ruled our lives in sin and resurrecting in us the new man, our spirit made alive in our repentance by Jesus Christ.

We pray for spiritual awakening and spiritual growth. For if our soul doesn't grow in the knowledge of God, then we are dead and there is no life in us. Our soul is who we are and not the body of flesh we live in for a set number of years. Our souls are eternal and must grow and be enlightened and this can only be achieved through prayer, for prayer is the key of life which connects us to God. We need to be living in a constant state of the spirit and praying continually through out the day. And when I say continually I mean that we should live and interact with everyone we meet as if we're communing with God himself, and we should treat them all with the love and respect we expect from God and give to God.

Through prayer we develop new habits, a new awakening of our spirit teaching us obedience and discipline in which to subdue our flesh, our dark side as we now begin life in the spirit or life in the light of God. In the spirit where we find God giving us power and faith to carry on in life and in which to believe. For man's faith has always been in what he can see, touch and feel be it for reward or be it out worry or fear. A person believing that diseases kill finds no victory when overcome with a disease for their reward is according to their faith, death. Where we place our faith, that's where we will find our reward. If our faith believes the inevitable of life is hopelessness and futility, then his reward in life is the lack of any success. In my life it was my faith in God and my prayer life that saved me and I survived one heart attack and two battles with cancer. I've undergone nine operations in my body and through it all survived for I had my faith in God to bring me through it all. Today I live a most precious and rewarded life received from God and I share it with everyone God leads me too.

In Matthew, chapter 7, the centurion asks Jesus to heal his dying servant and Jesus offers to go to his house to do so. Then the centurion says, *Lord I'm not worthy to have you come under my roof; but only speak the word and I know my servant will be healed.* Jesus then told everyone in the crowd that in all of Jerusalem, he had not found anyone with such faith. The servant was healed as Jesus, spoke the healing.

In Matthew, chapter 9, we find the woman who had been suffering from hemorrhages for twelve years came up behind Jesus and touched the fringe of his cloak, for she had said to herself *If I could just touch his cloak, I will be made well." Jesus turned, and seeing her he said, "Take heart, daughter, your faith has made you well.* She placed her faith and hope in God and God rewarded her with the healing.

The bible tells us that, *faith is the assurance (substance) of things hoped for, the conviction (evidence) of things not seen. By faith our ancestors received approval. By faith we understand that the worlds were prepared by the word of God, so that what is seen was made from things that are not visible (Hebrews, 11:1).* And again, *By faith Noah, warned by God about events as yet unseen, respected the warning and built an ark to save his household; by this he condemned the world and became an heir to the righteousness that is in accordance with faith (Hebrews, 11:7).*

So how does one get this faith from God that brings with it the rewards from God: His blessings, His healing and His miracles? The bible says in Romans, chapter 10:17, *So faith comes from what is heard, and what is heard comes through the word of God.* And once again how do we hear from God, but through prayer and in reading the word of God, His holy bible.

So my friends you can see that through prayer God immediately sets out to bring healing to our minds, setting us free from the enslavement's of the dark side. By prayer God brings new focus to our eyes and our minds, and the things of life that were so important yesterday no longer matter to you today. By prayer God brings you into the truth of Himself and His eternal Kingdom and begins a new focus on your life, that of your eternal soul.

Consequently when you pray give Him thanks for the things you need knowing fully that He knows what you have need of and what needs to be done for you before you even ask. Be diligent, always looking and seeking enlightenment from Him, and He will reveal wonderful and mysterious truths to you. Finally realizing that a wonderful union has opened between you and God, there will come that wonderful day when you open your heart completely confessing to God all your faults, but more importantly committing yourself before God to changing your life around. This is the day of your salvation, the day you ask Jesus into your heart as the Lord of your life, of your heart and soul freeing you from the enslavement of the old you which for so many years was tearing you apart. To do this you simply pray from all your heart with all your strength and all the truth you possess, Heavenly Father, I come to you in Jesus name, asking you to forgive me for all the wrongs and sins of my life. For I am truly sorry for them and do repent of them all. For I do believe in your son Jesus Christ, and that he died on the cross for our sins and rose from the dead on the third day having conquered all sin and hell. I ask you Jesus to come into my heart and live with me forever more being the Lord and Savior of my life. Thank you Lord, amen.

At that very moment Jesus, will baptize you with His Holy Spirit, and will be with you forever more. For some this day comes before they even develop a prayer life, for many people come to God the moment they hear the preaching of the word of God. The truth of God's word quickens in their spirit, and God's faith springs alive in them and they turn their lives over to Jesus at that moment.

I know this particular teaching of salvation is hard for many people of other faiths to accept. They believe in God, or Allah, or in God by another name but never in the name of Jesus. We are a big world with many people from all walks, all nationalities and from many different religious beliefs. This is all well and good and for all I say this, no matter how you believe you can't avoid certain truths. Prayer is the communication link to God, and we must exercise that link daily to be in communication with Him. From that point on simply trust in God, believing and He will guide and direct your lives to the truth. Once revealed to you, you will never depart from the truth given to you by God and you will begin a new life in the spirit. It is the light that gives life, which is the spirit within you and the darkness that kills life which is the world outside you. When God reveals himself to you, you will find that it is Jesus for he is the light of the world. Receive him into your heart and do not reject him because you are a Jew, a Muslim or a Buddhist, etc. Receive him and learn the truth he brings to you and follow the pathway he sets for you as a Muslim or as a Jew, etc. Later in the conclusion I will explain my beliefs in God and Jesus Christ, and why for me Jesus Christ is so important as my savior.

From this moment on God will bring you to your true self to live your life in the spirit and not by the flesh, where you at last can find true happiness, peace and fulfillment for your life. You will free yourself of that monkey on your back by no longer having to measure your self worth in terms of dollars, power or possessions, for now the measurement of your self worth is you and the love that flows within you, the peace that's filled your life and the knowledge that you are a child of God. From this point in your life you can begin to build the life for yourself and your family you've always dreamed of. You are free now no longer will you need to compete with every Tom, Dick and Harry, for every piece of the pie. Success can now be achieved without all the worldly stress and suffering. For now you've come to the reality of God in your life, and his grace and his salvation is free to all who believe in him and receive him into their hearts. Some of you are hurting and desperate to be set free from you situations in life, from the shackles that have kept you bound up for years. Others out there think they're already free enjoying all that they want out of life, living fancy free. Yet as we have witnessed constantly throughout life, even the rich and famous struggle daily with loneliness, unhappiness, dissatisfaction, and a host of other problems they feel not right in their lives. So is it so fancy free? Everyone living out of the spirit is not able to focus on the truth of their situations and that they have enslaved themselves unknowingly to the system. Their God is their wealth, their power base or whatever it is that keeps them separated from God. For both of you I say this, you need to set yourself free from within and let your spirits soar forward and take control over your lives bringing you into a relationship with God. Then and only then will you be truly set free and when you do you will truly realize that there is nothing like "real" freedom. This is the natural way to live one's life, in the spirit and not in the flesh. Life in the flesh is the cop out, it is worldliness, for the system needs your attention to things of the world if the world is to grow and enslave you. Satan had no power over Adam and Eve except to lure them with the lust of the eyes. This is the same snare the world uses to entrap us and lead us away from God. Therefore the jazz and glitter, the lure of the world must become more and more intoxicating, drawing you away from your spiritual self to a world of self indulgence, of fleeting promises and momentary fulfillment. Nothing the world has for you can you take with you when you die, and die we all must one day. All the wealth and possessions you accumulated in life are lost when you die, for the things of the world belong to the world and not you. But the things of the spirit remain with you beyond the grave and stay with you through out all eternity. And the love and joy and fulfillment and peace you felt while you were on earth living in the spirit will only be enhanced a hundred fold and more in your eternal life in the kingdom of God.

So now you've learned how to subdue the flesh, which has been running and ruining your life all these years, freeing you from the shackles of life, the torment, the sin, the bitterness, the loneliness, the lies, the hate and more. You have forgiven yourself and those who have hurt and offended you and you have rid yourself of that monkey that was on your back, bringing forth your spirit and giving it charge and control over yourself and letting God and His Holy Spirit and freedom reign in your life. For now you'll know what life is truly all about and how you can walk alongside of God, having Him as your friend and consul everyday of your life. And just as the Lord has saved you, in doing so you'll be an instrument of His on earth spreading the good news in your life. To use in leading others to the light, your family, your friends and the many people who interact with you everyday. For as your light of God shines in your life the overflow will touch everyone you interact with, bringing new life into them and a feeling of thanksgiving that you are a part of their life no matter how small or big a part, but a part indeed that brings joy and thanksgiving. You see the principle here of psalm 23, my cup runneth over. For all that God gives us He always gives in abundance, more than we need so the excess pours out to those we love and deal with everyday in life. As Jesus said, so let your light so shine before men, that they may see your good works, and glorify your Father which is in heaven, Matt 5:16. You will also by the display of fulfillment and contentment in your life plant seeds in the hearts and minds of others wanting to find the same answers to life that you found that changed you so much. When people see the changes, the joy, the happiness and success in your life, they'll want to rub shoulders with you and hope some of it rubs off on them.

So take ten minutes or more to pray today and everyday and add this time to your daily routine until you find your comfort zone and it becomes the natural thing to do everyday. Pray to Him and take time to meditate quietly with yourself, exploring your heart and soul, letting God speak to you. For when we are silent God speaks, so listen for God speaks within us. Let Him fill you with His presence until you cannot contain yourself then speak to God. And just don't pray babbling meaningless words, or repetitious prayers. Pray speaking to him all that's in your heart good and bad. Don't just come to him with a hit list of what's missing in your life and what you want Him to do for you. That's telling Him, He isn't a good provider and you're not satisfied. But come to Him in humility and humbleness, with a thankful heart giving Him thanks for your life and all that's in it. If you're life is in ruins ask Him to show you the errors of your ways and how to proceed from that point in your life. A good idea is the one left us by Jesus Christ himself in the book of Matthews, Chapter 6. He said, "And whenever you pray, do not be like the hypocrites; for they love to stand and pray in the synagogues and at the street corners, so that they may be seen by others. Truly I tell you, they have received their reward. But whenever you pray, go into your room and shut the door and pray to your Father who is in secret; and your Father who sees in secret will reward you.

When you are praying, do not heap up empty phrases as the Gentiles do; for they think that they will be heard because of their many words. Do not be like them, for you Father knows what you need before you ask him. Pray then in this way: Our Father in heaven, hallowed by your name. You kingdom come, you will be done on earth as it is in heaven. Give us this day our daily bread. And forgive us our debts as we forgive our debtors. And do not bring us into the time of trial, but rescue us from the evil one. For if you forgive others their trespasses your heavenly Father will also forgive you; but if you do not forgive others, neither will your Father forgive your trespasses."

We can no longer afford to ignore these situations ever again. We can no longer remain ignorant to the truth for we're paying too big a price for ignorance or for denial. We must turn to God and seek His truth before it's too late. For from this ignorance come indifference, separatism, bigotry, hate, conflicts, and wars. Fighting ignorance with ignorance, like the blind leading the blind and both winding up in the ditch, Luke, 6:39.

We are all to blame rich or poor, mighty or weak, worldly or innocent for the sinful and worldly ways of the world today. We must accept the fact that we're all to blame for the situation in which the world is today. We each need to take back control of our lives subduing the flesh within us and steering ourselves back to a spirit filled life, a life back onto the pathway of inner healing, loving God, loving ourselves, and finally loving one another. We each must turn to God and surrender our will to Him asking him to direct us, teach us and fill us with His wisdom and understanding so that we each can change. Asking God to lay out the footprints for us to follow which will bring us home. We need a good role model and let me offer the best one I know and that is Jesus Christ. Make Him your role model and you just can't go wrong, for his love is pure love, his advice will keep you always living in the light, living in the spirit. You'll have total control of your life through God and if each one of us does this we will take complete control of our countries, our governments and our planet through God. Surely then we would never have to fear an Armageddon.

We need to see not just our nation, but the whole world as one body in Christ consisting of the many members: white, black, brown, yellow, red, Jews, Christians, Hindus, Muslims, Buddhists, heterosexuals and homosexuals. Young and old, rich and poor, healthy and sick, from the mighty to the weak, we must live as one body, consisting of billions of parts of different colors, different sizes, different religions, different ethnic backgrounds and different sexual orientation. This is a natural order with God, and to violate that natural order is to disable the entire body. To cripple it diminishing its ability to function in it's fullness and complete health. That's what racism and hate do to a society cripple it with a disease that festers to all segments of society destroying the peace, the stability and the harmony that should exist in the land. To allow that act of racism to grow and multiply is to eventually kill America. For the body has need of all its parts to live and survive. Black or white, Jew or Gentile, Latino or Asian, straight or gay, the Indian and the Hindu, we all need one another to make the whole. This is a law of God we need to get hold of and place deep in our hearts. Can the leaf say to the tree I have no need of you or the tree say to the roots I have no need of you, absolutely not. For the one cannot live without the other just as the hand cannot say to the arm I have no need of you, they are vital to each other. The same rule applies to mankind. We have a need for one another and most important we are vital to one another. Planet earth is a melting pot of different peoples or different colors, different races, different religions and different sexual orientation, but all part of the one body in Christ Jesus.

Just take God's other creations and you'll see that this is true. Look at the universe, a whole body consisting of billions upon billions of stars, planets, moons, and galaxies. All of them separate bodies, individual worlds, all different from one another and yet living in harmony with each other to form the whole. The same law applies to our solar system, a body in space consisting of nine planets, many moons, asteroids, comets and meteors and again all different from one another, yet living in harmony forming the whole solar system. One more example of this law is the human body which consists of billions of cells which form all the different body parts that make the human body and all necessary to complete the whole body. And that is what we need to do with our lives here on earth. We need to live in love, in harmony, helping and caring for one another throughout the entire world. For each one of us is a cell and part of the whole body, which is the human race. We must live in love and harmony if the whole body is to survive and be healthy. Sharing, caring and lifting one another up regardless of color, gender or sexual preferences. And we the people of earth are fortunate for we have a glue to bind us together and that glue is Jesus Christ. We need to get hold of Him and hold on for dear life, if not then like a person dying from cancer or some other dreaded disease, we the human race will one day self-destruct and be no more.

So what can we do to change things from how they are? The first step is to begin a prayer life, opening a line of communication between God and you by setting aside ten, fifteen minutes or more everyday to be in meditation with your spirit and with God. Listening quietly to your soul and to that gentle voice within you, exploring your past life, the present and where you want to go in the future. Seek his help, his guidance and wisdom for you, being humble before Him, acknowledging Him and the fact that you are helpless to succeed without Him. Thus begins your new life, a life entering into the light of God. A new life bubbling up within you, filled with excitement, hope, joy and a peace like you never knew could be. You'll find a love for yourself and for God, and that love will fill you to overflowing. Now that you've found your connection with God, He begins by blessing you with faith to believe in Him, and in yourself and in all things. For faith is the builder of our lives and without faith we can do nothing nor accomplish anything for our belief system within us is dead. But God gives to all who believe in Him, and He'll renew your belief system within by giving you faith. This then will help to begin to restore and rebuild all that is wrong or shattered in your life, *To have faith is to be sure of the things we hope for, to be certain of the things we cannot see (Heb. 11:1), It is by faith that we understand that the universe was created by God's word, so what can be seen was made out of what cannot be seen, Heb. 11:3.*

One will find in the bible how all the great men of God operated solely on faith and from where came this faith, but from God. And what did all these great men have in common with God? They each had a daily time of prayer and meditation to communicate with their creator. In prayer you will learn to live a spirit filled life in union with God. It is in the spirit where man finds the yearning to know God, to love oneself and to love and care for one another. These are things too frivolous for the flesh to be concerned with. For the flesh is concerned only with the things of the flesh such as greed, money, lust, power, believing in only the things he can feel touch or see. The flesh of man cannot reason with wisdom, understanding and knowledge of what indeed is best for its host, for its concerns is with the now and not the eternal. Consequently the flesh has all the qualities in which to destroy man for it concerns itself with the now and to hell with eternity and God. The spirit or the soul within man is the eternal being, not your body that one-day will die and be buried and eventually waste away. But your soul is the eternal being which God created to live eternally. It is in the soul that man learns to conquer the lusts of his flesh, the sin or sins in his life. For in the flesh there can be no victory over sin for the flesh lives in sin. Saint Paul, said it best in Galatians 5:16-26, *walk in the spirit, and you shall not fulfill the lusts of the flesh. For the flesh lusts against the Spirit and the Spirit against the flesh: and these are contrary one to the other: so that you cannot do the things that you would. But if you are led of the Spirit, you are not under the Law.* To make it more contemporary and easy to understand, let's look at the Catholic, translation, *What I say is this, let the Spirit of God direct your lives and you will not satisfy the desires of the human nature. For what our human nature wants is opposed to what the Spirit wants and what the Spirit wants is opposed to what our human nature wants. These two are enemies; and this means that you cannot do what you want to do. If the Spirit leads you, then you are not subject to the Law. But if you live by the Spirit, you are not subject to the law (because you are under grace believing in Christ by faith and counted onto you for salvation. But he who lives by the flesh, must live by the written laws of the Old Testament before Christ, and is then subject to obeying all the written laws. To break one is to be guilty of breaking all). Now the works of the flesh (human nature) are obvious: fornication, impurity, licentiousness, idolatry, sorcery, enmities, strife, jealousy, anger, quarrels, dissension, factions, envy, drunkenness, carousing, and things like these. I am warning you, as I warned you before; those who do such things will not inherit the kingdom of God.*

By contrast, the fruit of the Spirit is love, joy, peace, patience, kindness, generosity, faithfulness, gentleness, and self-control. There is no law against such things and those who belong to Christ Jesus have crucified their flesh with its passions and desires. If we live by the Spirit, let us also be guided by the Spirit. Let us not become conceited, competing against one another, envying one another.

Then Saint Paul goes on to say a most prophetic statement in Galatians 6:7-10, he says, *Do not be deceived; God is not mocked, for you reap whatever you sow. If you sow to your own flesh, you will reap corruption from the flesh; but if you sow to the spirit, you will reap eternal life from the spirit. So let us not grow weary in doing what is right, for we will reap at harvest time, if we do not give up. So then, whenever we have an opportunity, let us work for the good of all, and especially for those of the family of faith,"* amen. I hope and pray this is reaching you the reader deep within where it counts. For it's never been said better or plainer than that. For us to know God, live by the love of God, have knowledge and understanding of God, and to know for sure that God has reserved our place in the eternal kingdom of heaven. We then must turn our lives around and stop the life in the flesh and commence the new life living in the Spirit. And this is where Jesus Christ is and has been waiting to meet with you. Revelations 3:20-22, Jesus says, *Listen I am standing at the door (to your heart) knocking; if you hear my voice and open the door, I will come in to you and eat with you, and you with me. To the one who conquers I will give a place with me on my throne, just as I myself conquered and sat down with my Father on his throne. Let anyone who has an ear listen to what the Spirit is saying to the churches (that's all of us).* That's it, you need go no further. That's the promise of God, your salvation guaranteed to you by no other than the Lord Jesus himself. Nowhere in this world can anyone give you that my friend. Death will come to each and everyone that's God's law, which we all accept for we can't change it. That's the way it is, but it's just the death of our bodies, which we shed. But we all go on into eternity and their remains but one question. Which eternity do you want, one of eternal loss and pain or one in the kingdom of God? The choice has always been on us, God never forces himself upon us. As we choose God and his love begins to fill us and He blesses us with his holy spirit, soon this love and spirituality of God that is in us will find its way in others. More and more till one day goodness replaces evilness in the world and man need not fear any more. May this day come soon for all of us, amen.

CHAPTER NINE

HEAVEN VS HELL, BELIEF VS DOUBT, THE RAGING WAR FOR YOUR SOUL

That's what is has been about all along since the beginning of time. It's why we have religions tugging at us in every direction. The battle between good and evil has raged on since Lucifer fell from grace and became Satan, which was before Adam and Eve. It has always been about you and me and the conquest of our souls. Satan trying so hard to lead us to destruction, tempting us with all sorts of lures picked especially for us knowing what will best appeal to our individual appetites. While God leads all who are willing to believe in him to an eternal life in the kingdom of heaven, Satan tempts us with lures, lusts and lies. God gives us his word, the holy bible, which is finite and never changing and his promise through his son Jesus Christ. So you see it's always been about you and me and it's up to you and me to decide whom we choose to follow. We have that promise from God not to intervene in our decision. It's as simple as when you go shopping except that in this choice one gives life and the other brings death. The choice has always been ours and God and Satan are the proprietors. Whom should we buy from?

So beloved I give you again the words of Paul, the Apostle, be strong in the Lord and in his mighty power. Put on the full armor of God as that you can take your stand against the devil's schemes. For our struggle is no against flesh and blood (ourselves), but against the rulers, against the authorities, against the powers of this dark world and against the spiritual forces of evil in the heavenly realms, Ephesians vs. 10-12.

So we can see from God's word, that there is a constant warfare being waged against us for our souls. All forces of the world from those in power and control over the wealth of the world and those of the darkened world of lust and evilness and the devil himself and his demonic hosts are doing their best to lure you away from God into the world of sin. So you must be on your guard everyday and you do this by meditating and praying everyday with God, taking time to read his holy bible so you can know God personally on a one to one. The more you meditate and pray and the more you read the word of God the more powerful you will become in the Lord. Sin cannot have you; the devil cannot make you do it as the comedian Flip Wilson use to joke around about. Only you have the power to give in to the dark side or to remain in the light of God. Only you can turn to a sinful life by taking your eyes off of God and giving into sin. The evil forces of this world and the evil forces of the heavenly realm including Satan himself have no power over your. Their job is to inundate you with all lusts and temptations to cause you to fall into sin, but you guessed it, only you can do the falling. You must take your eyes off of God and turn to sin and desire to sin and then sin overtakes you just like it did Adam & Eve. The devil tempted them, but they committed the sinful act. It says in Romans 6:23, *The wages of sin is death the gift of God is eternal life in Christ Jesus, our Lord.* We also find in the book of James, verses. 1:13-15, *when tempted, no one should say, "God is tempting me." For God cannot be tempted by evil, nor does he tempt anyone; but each one is tempted when, by his own evil desire, he is dragged away and enticed. Then, after desire has conceived, it gives birth to sin; and sin, when it is full-grown, gives birth to death.*

With this you now can now begin to understand what sin is and how it operates. How temptation and desire work to deceive us and weaken our souls. Left unchecked this process will destroy its host for sin is like cancer. It takes hold in your body and slowly like an unseen enemy as in cancer, begins the process of devouring your soul just as cancer devours the body. Like cancer it's only detected after a long period of time of doing damage to your soul, for sin like cancer spreads its seed throughout your soul becoming a habit, a way of life undetected. As so often is the case, it often results in the death of the host. Fortunately with sin unlike cancer, no one need die for it is curable and yet many do die from their sins for they remain blinded by the darkness all of their lives. For they allowed themselves to waste away, lost in the lust of their sinfulness becoming enslaved to the dark side where sin breeds and abounds. Over the years the darkness becomes the norm for your life and you don't see the sin anymore. It's then you begin to intellectualize life, no longer needing to pray then finally no longer needing God in your life.

Yet through all that, we all have a savior standing by, ready, willing and able to forgive us, heal us all and make us whole again and all it takes is a heart of repentance. The cost to you for this is nothing the holy bible is your insurance policy. The salvation or your soul has always been for free to those who turn back to God. Meditation and prayer will start the journey back. Unfortunately as it has always been with man, much too many of us find or put up excuses not to pray, not to meditate and spend some time each day with God. We're always too busy, have to work, have to cook or whatever. Worse yet too many are always bringing up those old familiar questions which they expect have no answers, thus giving them an excuse not to pray or meditate with God. They will put up popular barriers by asking challenging questions such as does evil really exist in the world? Is there really a Satan or demonic spirits? Or is it something inherent in all of us? Is there really a heaven or a kingdom of God? Is there truly a God? And where does one go to find all these answers?

The answer is yes to all. For we must always remember that darkness existed before there was light and light was brought out of the darkness. In Genesis 1, 1-3, the bible confirms what scientist have discovered and that is that "In the beginning when God created the heavens and the earth, the earth was a formless void and darkness covered the face of the deep, while a wind from God swept over the face of the waters. Then God said, "Let there be light"; and there was light. The darkness represents sin, for it was present before the light. Then out of the evil of darkness God brought all that is good, and that was the light. The light of God, for it wasn't the sun or the moon or the stars for they weren't created until the forth day. But it was the light of God, the light of "all knowledge, all good and all understanding". Just like man when he repents to God of all his sinfulness and turns his life around. He has stepped out of the darkness of his life and entered the light of God, the light of all understanding, the salvation of his soul. Jesus said in John 8:12, *I am the light of the world whoever follows me will never live in darkness but in the light of the world.* So there is a parallel here with our personal lives. For Romans 3:23 says, *that all have sinned and fall short of the glory of God; they are now justified by his grace as a gift, through the redemption that is in Christ Jesus.*

Therefore sin was here first before righteousness could enter the world. For how could there be redemption if there were no one to be redeemed. Same with the creation of the world, as first there was darkness then God brought the good out of the bad by bringing forth the light out of the dark. It was a way that God used in preparing us to know Him and His work in our lives. For since the sin of Adam and Eve, all men have been born in sin. So sin entered the world through the first Adam. And out of the darkness of sin God reaches out to each and every one of us by bringing us his light through the second Adam, Jesus Christ to redeem us, if we repent of our ways. That's the secret that escapes most people through out the ages. It was so simple that it eluded man down through the ages. Surely one should have to work hard and do good deeds and be very religious to enter the kingdom of heaven. This was the thinking of most people then and still is to this day. When in fact it was just the opposite, for what God has sought for in man is for man to believe in God and to love God and his fellow man. Consequently as man couldn't accept the simplicity of God's plan of redemption and he finally had to send us Jesus Christ, his son, the light that comes out of the darkness to show us the way home, to shine his light upon us so that we could see our sinful selves and repent and receive him into our hearts.

It is pure and simple, so filled with love that the solution seems improbable to most and too simple. Surely the thought of most men is that if one is so sinful and impure it should take a lot more than a simple act of repentance, yet I'm happy to bring you the good news that is the mystery of salvation is just that pure and simple. The complication of understanding God and his plan of salvation comes out of religious teachings and not from God. As it was man and his religions that have boxed God in and the laymen could do nothing but follow for in the early church there were no bibles. For what is religion but man's attempt to understand God and interpret his word as man sees it or often as many used it and twisted its meanings creating doctrines of their own in order to control the masses and not so much as to follow his word as God inspired the writing of his word. Consequently we end up with a world filled with hundreds of different religions, each with its own interpretation of who God is and the interpretation of His holy word. Furthermore is the myriad of rules, doctrines and definitions telling us what sin is, and that the way to repentance and salvation that many religions teach is that their way being the only true way to God. It just boggles the mind. Then when you read the bible for yourself you discover how the word of God is different in many ways from your religion. Why do you suppose? If as the Christian faiths as well as the many other religions of the world tell us and we all seem to believe it, that the bible is the absolute word of God. Why then do we find it necessary to change it to satisfy so many different religions? Much too often man is twisting the word of God around to suit himself and how he wants to serve and believe in God. Or could it be a way to exert their control and influence over the lives of their membership, but whatever it just won't work and has never worked. You see religion cannot save you and enter you in the kingdom of heaven, only God can. God is not a religion, he is God and we each must come to him on a one to one basis to seek his help and forgiveness.

This battle of one religion verses another, one country verses another is one of the reasons the world has had so many wars and been filled with so much hate. We separate ourselves from one another, create borders, territories, new religions and try to lord it over one another. Yet man must always keep in mind that he is not God nor are the leaders of his church. They can't forgive sin and can't give eternal life. They can't help anyone change the circumstances of their lives, nor heal the sick or raise the dead, nor bring food down from heaven. Yet all this and more can God do for you. I know, for he's done that for me, and the miracles and blessings of God are still going on in my life. How can I make you see or understand what beauty there is in real faith? For in faith we turn away from the ways of the world and turn within ourselves to free our spirits in pursuit of a spiritual life with God. We turn our confidence to God seeking his peace and joy for our lives, knowing that he will bless us with his "perfect will." In his perfect will we will have all that we will ever want and be fully and completely happy with that. Whether it be obtaining the best paying job, a position of influence, money or even fame or maybe none of the above. Maybe it'll be just the blessing of great health, a solid job, a happy and united family and children that truly love and respect you, let God work for you to reveal to you your true happiness in life.

Nothing we do on our own leads to fulfillment and total joy. For we act out of human nature via our carnal minds and make decisions or choices that last but for a season and then we hunger again for more. Our goals in life are short term, having conclusions with the delusion that they will bring total bliss to our lives. Yet when you achieve the goal, the happiness is temporal and soon fades away. Whether it meant landing the best job in the world that you worked and studied hard for many, many years to achieve it. Or it was the half-million dollar house on the hill. Whatever it was doesn't much matter because for much too many people, once the desire becomes a reality, the thrill of having it is gone. It's back to square one and soon you find dissatisfaction with something else in your life. How come, didn't you just find total joy and all that you ever wanted with that wonderful job or that big house? What you need to understand is that no matter what your desires in life are, they are just ends to a means and nothing more. You still have to deal with you and you've avoided that truth all of your life. Where is your real happiness, in money, great jobs and fancy homes? They'll all nice and good but the happiness they bring is temporal. You need to find a permanent peace with yourself, an inner joy that's everlasting no matter what your circumstances in life is. That's the true prize in life, inner joy, and inner peace with oneself and with God that will stay with you through all eternity. That's the nirvana of Buddhism. Not letting the outer things in life own you but you owning control of yourself and finding both your truth and God's truth in your soul. Then whether you're rich or poor, married or remain single, physically fit or disabled, all is unimportant for you have complete inner joy and peace with self. Funny in Buddhism, they say the first principal in life is suffering, and we all experience suffering be it inner suffering in our personal lives or outer suffering affecting the world at large. We suffer because of motivation in life is "desire" causing us to chase after the golden rainbow, the ever escaping lottery, the pie in the sky that will bring us eternal joy. But life has shown us it never does. Many lottery winners have lost their families and divorced over the pot of gold. That's real suffering and the joy of gain was quickly lost.

The truth pathway to a joyful and peaceful life is to remove the stress, and the pressure that life brings, and to end the suffering within and without, regardless of the influences or temptations, by grounding ourselves in Christ. It means changing the focus of our lives from "desire" or the flesh to a spirit filled live within oneself. It means finding the middle ground in which to live your life, not dependent on the things of the world that bring temporal joy and peace and not on the negative aspects of life always seeing the world and oneself from a losing proposition. None of these do anything to improve your life and can and are very harmful to one's well being.

Then what is the answer? We must accentuate the positive with positive thinking and positive actions. To begin one must stop, take a deep breath and walk away from the daily routines and take sometime out each day to evaluate and examine your life, to meditate quietly seeking God for His word and to pray seeking help and guidance. Then allowing your spirit as God reveals the real truth to you, to correct what you discover to be wrong with yourself and repenting of your sinfulness and them being able to make then necessary changes in your life now that God has revealed this truth to you and has supplied you with the wherewith to do what is necessary. You will find that your life will change dramatically with a new joy springing up from within as the Lord begins teaching you and showing you the way and the will of God for your life. Believe me nothing can be sweeter. It will change you the moment you open your heart to him and he fills you with faith, for faith is a gift of God free to all those that seek him. Faith is the opposite of religion as we see religion in the world today. Religion is made by man faith is a gift from God.

No wonder the world is in disarray, confused with huge masses of people just straying away not wanting to be bothered by it all. Too many churches aren't teaching faith, redemption and inner peace and spiritually filled living. They're too busy playing church and religiosity and giving orders and church doctrines on the proper way to live. Too many churches in lieu of helping one find and search for true inner peace with God instead fill you with church doctrines and dogma to further stress you life. They force you to always focus on the negatives about yourself and what an awful person we all are instead of just showing us the way to the cross, to Jesus the author and finisher of our faith. Even to this very date many churches still teach the "fear of God" when in fact this old doctrine needs to be done away with. We should be teaching each other the love and mercy of God and the wonderful grace He has for each one of us.

Too many religions will preach their countless sermons condemning us and condemning the world as to the wrongs and ills we have. Yet offer little by way of finding healing and inner peace. All too many churches want you to live your life and make your salvation according to their religious doctrines ignoring the written word of God. Neither does it matter how God is working in your life, for if it doesn't match with their teachings then it can't be from God they tell you. What arrogance and yet it's done all over the world that way. Think seriously about this, is it more important to please your church or to please God? Who knows you best and who is it that will usher you into the kingdom of God? As much as churches are well intentioned they can't save your soul only God can. As well intentioned as they are they don't know you, and the pastors, rabbis and priests don't know you and don't know what's right and good for you, but your creator does know you and does know what's best for you. He also knows the pace of change best suited to you and how best to bring the truth to you that you will respond and awaken to. So you owe it to you to place all your trust and faith in God and let him work out your daily walk in life, your salvation.

Trust me in this, when we each whether we are Christian, Jew, Muslim, Buddhist, Hindu or whatever find our way in God and become one with Him, then religion as we know it will fade away and we will all become one with each other as we are one with Him. All religions will fade away as they will no longer be needed, for we will have the one God living in all of us.

Love will flourish and hatred and wars will end and the Lord will come to live among us. For then we are all a spiritual people, fully enlightened by God. In First Corinthians, chapter 13, St Paul tells us that love will last forever! But that our knowledge is partial, incomplete and the gifts of prophecy and speaking in tongues are all partial and incomplete. But when that which is perfect comes then we will know in truth and all that is partial will fade away. When we were children we spoke and reasoned as children, but when we grew up we put childish things aside. We now know things in part, confused and puzzling but when that which is perfect (Jesus Christ) comes then we will see everything with clarity and complete truth. What I know now is only partial and incomplete but then when Christ comes I will know everything completely just as God knows me completely. Three things are eternal faith, hope and love and the greatest of these is love.

How can you expect a person who is lost to God for whatever reason, have any opportunity to reunite themselves to God when they have to swim through the myriad of rules, doctrines and regulations of the many religions? Having to often debase themselves publicly for their godless lives and do pennants before they can find approval with God. Multiply that number by the tens of millions of people who have to go through this all for the sake of religion, for it isn't the way of God. God looks for a repentant heart not for physical sacrifices or public displays seeking public pity and forgiveness otherwise we would be sacrificing animals at the altar again. The religions of the world need to reassess themselves and their purpose in this world. Too many religious orders act today not as places of worship and redemption but more like places to display one's self-righteousness, self importance or just to go through the motions of religiousness. Too many others lost the word of God long ago and became religious banks hoarding the millions of dollars people give only for the purpose of making themselves rich. What we see all over the world today is the same religiosity that existed in ancient Israel, religions with rituals, rules, dress codes and seating arrangements but little or no faith. Like the Pharisees of ancient Israel hypocrites practicing religiosity instead of real faith, their main concerns centering on power, control and wealth. All too many ministers of the faith and religions, arguing over which one's interpretation of the bible is the right one, pitting the Old Testament against the New Testament against the Koran and so forth. Always the same old arguments, the same old disputes and finally we're still fighting the same old wars as thousands of years ago. Wars founded on religious hatred. Only today this senseless fighting is bringing the world to the brink of total destruction. I for one believe it's time to end all these so called "religious wars" for they serve only to divide the children of God. This then can only be considered as a victory for the enemy Satan, who uses the churches own religiosity to confound it, confuse it and keep it separated in these disputes. The world has endured thousands of years of religious wars while whole purpose of church was missed, and that is God.

A good question one should ask oneself is why do you go to church or temple? Is it to worship God or to show off which church is the best or how religious you are? You might as well know it now, if you think yourself to be a very righteous and religious person, you are probably far off course and lost in self-righteousness. For only God can judge who is righteous and who is not. Better to be righteous in the eyes of God then approved by men. For what man can save your soul? Then the question we should all be asking is this: are we being fed in our spirits when we are attending church? Are people turning their lives around and walking away from their worldliness and sinfulness? Are people being healed and miracles happening to the people in the church? The answer to these and even more questions is usually no. And on the opposite end we have many churches that are so called bible believing, tongue talking born again churches. Yet much too many of them are not truly worshipping in the word of God as much as they are caught up in a religious hype of copying and mimicking one another. They do this when they talk in tongues, dance in the spirit, give prophecies, and the most abused of all gifts is the healing services.

Now these gifts of the Holy Spirit do in fact exist and God does work them through his people as He sees the need. Yes God is healing many sick in the churches and those given the gifts of healing should be doing the work of the Lord as it was given for them to do. This is beautiful and happens all over the world not just in born again churches. People do get healed by God and it is a most wonderful miracle from God, but too many evangelicals abuse the gifts of the Holy Spirit. You attend their services and constantly you see the same results, no healing, lots of speaking in tongues, and the laying of hands and shouting and jumping and excitement, but very seldom one sees anyone healed. Week after week, they have healing services at the end of their normal service. You see dozens and dozens of people going forward and having hands laid on them for healing, and you guessed it no one receives healing. To add insult to the situation this is repeated in many churches two, three times a week and the same people going forward each service having hands laid on them but no healing. What is it that God is short on healing or are these people acting on an act or religiosity void of faith and belief in God? I believe it is the latter.

To make matters worse there are many well-known evangelists doing the same and also duping the public by performing fake healings. They pay people off to claim illness on stage, have the evangelist pray and lay hands on them and suddenly they are healed. All this nonsense is sin at its worse, for its sin against God and against his Holy Spirit. It misleads people to a wrong faith in God, and when they don't receive their miracles, lose their faith in God and seldom return to God. Does this mean that I don't believe in miracle healings? Absolutely not for I've been healed miraculously by God on many occasions. I know it sounds crazy, but it's the truth. My first healing miracle was a massive heart attack when I was forty years old. I was rushed by my family doctor in an ambulance and rushed into intensive care as I was undergoing a massive heart attack. Three days later the heart specialist comes to visit me on a Saturday night at about 2 a.m. in the morning all dressed in a tuxedo with a white silk scarf and tie. I will never forget that night as I was still awake and saw him entering and I took a deep gulp figuring this was bad for me him coming this late at night. I was sure it mean surgery for I was dying. He approached my bed with another doctor and the intensive care nurse. He looked down at me with tears in his eyes and I remember saying to him ok let me have the bad news. At that moment he leaned over and hugged me and gave me a kiss on my cheek saying its good news, not bad. You're miraculously healed and we can't explain it except that your faith in God has made you whole, which is a much more powerful medicine than anything we have to offer.

The next two miracles was just a miraculous as I was healed from a brain tumor that had paralyzed my entire body from the neck down. Thanks to God I was healed as the tumor was removed surgically and suffered no ill affects and got all my mobility back and again another miracle that left the doctors speechless. Then the third time happened six years ago and as it turned out very serious. I had prostate cancer and was rushed into surgery. The surgery was a failure as the doctors told me they could do nothing for me. There was too much cancer spread inside me and too many lesions from previous operations and furthermore the cancer was reaching my spine. They could do nothing for me but for me to get my affairs in order for I was going to die. Needless to say I was shocked and horrified at the news. Me dying how could that be I feel fine, no pain? Oh how I prayed turning to God and asking him what went wrong in my life to cause this to me. I remember telling God that I was being selfish but felt I wasn't ready to die yet, that I had a lot more to live for and a family to take care of especially my partner in life whom I loved with all my heart.

A few days later more bad news, my urologist handling me took ill from a massive heart attack and was forced into retirement. Now what was I going to do? I held onto my partner for dear life and him to me for I wasn't ready to leave this world yet. I then get a phone call from a urologist who worked with my former doctor. He wanted me to come in to talk to me. I went with my partner and we sat down to discuss my situation with prostate cancer. He first asked me if I would trust him to treat me that he believed he could help me get through this. No guarantees, but he believed he could help me. I said yes right away as my heart knew this was an intervention from God, and help was right at hand.

This wonderful young man put me through radiation therapy, forty eight treatments for a ten week period. He had cautioned me that my hair would probably fall out and not go to work for I would be nauseous and vomiting a lot from the treatments. Well I went in every morning for my treatment and then went to work and never missed a day of work. When it was over the cancer was gone and it's been six years and no more cancer thanks to God and a wise young doctor.

So therefore beware you who pervert God's word and his Holy Spirit. Jesus said in Matthew 12:31, *Whoever speaks a word against the Son of Man will be forgiven, but whoever speaks against the Holy Spirit will not be forgiven.* Those words of the Lord speak for themselves, beware and don't get caught up in anything fake misusing God or using God to deceive others. If you see such things, turn the other way and leave. There are and will be many false prophets, test every spirit that it be from God. Use common sense and keep your eyes wide open you can smell a rat from far away. For many look good and righteous, but in fact are raging wolves inside looking for whom they may devour.

See 1st John 4:1-6 where the bible reads *beloved, do not believe every spirit, but test the spirits to see whether they are from God; for many false prophets have gone out into the world. By this you know the Spirit of God; every spirit that confesses that Jesus Christ has come in the flesh is from God, and every spirit that does not confess Jesus, is not from God. And this is the spirit of the antichrist, of which you have heard that it is coming; and now it is already in the world. Little children, you are from God, and have conquered them; for the one who is in you is greater than the one who is in the world. hey are from the world; therefore what they say is from the world, and the world listens to them. We are from God. Whoever knows God listens to us, and whoever is not from God does not listen to us. From this we know the spirit of truth and the spirit of error.*

This scripture is even more vitally important to us all today than it was in the days it was written. For we are the End Time generation that will see the end of this world as we know it, and the second coming of the messiah, Jesus Christ. Don't be duped by fancy talking preachers demanding money and allegiance to their churches or scream and shout God in your face. Don't turn over all your income and wealth to any Church that just isn't the word of God. Pray when you are to give and let the Holy Spirit guide your heart to giving. You give with joy not with obligation. You give cheerfully of your heart not because you were ordered too.

Most important if you are confused about anything, especially matters of the church, then "wait". Be still and quiet and talk to God quietly in your room (your heart) and ask God for his truth and his guidance in the situation you are in. Then just be quiet and wait for the Holy Spirit to talk to your heart. It's a promise of God in Isaiah 40:31which says, *Those who wait upon the Lord shall renew their strength, they shall mount up with wings like eagles, they shall run and not be weary, they shall walk and not faint.* Be alert and stay alert and guard your spirit from all that would tear you down and mean you no good. From such flee and trust only in the lord who helps you to discern the spirits that come from the truth and those that come from evil, amen.

So then where is the heaven, the kingdom of God? Where is hell? Where would you think? You need look no further than yourself. For where you heart is there is the kingdom of heaven or hell. We create our own hell here on earth, we create our own suffering by the type of lives we chose to live and by those desires we chose to motivate ourselves with. Life bears enough suffering of its own in each of our lives with its ups and downs that we shouldn't have to add to it. We are so concerned with tomorrow and what it will bring. Leave tomorrow to itself enough is the evil of today for one to deal with. Live and handle the things of today, for that is the rest of you life, today.

There lies a second battlefront where a war rages on for the control of your soul. This one is outside the body in the spiritual realm, where the forces of God fight the forces of evil from devouring your mind and soul. For here is where your biggest problem lies in your flesh. For here is where man lives life everyday life, by human nature and by sight. It's where most men have placed all their belief system in. Your spirit (your eternal soul), lies dormant, asleep and dying while you engage life by the flesh, living by all the worldly standards. For you to find eternal life you must resurrect your spirit for only through your spirit can you find eternal life, repentance before God, a communion with God so that He can fill you with His Holy Spirit, so that you can begin "Living Life in the Spirit".

For this reason you must begin to develop a prayer life for it's the only way we can communicate with God, showing Him the all and all of ourselves. Although He already knows it, yet we must for our own belief system confess it with our hearts and our mouths. Romans 10:10 says, *For with the heart man believes unto righteousness; and with the mouth confession is made onto salvation.* Here is where God examines the true intent of our hearts and salvation is made complete, for once saved, will always be saved.

Oh sure you may slip and fall back into your old ways. I know that road so well myself. For surely I've been there and did that very same thing. Remember once saved always saved and no matter how far our Lord Jesus, must go to get you back He will. After all didn't He die on the cross to take our sins away, all sins past, present and future sins? Jesus says in John 6:35-40, *I am the bread of life. Whoever comes to me will never be hungry, and whoever believes in me will never be thirsty. But I said to you that you have seen me and yet do not believe. Everything the Father has gives me will come to me, and anyone who come to me I will never drive away; for I have come down from heaven, not to do my own will, but the will of him who sent me. This is the will of him who sent me that I shall lose nothing of all that He has given me, but raise it up on the last day."*

So you can see right there that once you truly belong to Christ Jesus, He will do everything needed to be done to keep you saved. If you slip back into your old ways, He'll go there to get you like He did me. I had slipped way back into my old life and had no dealings with God for over a year, and one day accidentally almost killed myself from an overdose of drinking. I had just moved into a new home and feeling very lonely and broken hearted from a break up with a former partner and proceeded to drink three quarts of rum and vodka. I drank out of my depression for I couldn't get a grip on my life. I had no idea the danger drinking that much alcohol could do, but Jesus did. He went to the work places of three of my friends and spoke to them in their hearts, *Stop what you're doing for your brother Ray is in severe danger and may die this very day. Go to him and help him that he may live.* And so the three left their jobs, got into their cars and began driving, but they knew not where to go. I had just moved and hadn't given anyone the new address yet or the phone number. They each cried out in their cars "where to Lord, I don't know where he lives". And Jesus directed each one onto the highway and to the town and to the very street where I lived. As they parked and got out of their cars, they saw one another and immediately realized the severity of the situation. They asked Jesus, which house to go to and he showed them the house. They knocked and no answer, for I was already unconscious on the floor. In faith they just kicked the door in knowing that if God brought them this far then this had to be the house.

They found me on the dining room floor unconscious and the rest is history. They worked furiously on me to bring me back to consciousness, and for the next twenty-four hours it was black coffee, food and ice showers until I was fully recovered. Jesus went to the far extreme to recover me from my destitution. He wasn't about to lose me, for I was his child, and if you become a child of God you too can rest assured He'll do the same for you. Jesus said gave the parable of the shepherd with his sheep who had one hundred sheep and one went astray. The shepherd then left the ninety nine alone and went after the one and brought him back into the fold. This is was the Lord will do for us when we stray off course.

This is the hardest place to win the battle for your salvation, for your spirit is willing but your flesh isn't. For all of us when in the worldly life, live by our flesh, where we do all our thinking, wishing, have desires, use our logic, solve problems and come up with solutions to our daily lives. It's here in our flesh that we desire all that we see, hear and feel. It's here where man lives by his senses always the victim of his near sightedness. Enjoying short terms of happiness and having constant and renewing battles with stress and suffering. How does one learn to enjoy life, and find true satisfaction as opposed to the things that drag us down from day to day? The dark side of life (worldliness) has always brought hopelessness, dreariness, and despair, always a series of repetitious and constantly worrisome problems, suffering from both internal and external forces. All brought on by the senses and their desire to cling to the worldly life and its possessions and relationships. Instead of learning how to live a fulfilled spiritual life with God and learning to love one another and enjoy all that life has for us. Unfortunately we're raised up in a world whose motto is desire and lust and instant satisfaction and gratification always struggling to reach for the stars whether or not your happiness lies there. All too often we see people pushing themselves into careers and studies way beyond or outside of their level of happiness or interest brought on by all too many outside influences both parental and otherwise. Is it that important that all chase after the doctorate, become lawyers, politicians, movie stars, and politicians? Some are called to do those things and that's fine for them, they'll find their happiness and satisfaction there as they should. But then there are the other occupations in life, such as: banking, insurance, financial services, public service, civil service, factories, restaurants, cooks, etc. Is there any disgrace in doing those jobs? Of course not and those best suited for that should be just as happy as the one who becomes a doctor. God's purpose is obviously that all the needs of the entire body be met. All cannot be millionaires, even though they would love to be. Life is not measured nor valued in how much materialism you career can afford you, but in the fact that in the right career you will definitely enjoy the many years ahead of you, both in work and achieve all the success God intended for you. If you're happy in your work how much happier won't your family be when you come home in the evenings after work happy and fulfilled and ready to socialize with your family. Life should never be measured by what we can accumulate in life yet unfortunately that is the way we do things today. Sure we want to provide the best for our families, but even the rich and famous suffer as much as those without. Obviously money isn't the end all and be all to our problems. Each person should be focused on the best talents they have, on that inner desire to be the one thing in life they have always wanted. No matter how improbable or impossible it may seem, with God all things are possible Pray, meditate with God and petition Him for help, guidance and direction. You will surely get it from Him. Proof alone is this book being written by one who's never written anything creative in his entire life. Yet through daily prayers and meditations with God, he revealed to me His calling for me to write this book. A hidden talent you think? I would have never suspected that this type of talent ever existed within me, yet here is the book. It so often takes the work of God to awaken us to who we are and to who we can be.

Unfortunately we've allowed our carnal minds to govern our lives and the functions of our bodies. Consequently human nature rules the man using desire as the catalyst to obscure man's vision from the truth to the lusts of life which is why the word of God states that all men are sinners and fall short of the glory of God. For the inherent nature of man from birth is sin although as a child man knows no sin for as a child man has no knowledge of what sin is. Worldliness and sin is not what God had intended for us or for Adam and Eve, when they committed the first sin of man. He made us each his holy temple for him to dwell in us and thus commune with us. To teach us to live life in the spirit, living through the fullness of God, and not the fleshly lives we ended up living.

It is here in your soul where God comes to effect a change in your life. For it is here in the soul, which is the only eternal part of us that God is concerned with saving for why bother with the body which is flesh and will one day die and be buried, but the soul of man goes on forever. Problem is most of us are dead in our spirits and can't tell or identify from whom the help is coming from or to whom to go for help. As our carnal minds can't perceive the things of God, nor can we conceive of God helping us directly, consequently instead of looking within our spirits for God's help, we look around at the soul level to see which man or institution can help us. We look to the government, to science, to technology or the medical and intellectual wizards of our world with all expectation for the help we seek. Seldom does anyone think to look within themselves into their souls for the answer. Why do you think that is? Mainly because we've become trained and brain washed in school, by our families and friends and by society into resolving everything in life at the soul level (the outer man, our flesh). More and more today we've become addicted to this way of thinking and this perception of life, and television more and more has added to this addiction of fleshly living. We are a people who live by sight and not by faith or spirit. If it feels good do it. So today we've become thoroughly brainwashed into living and thinking and perceiving all by the fleshly desires of our hearts, the carnal mind of man.

We can all stop this madness now and take a deep look at life in the world, in our communities, our towns and the street where we live and most importantly a look at the life we ourselves are living. What makes us tick, what is our true ticket to success? Note that I say success for I truly believe that success is not measured in dollars, but in one's total happiness at home and at work and in one's daily life. A person living life in the spirit in oneness with God and their family is a most successful person. With success will come all the financial needs of that individual for God gives cheerfully to His children and besides what has this carnal type of living produced for man over the centuries? Wars, hunger, strife, bigotry, hate, murder, drug abuse, dishonesty, and need I say more. It's amazing to me that man has managed to survive in this world to this date in spite of all this.

Again, the question, how can I make such a change, I'm just one person? By first understanding the battle that rages in this world is also raging within you. By understanding that we each must start to change regardless of the next guy, we can't wait for the next guy to start first or nothing will ever get done. Good habits are contagious, and if you begin on your part and show the good that comes from you to the world, then the next guy will take notice and start to do the same and so on. If we want to see an end to wars, we must first each one of us must stop the hate and the bigotry that separates us. If we want to see our children free of addictions to lust, drugs, booze, sex, perversion, we must set the example for them. All of us have the answer to life and it is within us and God is ready and waiting for us to make the first move. It's not in the universities of the world, or in the great halls of our governments. It's in your spirit, in mine and we must stop and take a look within for the free gift of God is in you and that's eternal life and faith. We all not only a chance, but the right to an eternal life and we don't have to earn it or work for it for it was in us all along as a free gift from God. It requires only that we believe in God and repent of our worldly lives and enter into a life in the spirit with God. Therefore what we need to do is change our commitment in life from living by our flesh to a life lived and controlled by our spirit. You need to bring forth the spirit to govern and rule your life in order that you can liberate yourself from the flesh. But your soul and flesh rage this war with your spirit keeping the spirit subdued. Thus we end up living by worldly standards, controlled by our flesh. I used to hear preachers and evangelist preach this message saying we must put our flesh under our feet and subdue it there and let our spirits come forth and take control of our lives. Well funny as it may sound this is exactly what each of us must do. God can't do it for you, this one you must do for you. This is where the rubber meets the road as they say. This is where you must say no more, I will sin no more. I will end the hurt and self-inflicted pain and the death in my soul and commence a new life in the spirit. No more will I live by the flesh allowing myself to be separated from God because of my selfishness. Here is where you must come to the God, and ask for his forgiveness by repenting of your sins and your wrongful ways and then asking Jesus into your life to be your savior. Then and only then, can God come into your life and help you and heal you and most important forgive you. He will never impose himself upon you, YOU MUST ASK HIM IN. By doing so you declare you love for him and give him the right to come into your life and help you. It's your life, you can do with it as you choose to, and God will not interfere. If it's hell you want then its hell you get. If it's God you want and his eternal kingdom of heaven, then it's God you'll get and his eternal kingdom of heaven. It's that simple and true. God stands at the doorway to your heart, knocking to see if you'll let him in. You've tried all the rest and nothing has worked in your life don't you think it's time to give God a chance.

As if life wasn't tough enough with man having to battle all his life between his flesh and his spirit. Then as I had mentioned before comes that other battle, the one that's waged for your soul by the spiritual forces in high places. How do I know this? For it's in God's word, Ephesians 6: 10-18, where the Apostle Paul, encourages us that in our daily lives we must live a spiritually strong life. Paul writes *Finally, be strong in the Lord and in the strength of his power. Put on the whole armor of God, so that you may be able to stand against the wiles of the devil. For our struggle is not against enemies of blood and flesh, but against the rulers, against the authorities, against the cosmic powers of this present darkness, against the spiritual forces of evil in the heavenly places. Therefore take up the whole armor of God, so that you may be able to withstand on that evil day, and having done everything, to stand firm. Stand therefore, and fasten the belt of truth around your waist, and put on the breastplate of righteousness. As shoes for your feet put on whatever will make you ready to proclaim the gospel of peace. With all of these, take the shield of faith, and with which you will be able to quench all the flaming arrows of the evil one. Take the helmet of salvation, and the sword of the Spirit, which is the word of God. Pray in the Spirit at all times in every prayer and supplication. To that end keep alert and always persevere in supplication for all the saints."*

Wow, imagine that! We have the weaponry in us to defeat the devil and should be using it everyday. Yet we don't. Why do you think? It's because like most people we don't read the word of God to know that this power of God exists within them. We have no understanding and no knowledge because we don't read the word of God, his holy bible. All the weaponry needed to defeat the devil are available to all, provided to you by God in his holy word. The mighty weapons are these:

First is TRUTH, for it's one of the most important characteristics we possess and that is the truth in us, our honesty. The devil can't stand next to the truth, for he is the father of liars. So everyday of your life you must always live you life in truth. Be honest in all things never lying or giving false witness. Jesus says in Matt 5:33-37, *Again, you have heard that it was said to those of ancient times, 'You shall not swear falsely, but carry out the vows you made to the Lord.' But I say to you, do not swear at all, either by heaven, for it is the throne of God, or by the earth, for it is his footstool, or by Jerusalem, for it is the city of the great King. nd do not swear by you head, for you cannot make one hair white or black. LET YOUR WORD BE YES OR NO, anything more than this comes from the evil one.* So you can see how terribly important it is to be truthful at all times, it's for you own good, for your own welfare. In truth the devil is defeated every time he tries to tempt you. And he won't stop trying to get to you, so beware.

Second, put on the breastplate of righteousness. Only God can make us righteous, for no man sees himself righteous unless God makes him righteous. As the children of God, we are all made righteous in him. Thus live you life righteously every day, it's your garment of son-ship with the Lord. Wear it daily by always being a righteous example of Christ on Earth wherever life takes you. In doing this you'll keep the enemy at bay but also draw people to you to seek the good in you. Thus you can point them to Jesus, the Lord and Savior of the world. That what he has done for you he will do for them also who diligently seek him and open their hearts to him.

Third fasten on the shoes of the gospel of peace. This naturally would follow righteousness, for it's the next obvious step for ones life. If you live your life righteously as God has made you, you become a daily example of Christ on earth. You'll never have to preach to people to show them the way; your life will be all the witness God needs to win souls into the kingdom of heaven. Besides this same witnessing you make with you life also witnesses to the love and peace within you and how others who meet with you also can obtain this peace and tranquillity that you possess. It also says to put on whatever shoes that will make you ready to proclaim the gospel of peace. I believe this means that the different religions and churches that we each go to doesn't matter as long as we're being fed the word of God and the truth, that we've been completed as children and God, and go boldly forward into the world proclaiming God, and the gospel of peace.

Fourth stand in your faith, the faith that God gave you. No matter how stressful the situation gets and it will many times be very stressful as the enemy is trying to defeat you and make you his. Stand firm in the faith of God, and God will get you through it. A confirmation of this is found in 1st Corinthians 10:13, where the St. Paul writes in the bible, *No testing has overtaken you that is not common to everyone. God is faithful, and he will not let you be tested beyond your strength, but with the test he will also provide the way out so that you may be able to endure it. So above all things always be strong in the faith that the Lord Jesus, gave to you. For he will always provide for you in all things.*

Fifth take the helmet of salvation and the sword of the Spirit, which is the word of God. This is the ultimate weapon of warfare against the devil and all the dark forces coming against you. Use it against the enemy and he will flee from you for he cannot stand in the face of God's word. For it was the word of God alone, that banished Satan from heaven and doomed him into hell for all eternity along with one third of the angels who also fell from grace as they worshipped Satan.

So this is a major example of living life in the spirit. It's a spiritually centered life, which we can freely live day after day. A life centered in truth, righteousness, peacefulness, faith and salvation. Where once we lived in the flesh, doing the things of the world and being rewarded to keep us blinded from the truth we now live a new life in the spirit. No longer does the flesh rule our lives but our spirit now has control. No longer will you have to suffer from a worldly life where things are temporal including the happiness the world brings to you which fades away so quickly. For the gifts of God are permanent and eternal. The love you find will be with you always and forever as will all the happiness, success and joy you find, for God will never leave nor forsake you as the world will and in fact does. The ups and downs of your life in the world will have little effect on you and bring you little or no stress. For you will have the wisdom to know the world for what it is, temporal in all things and your spirit will always seek the solace of the Lord where there is always stability and safety for your soul. God always gives us the peace to stand in whatever situation life puts us in and to stay firmly grounded and withstanding the storm our lives maybe involved in. Therefore we stand still and wait, and study the situation giving God the time to speak to our hearts and give us a solution. The best part is that he does to those who wait upon him. There's a wonderful verse in Isaiah 40:28-31 says it best, *Have you not known? Have you not heard? The Lord is the everlasting God, the Creator of the ends of the earth. He does not faint or grow weary; his understanding is unsearchable. He gives power to the faint, and strengthens the powerless. Even youths will faint and be weary and the young will fall and be exhausted; but to those who wait for the Lord shall renew their strength, they shall mount up with wings like eagles, they shall run and not be weary, they shall walk and not faint, and amen to that.*

Why once you realize all that awaits you, death isn't the end of everything but the beginning. It's just the removal of you flesh body, a weight that holds you spirit down from being eternally free to grow as God intended us to grow. Death only removes the mortal body, which must die, but God then gives us an eternal body that never dies. We will come back to this world to live here once again, but in our new eternal bodies, without death and without decay. Therefore death is our last act on earth that then brings us to be with our eternal self and with the Lord.

A good question to ask now is does the devil really exist? Is this just all a Hollywood hype to sell movies? Are there demonic spirits working on earth to defeat us? I know it all sounds spooky and has the makings of a horror story, but let's look into the bible, at the word of God for more proof. We find it in the Old Testament, in Isaiah 14:12, which tells of the fall of Lucifer, the angel of the Dawn, the Day Star. Isaiah writes, *How you are fallen from heaven, O Day Star, son of Dawn. How you are cut down to the ground, you who laid the nations low! You said in your heart, I will ascend to heaven; I will raise my throne above the stars of God; I will sit on the mount of congregation, in the uttermost parts of the north; I will ascend to the tops of the clouds, will make myself like the Most High." But you are brought down to Sheol (hell), to the depths of the pit."*

Then in Luke, 10:17-20 the bible says *The seventy returned with joy, saying,"Lord, in your name even the demons submit to us!" Jesus then said to them, "I watched Satan fall from heaven like a flash of lightning. See I have given you authority to tread on snakes and scorpions and over all the power of the enemy; and nothing will hurt you. Nevertheless, do not rejoice at this, that the spirits submit to you, but rejoice that your names are written in heaven.*

Then one more example in Matthew 4:1-11,"*Then Jesus was led up by the Spirit into the wilderness to be tempted by the devil. He fasted forty days and forty nights, and afterwards he was famished. The tempter (Satan) came and said to him, "If you are the Son of God, command these stones to become loaves of bread." But he answered, "It is written, one does not live by bread alone, but by every word that comes from the mouth of god.*

Then the devil took him to the holy city and placed him on the pinnacle of the temple, saying to him, "if you are the Son of God, throw yourself down; for it is written, 'He will command his angels concerning you,' and 'On their hands they will bear you up so that you will not dash you foot against a stone.'

Jesus said to him, "Again it is written, 'do not put the Lord your God to the test." Again the devil took him to a very high mountain and showed him all the kingdoms of the world and their splendor; and he said to him, "All these I will give you, if you will fall down and worship me." Jesus said to him, "Away with you, Satan! For it is written worship the Lord your God, and serve only him." Then the devil left him, and suddenly angels came and waited on him."

Can you imagine, before being tempted by the devil, Jesus goes through forty days and forty nights of fasting. He was preparing himself in the Spirit to be ready to stand against all evil than could come against him. Yet in the weakened physical state of hunger and thirst and dehydration, he took truth, his righteousness, his faith, his gospel of love and peace, his salvation and the word of God and quickly defeated Satan, once and for all.

Please be aware at all times, that nothing bad can happen to you when the evil one comes to tempt you and or to defeat you. You only need to stay in the spirit, fully dressed in the armor of God, and nothing they can do can hurt you. You don't have to worry, fear, or run from anything, for God is on your side, and if God is for you then who can be against you. Isaiah 54:16-17, says: *you see it is I who has created the smith who blows the fire of coals, and produces a weapon fit for its purpose. I have also created the ravager to destroy. No weapon formed against you shall prosper, and you shall refute every tongue that rises against you in judgment. This is the heritage of the servants of the Lord and their vindication is from me, says the Lord.* I for one am proof of these scriptures for every weapon waged against me in my life have failed and God has held me firm and strong and brought me through all of them: a heart attack, two battles with cancer and five kidney operations. I've survived several auto accidents which by all understanding could only be defined as miracles of God for surely I and all those with me should have been killed in them. So my word for you is to hang tough with God for He is on your side and Satan has no power to defeat you except to tempt you with the temptations of your flesh. He knows where you are weakest but with a spirit filled life you now have the weapons of your warfare.

Imagine that, God created even Satan himself and all his evilness to be there in the world to tempt, cause havoc and destroy the lives of men "who refuse to serve God." Remember Satan has no power over man but that power which man allows him or gives him, for Satan is powerless otherwise. Like the song of Santana says, he's the monster living under your bed whispering in your ears. He's a tempter but he can't make you do it.

It's this same Satan, who's dared to promise the Lord all the riches in the world if the Lord will bow and serve him. Remember in Matt. 4:8-10, Satan took Jesus to the highest mountain and said to Jesus, all this will I give to you if you bow down and worship me. How could he offer this if it wasn't his to offer? Satan can never offer something eternal and everlasting, but can offer you momentary pleasures that are here today and gone tomorrow.

He rules all that is evil in the world and worldliness is the kingdom of Satan. So when you live your life governed by your flesh, by the world (human nature), you are living outside of your own spirit, a life in worship of Satan without knowing it. You're doing all the things and committing all the sins that give worship to him and keep you separated from God. You are destroying yourself because of this alliance you're in knowingly or unknowingly you're in league with the devil and not walking with God. You are doing his bidding.

On the other hand when you love the Lord, and truly worship him you will do all that is right in the sight of God, especially taking care of your body which is the temple of God. We see this confirmed in 1st Corinthians 3:16, *Do you not know that you are God's temple and that God's Spirit dwells in you? If anyone destroys God's temple, God will destroy that person, for God's temple is holy, and you are that temple.* Every soul is created by God and is holy onto God, and that includes all six billion or more people in the world today. We are holy temples onto God, and if we destroy the temple of God, which is our souls then God will destroy us. As Jesus said what good is salt if it has lost its saltiness, it's good for nothing and you throw it out. Well what good is a soul to God if you destroyed your soul and refuse to believe in God? You're good for nothing and God will no longer have anything to do with you. You are in fact then Satan's child and he becomes your reward. It is the only way a person can become permanently lost to God by committing the unpardonable sin which is the total rejection of God for the things of the world.

Now that is probably one of the most important messages in the bible for all of us second to the gospel message of Jesus Christ. We are the temples of God, made holy by God. So then how can we live defiling the holy temple of God, which is in us? Think about it for a moment. The bible reminds us that the reward of sin is death. It destroys you slowly day by day, destroying the temple of God. How can God live in the defiled sinful temple that you have created or have allowed to exist within you? In this defiled state God has to remove himself from your temple leaving you void and unprotected. You become free for any demonic spirit to inhabit your temple. Satan takes over you life and before you know it you've surrendered it to him and all that remains is your ultimate destruction. For if you let your temple get destroyed by your sinfulness then the result is the death of both your body and soul. Now note the consummate word here is let. You are the one who must make the choice. You are the person that chooses the life you want to live. Choose a life of sin and you will destroy your holy temple forcing God out of your life. I'm sure most don't know this but it's true. You force God out of your life by the choices you make. And without God to protect you for he no longer resides in you, then what? I rest my case.

Remember this and I think it also is one of the more important messages from God in his holy word. God doesn't destroy us, bring wars upon us, he doesn't annihilate us when bad. God doesn't bring the end of the world or the threat of Armageddon, but what God does do is to warn us what will happen to us if we pursue certain sinful courses in life. It's the inevitable results for the life we choose to live by or better known as karma. Same applies with the end of the world; it also is the inevitable results of the life we all chose to live here on earth by. Lives filled with hatred, bigotry, selfishness and greed, laziness, inhospitable, worshippers of money, lust, worldliness and whoremongers. How can the world not eventually come to an end? We're a reckless society with no love for one another and a total disregard for God. For the world to survive into the next millennium we all have to change to a God fearing, spirit filled people whose foundation for living is LOVE, not greed, power and recklessness. That's the message from God. That isn't to say there aren't wonderful people in this world, the world is full of wonderful people. There are six billion people in the world, more or less, but there aren't that many who have dedicated their lives to living in the spirit and to God, ready and willing to repent of their faults, their evilness, their sinfulness and adopting a new life, a son-ship with the Lord Jesus Christ. Surely there aren't enough righteous people to save this world from Armageddon. The world wars or the final conflict of man will come. Just like Sodom, God removed all the righteous (Lot and his family) and destroyed all the rest of the men, women and children because their sins were so grave. Note I said men, women and children for the five cities of Sodom and Gomorrah, weren't gay or homosexual cities as preachers have made us to believe. They were cities primarily inhabited by heterosexual men and women and married families with children as well as by homosexuals. The sins of Sodom and Gomorrah were the sins of the world. The accounts of Sodom and Gomorrah, is a precursor of the destiny of man for what happened there will happen again in the end to the entire world. Why, because we are committing the same sins today as they did then?

Yes there are demonic spirits at work trying to destroy us; we see it in Mark, 19:20-28, *and they brought the boy to him. When the spirit saw him, immediately it convulsed the boy, and he fell on the ground and rolled him about, foaming at the mouth. Jesus asked the father, "How long has this been happening to him?" And he said, "From childhood. It has often cast him into the fire and into the water, to destroy him; but if you are able to do anything, have pity on us and help us." Jesus said to him, "If you are able! All things can be done for the one who believes." Immediately the father of the child cried out, "I believe; help my unbelief!" When Jesus saw that a crowd came running together, he rebuked the unclean spirit, saying to it, "You spirit that keeps this boy from speaking and hearing, I command you, come out of him, and never enter him again!" After crying out and convulsing him terribly, it came out, and the boy was like a corpse, so that most of them said, "He is dead." But Jesus took him by the hand and lifted him up, and he was able to stand. When he had entered the house his disciples asked him privately, "Why could we not cast it out?" He said to them, "This kind can come out only through prayer."*

Remember this always, the battle for your soul rages on daily. As I said before from the book of Ephesians, we wrestle again spiritual forces of darkness in high places. This isn't a joke; it's most serious, if Satan tried to tempt Jesus Christ, how much more won't he try to defeat you? Folks, this is out and out spiritual warfare and you are the prize. A major war is being fought for our souls, with angels fighting off demonic forces daily to help us. But we must do the main fighting for our souls. How by changing the way we live from our worldly fashion to a life in the spirit. We need to embrace Jesus Christ as Lord and Savior of our personal lives. Repenting and becoming truly reborn spiritually in our hearts and souls. Then and only then can the forces of darkness and Satan be defeated forever.

Are you ready to battle for your soul? Are you ready to battle for the souls of your children? Are you ready to battle for the salvation of life on earth as we hope for it to be someday? A life filled with love caring, harmony and peace, a world free of hatred, wars, famine and abuse, where we do care and love one another, centering our beliefs and our way of living to a life lived in the spirit and the in the Lord. All this is so very possible. But we must each take the first step. The Lord leaves us his footprints, the pathway home the day he took the cross and defeated all sin and death for all time. We each must decide whether or not to take it. God will never force himself or his will upon you. Love will never force its way upon you. We are all free to choose the life we want to live and God then will judge us for our decisions and how we decided to live our lives. If we chose to live a life by the spirit then we must begin today to subdue our outer man, our flesh and bring him to the cross and crucify him. Then and only then can our spirit come forth into the daylight and out of the darkness. Only then can we truly know God and His divine love and plan for our lives.

Finally in closing the choices again are ours. We can change bring God back into our lives and in doing so save ourselves as well as the world. Or we can remain status quo and change nothing. The results of this being that the end of this world will surely come and come very soon. We now live in a world of terror and hate at a heightened level beyond our wildest imaginations. Third world nations today are studying and preparing to build for themselves atomic weapons. In the hands of a few maniacs it wouldn't take but a small spark for the launching of the first of the atomic weapons and then what, World War III? The bible tells us that in the end times two thirds of the world's population will perish in the wars, famine and natural disasters that will come to the world and all this because of the choices we chose to make. I think this is the time for each and everyone of us to sit quietly with our souls and with God and begin a life of prayer, meditation and self-examination and decide what outcome we want for ourselves, for our families, our friends and neighbors and for our world. Again God is giving us the warnings of where we're headed if we don't change. The choice is ours a life everlasting or the end of this world because of our selfishness. I pray we all make the right decision, amen.

THE POWER OF FAITH AND A POSITIVE MIND

Now you know the truth of the battle that rages on to win your soul and doom you to destruction. Then the question arises in one's mind, what can I do on my part to help save my soul? Well now that you have turned your life over to God, you've put on the whole armor of salvation as Paul the apostle calls it, then comes your part and here is where many are weakest. We don't want to have to do anything but sick back and let God do all the work. It is human nature for man to look to others to pull him through. We look to the government as if they were god to provide us with our daily needs. Too many live by the motto, give me, get me and I want. Well it is time to realize that we too have to get up and move our rear ends to do some work ourselves, and this is where positive thinking comes in. For we must believe God beyond everything else and know that what he promises to do for us, he will do!

We must learn to trust only in the Lord as it says in proverbs 3:5-10. Trust in the Lord with all your heart; and lean not unto your own understanding. In all ways acknowledge him, and he shall direct your paths. Be not wise in your own eyes: fear the Lord and depart from evil. It shall be health to thy navel, and marrow to your bones. Honor the Lord with thy substance, and with your first fruits of your increase. So shall your barns be filled with plenty, and your presses shall burst out with new wine.

We are living in very tough times and many have lost their jobs and are worrying how they going feed their families, pay mortgages and rents and meet all their financial obligations. Our country is in a recession and it seems more like a depression. Our government is claiming recovery and that the fat cats of Wall Street are making money once again. Well the problem here is it did not trickle down to the average American. Unemployment is just under 10% which is the figure of those actually collecting checks from the unemployment system. It doesn't account for those who benefits expired and no longer collect, it doesn't account for those who just gave up looking for work or for those who with their unemployment benefits expired are forced to grab part time jobs and minimum wage jobs to stay alive. The real unemployment is probably more like 20% or higher.

So what can you do? Continue to have faith in the government that doesn't recognize your plight and shows no intentions of caring or doing anything about it? Continue to have faith in a worldly system that is geared for the enrichment of the big corporations of this country or the fat cats of Wall Street, whose only concern is buying and selling of stocks and commodities? Or is it time to bring your faith and trust to the one who can help, to God himself? When all else failed me in life, and my life had reached its end I chose not to turn to desperation, but instead I turned to God. I was a new child of God, saved by Jesus Christ, by his visitation to me in my home, and now just a year after coming to Christ, I encountered my first test, I suffered a heart attack. I was rushed into Smithtown General Hospital, in Smithtown, New York. I was in ICU for three days waiting for a decision from the surgeon as to when they were going to operate me. I'll never forget the scare the heart attack at first gave me, but within a day or so I realized that the scare was a justified human reaction. After all no one wants to die and I had no understanding of eternal life or life after death at the time. I was a new babe in Christ Jesus, just beginning to learn who and what God was all about. All I knew at the time was that life seemed to be running out on me and I was facing a early departure from this world. I was only forty at the time of the heart attack and did not know how to face this crisis. Death, the word kept pounding in my mind, but somewhere deep inside of me I wasn't ready for death. I knew somehow that I knew I had to survive this. Why would Jesus come to me and lift me out of the mire, just to snatch me away from earth a year or so later. I had things to do for God, to serve him, to help people out, this I knew deep in my heart. In thinking this it started to build my faith, until I could nothing else but stand on the promises of God.

What I did do when the reality of my condition sank in was turn to God with all of my heart and I remember praying and saying to him, "Lord I put all my trust in you. I don't think it is my time to leave this world for I feel there is a lot for me to do and to learn. When the time is right I will know it in my heart and you won't have to call me for I will come running to you."

The following night which was Sunday morning about 2 am, I was woken from my sleep and standing before me was the night doctor on call and my heart doctor dressed in a tuxedo. I remember thinking "oh God it must really be bad if he had to leave a party to see me on a Sunday morning. At that moment I noticed he was crying and he leaned over to hug me and kissed me on my cheek. I looked up at him and said "ok doc, give me the bad news." He looked down at me smiling and said "oh no, it is good news. We cannot explain what's happened to you, but you are healed. The one section of your heart is dead and will remain dead, but the rest of your heart is fine and strong. You must have a doctor better than us on earth." I took his hand and said "oh, yes and his name is Jesus."

That was my first encounter with death, but it wasn't going to be my last. My faith was reaffirmed after that and my positive attitude towards life, towards myself and to God got stronger with each passing day. Within the next six years, I suffered severe attacks from kidney stones which resulted in five surgeries and one stone crushing. The first five surgeries was because the stone crushing machine was not yet accepted in the United States. Consequently I had to undergo five surgeries and hospitals stays of 30 days for each operation.

Every time my faith was solidly in God and I knew because I just knew God would bring me through. Thank God for that faith, for the fifth operation turned out to be more difficult than expected, and I went into a coma which lasted for three days. The doctors had told the family to get me a priest for they did not expect me to make it through. Three days later God did another miracle for me and rose me out of my coma.

What is really exciting about this is what happened afterwards. I would make rounds of the hospital floor walking with my IV pole for exercise. As I was walking down the hallway of the hospital I passed a room with an iron lung. I had seen them in movies, but never in real life. Someone said hello which startled me for I did not see anyone in the room, but in looking carefully I saw the man's reflection in the mirror above his head in the iron lung. I said hello and he asked me if I had a few minutes to keep him company. He was lonely, had no family or friends to visit him. I said it would be my pleasure and I entered the room, taking a chair by the wall and moving it over to the iron lung.

We talked and laughed for quite a while. He explained to me he was born a hunch back, and that every six months he comes into the hospital to be placed in the iron lung to oxygenate his lungs as they are folded from his hunch back position. I felt so bad for him and felt the need to pray for him. I knew I had the faith, but did he have the faith to receive prayer. I asked him if he would let me pray for him. He said "oh yes, and pray in the name of Jesus, as I know you are a Christian. I am Jewish, but do believe in Jesus also." So we prayed together, I laid hands on his forehead, and we believed God for a miracle. And a miracle we got the very next day. When the doctors opened the lung to let him out, he was no longer a hunch back. God had healed him and straightened out his body. He now stood upright for the very first time in his life. I never saw him again, but know that he was a great testimony for the power of God.

What I am trying to convey here is that we must exercise our power of faith and positive thinking for miracles, healings and the likes to happen. Jesus does perform miracles and healings that in his mercy and by his grace he just blesses some with, but when you check the word of God, one must exercise one's faith and positive thinking to receive the miracle. We see this in the New Testament, in the gospel of Matthew, chapters eight and nine we find three healings performed by Jesus, and in all three cases, faith was necessary for the recipients to receive the healings. In chapter eight, a Roman centurion, comes to Jesus requesting that if Jesus, just gives the word his servant who is dying will be healed. Jesus marvels at the faith this centurion soldier has in Jesus, and because of this faith Jesus heals the servant. He tells the centurion "go thy way, and as thou hast believed, so be it done unto thee."

In chapter nine a ruler came worshipping Jesus, expressing his faith that if Jesus comes to his house, his daughter who has already died will be raised from the dead by Jesus. Jesus proceeds to follow the man to his house. On the way a woman who has had a bleeding issue for twelve years, came up behind Jesus and touched the hem of his garment. She believed that if she could just touch him, she would be healed. Jesus sensing that someone had touched him turns around and see's the woman and says to her "Daughter, be of good comfort; thy faith has made thee whole."

Following this healing Jesus enters the ruler's house and funeral proceedings were under way.

Jesus asks for the mourners to step aside, that the child is not dead, but asleep. But they laugh and scorn him for they know when one is dead (they showed their lack of faith). Yet the ruler maintains his faith in Jesus, and Jesus goes in and takes the daughter by the hand and immediately she is healed and raised from the dead. Once again the father's faith and positive thinking worked to complete the healing.

Following that healing, as he left the house of the ruler two blind men begged him to heal them. He went into the house to speak to them and asked "Do you believe that I can do this?" They answered oh yes, Lord. Jesus then touched their eyes and said "According to your faith, be it unto you." And their eye sights were restored.

There were four major incidences in my life where Jesus performed miracles that one changed my life and two saved me from certain death. These occurred years after my salvation. I was in my mid forties when I had lost my home through a break up with my partner, and was living in a rented house. I remember that as hard as it was for me to go on without my partner, I knew that I had my health, I had God in my life and life somehow would go on. I would stand on the word of God knowing that somehow he would get me through this. After all I was sure that he did not waste his time saving me when he made his first visit into my home.

During these months I had become a faithful member of a Christian Church. Once again it took another miracle to get me there. I hadn't been inside of a church in over twenty five years, but the Lord felt I needed the companionship of other Christians to help me in my new walk with God and to learn his holy word. So one evening while having dinner, it was a Wednesday, the Lord spoke to me that he wanted me to start going to church. That this night was a perfect night for me to start and he had a perfect church in mind for me. I said to myself this is crazy, no one has church on Wednesday, so I said to the Lord, yes I will go on Sunday thinking of a nearby Catholic church. I was born a Catholic, and figured that's what the Lord would want. But no he said it had to be tonight. So I got dressed and drove off in my car to where I had no idea.

The Lord gave me directions to a church that was about twelve miles from my home, a church that I had never heard of. It was a small New England type chapel or colonial, all white clapboard. Looking like it was on a Hollywood set. I parked my car and went inside and the church was packed with parishioners. So I stayed in the back with the standing room crowd, but the members turned around and saw me and insisted I sit. I tried to say I was ok standing, but everyone including the standing room crowd insisted I sit and enjoy the service. They all somehow knew I was a new comer, and they wanted me to feel as welcome as they could possibly make it for me.

As the service began I remember that I was shaken almost out of my skin when the congregation began singing. The music was blaring and they sang with an enthusiasm and an excitement I had never seen before. They raised their hands praising God. They danced in the aisles and in their seats, shouting hallelujah, hallelujah. Then the most frightening thing of all, some spoke in a strange language which didn't make any sense to me. It wasn't Latin, but neither was it any language known on earth, for this I was sure. I began to cry wondering why Jesus would bring me to such a place. I was just about to get up and leave, run for my life it seemed, when a brother reached out to me and grabbed my hand. Someone else put a hand around my shoulders, as they comforted me and then the music changed. It was quieter, slow and moving. It was Amazing Grace, and it caught my attention instantly. My past came before me as I heard the song, I cried and cried like a baby listening and viewing my sinful life.

An evangelist got up to speak, whose name escapes me, but I believe her name was Mary. She looked into the congregation and asked everyone to be still and quiet and instantly the place was like a tomb. She then put out her arm and said young man, you in the rear you are new to our church. Please come forward for God brought you to us to become a member of our family. I didn't pay any attention to her, as I thought she was talking to someone else. At least I was hoping she did not mean me. I was wrong, it was me she was calling and finally one of the brothers said to me, "it's you she wants, if you want I will walk with you up to the altar." I got up and two brothers walked me up the aisle. I got to her and she immediately began to pray over me. She saw my life exactly the way it was and said God had sent me to her for a healing of my soul. I knew she was right on, for it was Jesus who directed me that night to this church. I began crying and once more repented to God and asked Jesus for his forgiveness for the terrible life that I had lived. She then laid her hand on my head, just barely and I collapsed onto the floor. I was out for almost fifteen minutes and when I awoke the helped me to my feet. It was explained to me that truly I was slain in the spirit, and baptized with the Holy Spirit at that moment. We prayed and I instantly began praying in tongues. This I must say, was a most incredible experience for a young man who only a week ago didn't know who God was, nor did I care to know. Now a week later and here I am a born again Christian, not because of any religious indoctrination or religious brain washing, but because Jesus Christ led me to this salvation. I confirmed it and you can too in the New Testament, John 3:3, Jesus says "Verily, verily, I say unto you, except a man be born again he cannot see the kingdom of God."

So I was now set on my new life with God. I had moved into my new home that I was renting and hoping this would be a good change for me.

However still in my heart was the anguish of the break up and the fact that my ex kept creeping back into my life sort of like putting salt on the wound. It was a battle for me to have him come back and then leave again, then come back and once again leave again. I became distraught and a total wreck and one day without realizing what I was doing almost committed suicide. I sat down on the floor in my dining room, and opened three or four quarts of vodka and proceeded to drink them all. I don't know at what point I blacked out, but later found out that all four bottles were consumed. I was going to die of an overdose if I didn't get help right away. I was totally unconscious and death was knocking at my door.

I was new in the house and no one knew where I had moved too. I had told everyone that I would call them when the phone was installed and give them the new address and phone number. Thank God for the one who could save me and that was Jesus Christ. He went to the jobs of my three closest friends, Mike, Mike and John. He said to them to stop working for I had an emergency and they needed to get to me or I would die that very day. Without questioning they ran to their bosses and explained the emergency and were given the day off to find me. They each had no idea where I was or where I had moved too. Jesus then spoke to each one in his car and led them to the block I had moved to. When they parked their cars and got out of the cars, they were in shock to see one another. Apparently this was more serious than they had imagined for Jesus to send all three of them there.

John asked the Lord, which house and Jesus showed him. Without even knocking to make sure they had the right house, they kicked in the door and ran inside and found me unconscious on the floor of the dining room. They saw the empty bottles and knew that I was dying. Somehow they didn't want to call the police and believed in God to let them help me back to health. Here is where faith and a positive mind is an absolute must if this is going to work. They knew Jesus brought them here to save me and save me they were going to do, no doubts just unconditional faith in God.

They lifted me up onto my feet and for the next day and a half, with each one holding me up on each side of me, they walked me back and forth never letting me sleep. They bought all the ice bags they could find in supermarkets and 7-11 stores, and filled my tub with ice. They undressed me and gave me ice baths almost every hour. Black coffee, more ice baths, walking back and forth, each one taking terms in carrying me back and forth. As I said this went on a day and a half, maybe more until I became coherent, making sense. I looked at them and cried in their arms, thanking them for the obedience to God in saving my life. That I had no idea this would happen to me. They hugged and kissed me and said we wouldn't never let you die and we all cried together over the joy of saving my life.

They knew the weakened mental state I was in, although I tried to deny it and say I was fine. One of my three friends, Michael, insisted to move in with me and care for me. He stayed with me for one year. I can never thank the three of them enough, for without their love and obedience to the call of God, I would be dead today. Once again faith, a positive mind brought this miracle to a successful conclusion.

Months went by and my pain was diminishing, and my joy was increasing as I leaned more and more on Jesus. One evening Jesus came to me in an audible voice (most of his visits were audible ones and only one was visual) and he spoke out to me in my bedroom "behold I bring good news for you my son. In twelve months you will buy a home that presently is under construction. Behold the woman who will sell you the house." Instantly there appeared a vision in my room of this older woman sitting at her desk, in her office. She was heavy set, in her mid fifties, grey haired and tied in a bun. "This is the woman who will sell you the house." I cried out to the Lord," but Lord Jesus how can I buy a home? I am broke and have no credit". And the Lord replied "trust in me, all things are possible to those who believe. In six months you will receive two credit cards in the mail compliments of American Express and Sears Roebuck. Take them and you will re-establish you credit instantly."

I believed in the promise Jesus had just given me and stood faithfully on it. Six months later to my surprise for I had forgotten the promise from Jesus, I received in the mail the two credit cards from American Express and Sears Roebuck. I sat down and cried as once again Jesus has stepped into my life with another miracle. I then kept track of the days and months faithfully waiting to meet the woman in the vision, but no luck we never crossed paths with one another. On the night prior to the anniversary of the twelve months the Lord had promised that I would be buying the home, I went to him in prayer. I said to the Lord, "please forgive me but I don't think this promise will be met by you as I have never met the woman you showed me in the vision." Unfortunately I had lost my faith that this promise would come to pass. I had become like the apostle Thomas, doubting the Lords word. You must show me for me to believe you. Yet Jesus in his mercy spoke to me audibly once more "my son of little faith, tomorrow Saturday take your mother with you as a witness. I will direct you to the woman." I ran to my mother and told her what Jesus has told me. She promised to be ready on Saturday morning.

The next morning both my mother and I got into my car and drove. I didn't know where to go and asked the Lord where do we go from here? He spoke to me in the car and strange enough only I could hear him. My mother never heard his voice. He directed me onto the Long Island Expressway, heading east. We drove from exit 60, where we lived to exit 68, William Floyd Parkway. He directed to get off and head south to Montauk Highway. I did so and then he directed me to turn left onto Montauk Highway. As soon as I turned I immediately saw the real estate office shown to me in the vision. It was across the street, so I turned on my signal and waited for the traffic to clear so I could turn into their driveway. Needless to say I was crying like a baby and my whole body was trembling, as once again I was in the midst of another major miracle from God. I parked the car and went inside the real estate office. As soon as I went inside, sure enough the woman from the vision was sitting in the front desk. She looked up at me and asked if she could help me? The tears were uncontrollable as I told her of the vision and that I was there to see if I could buy a house." I also told her that I had gone bankrupt only a year ago, so that my credit was pretty bad. She looked at me and said and I will never forget it "Ray, if the Lord sent you to me, so let's get a move on for I have many houses to show you."

She showed me many homes that day and whatever I bid was out bided by other buyers. I was exhausted and it was late afternoon. My mother was hungry and so was I and we decided to call it a day. If there was a house for me to buy it would have to wait for another day. We were headed back to the car when Bridget, the realtor of the vision, ran out and called me back. She apologized and said "listen I forgot I do have one more house I can show you. I didn't think of it for it's not quite ready. It's been under construction for twelve months now. I must also tell you that I own fifty percent of the house and my brother owns the other half. The house belonged to my father and he left it to us when he died. My brother has been coming down on weekends from his home in Maine, to renovate the house. It is almost done, if you let me show it to you?"

She took us to the house and immediately my first thought was unaffordable. The house was Mastic Beach, which would be affordable however this was a water front house on the Great South Bay, with it owns dock. This was way beyond what I would ever be able to afford. I expressed this to Bridget, and she replied "nonsense, you don't know what you can afford. Look at the house and see if you like it and then we will talk."

I went inside with my mother and oh my, the house was beautiful. Everything was new, new wood floors, new kitchen and new appliances, a new Italian marble fireplace and beautiful French doors. It was gorgeous to say the least, but afford it was an impossibility in my mind. We went back outside onto the driveway to tell Bridget, sorry for wasting your time. She looked at me and said "you did not waste my time, this house was meant for you and you will buy it. I have written a price on this piece of paper, and I don't want a dollar more and not a dollar less." I said again to Bridget, "I love the house but it is way out of my league." She said "nonsense, you don't know what you can afford. Look at the paper then you tell me what you think." I opened the paper and it read $37,500. My eyes popped, my heart leaped into my throat. Could this be for real? This was easily at least $100,000, below market. She looked at me and said "you see, God did keep his word for you and here is your new home." I signed papers, she found a company to give me a mortgage even with my bankruptcy, and the rest is history. Once again faith, belief and positive thinking played a major role in the fulfillment of this prophecy. For without faith, without believing in Jesus, I would have never pursued this to its fulfillment.

But the miracles of God did not stop here. As I said there have been many visitations that I have had with Jesus and once again all of them with one exception were audible visitations and one was visual where he actually stood before me.

The visual visitation came when my grandmother was dying from a heart attack. She was eighty five years old at the time and this was not the first heart attack she had suffered from. But this one was as the doctor's told us was the one that would take her. She was too old and frail to be operated and there was nothing more they could do for her.

That Sunday, I went to church with my mother and my ex partner Billy. We got to church late and there were hardly any seats as the church was packed with the members of the congregation. The pastor seeing us entering the church, stop the service and called out to me "Brother Ray, you and your family are welcome to sit up front, we have three seats open for you." Gosh I hated sitting up front in church I thought, you can't sleep. Everyone including the pastor can see you, but as there was no where's else to sit we sat up front.

The service went on as normal until our pastor began preaching his sermon. Then the strangest thing happened, a cloud was coming through the wall of the front of the church at the altar. Everyone was startled and whispering and the pastor saw it and stopped his sermon. He asked everyone to be still and to pray as we were being visited by the holy spirit of God. Just as he spoke the cloud came down to where I sat and engulfed me and when I looked up there was Jesus Christ, standing before me. He was beautiful to behold in his white garment that was so white it blinded you. He wore a gold sash around his waist, and his blue eyes were the bluest you had ever seen. You could see eternity in his eyes. He stood before me and brought me the following message: "my son, tomorrow go to the hospital and visit your grandmother. Be there at 2pm sharp, and give her this message. Tell her that she harbors an old sin in her heart that she needs to repent of and that if she does repent that I will save her and bring her into the kingdom of God. That I will heal her now and in six months I will take her with me in her sleep. That there will be no more pain and suffering."

The next day I went to work and spent the morning trying to figure out how I could approach my boss for the afternoon off to see my grandmother. Well I never had to for he came to me scratching his head. He said to me he couldn't sleep all night with me on his mind and some kind of emergency I was having. I explained my grandmother's illness and the visitation in church with Jesus Christ. He said leave, go quickly to your grandmother's side and gave me the rest of the day off.

I got to the hospital at 1:50 pm, and could find no parking. I was panicking for it was getting close to 2pm. I called out to Jesus, "Lord I am here, but there is no place to park the car." Jesus then speaks to me and says "my son of little faith, look just six cars in front of you and one is pulling out." I look and sure enough six cars in front and I see the tail lights go on, and the car pulls out. I park and run inside the hospital to see my grandmother and bring her the good news.

When I get there my mother is in the hall crying and I run up to her afraid that my grandmother had passed away. She says no, but you are supposed to see her at 2pm, and the doctors won't be finished with the patients until around 2:30pm they said. I looked up and said "Lord I have kept my promise and I am here, but they won't let me into CCU to see her." Jesus then replied "my son, behold the power of God." At that moment the pa system goes on and a voice is calling every doctor in CCU with an emergency with other patients of theirs on other floors of the hospital. All of a sudden the CCU door swings open and all the doctors come running out to answer their emergencies. I started to go in, but the Lord said to wait and again the door swings open and all the nurses come running out holding their heads. Seems like they all came down with severe headaches and abandoned the unit. Jesus then speaks to me saying "now go in and talk to your grandmother."

I go in and kiss my grandmother hello, and bring the message from Jesus. She looked at me and said "it had to be you to bring the message to me, for I wouldn't have accepted it from anyone else." She repented, we prayed together and I left the hospital with my mother. The very next day we get a phone call from the hospital to hurry and come down. A miracle has happened and my grandmother is healed and completely cured from her heart attack. When we got to the hospital, we found her sitting up in bed with lunch and laughing with the doctors and nurses who were all laughing and crying with her. They couldn't explain it but that she was totally healed. I knew how it happened and she did too and so did my mother. Jesus kept his promise to heal her.

Six months later my grandmother went to bed with my mother, and she quietly died in her sleep. Jesus had kept his word to the very end.

God wasn't finished with me yet. There would be more tests of faith for me. They came when a turned sixty years old. It started with a pain and paralysis that started in my right arm and then as the days went on progressed to my left arm. The doctors were baffled and could only prescribe pain killers for me. But the pain grew and traveled down by body until the pain took over my entire body and I could not use my legs or arms. The doctors were examining me with every test in the book, but could not figure out what was wrong. I was heavily sedated to control the pain and in the meantime I was busy praying, knowing that somehow God would bring me through this. Finally one morning I woke up, and as I laid in bed the room began to spin around. Slow at first and then the spinning got faster and faster until I was inside a vortex. I screamed out for help and my partner Eric came to help me out. Finally after some time the spinning stopped. I went into the shower to bathe and the spinning started again. Only this time it was furious and I lost all control of myself. I screamed and screamed and Eric came and got me out of the shower. He dried me up and clothed me and rushed me to the emergency room at the local hospital.

The doctors from giving them the history of my paralysis, the pain and now the vertigo suspected a brain tumor. They gave me a pain killer and a drug called anti-vert to control the vertigo. Then they did a cat scan of my brain and sure enough they found the tumor. It was right on a main blood artery and pressing down on the area of my brain causing me the pain and paralysis. I was scheduled for surgery and sure enough as soon as the operation was over I was totally healed from the vertigo, from the pain and from all the paralysis. Needless to say my family was so grateful to God, for once again delivering me out of a terrible situation.

But as life would have it I wasn't out of the woods yet. Two years later I went for a routine physical exam and as luck would have it, the results were pretty bad. My doctor called me into his office when he got the results and my PSA he told me was 14. I didn't understand the significance of the number 14, until he told me you have prostate cancer. I am sending you to the best urologist in Long Island, so that he can examine you and confirm the cancer and decide on what treatment they can give you.

So I go to the urologist who from the onset tells me that surgery of this type for a man over sixty is very risky. He said that I would have to be in really strong health to undergo such a massive operation. I looked at him and said what choice do I have, and so they scheduled me for surgery. The operation was long and when I awoke from the operation my partner Eric, was at my side. He said to me the operation was a failure, that there was too much cancer and they decided to sew me up and do nothing. This frightened me and I began to fear the worst. I remember the tears were swelling up in my eyes, and Eric hugging me and trying to consol me that we would find an answer.

Finally when I saw the doctor, it was worst than I could ever have imagined. He told me that there was nothing they could do for me, that there was too much cancer and I had about six months to live, that I needed to get my affairs in order. Ouch, after all I have been through in my life this was it, I was going to die from prostate cancer. But I didn't want to die, I felt it was wrong and not my time. I held onto Eric for support and he kept consoling me and reaffirming me that we would find an answer. I prayed to God for I felt lost and helpless and afraid. Through this God showed me to hold on to my faith and trust him for everything. I also during these weeks of fear somehow found a way to accept death as a possibility. I was after all 62 years old and my father had died at 54 years of age.

Thank God, for he had other plans for my life. Shortly thereafter my urologist suffered a massive heart attack that left him so weak that he was forced into retirement. Seems like God needed to remove him as my doctor as he was too negative and shortly thereafter his assistant, a young urologist calls me. He says he was reviewing my case and would like to see me in his office. I agree to see him and we go to see him. We sit in his office and he opens my file and says to me, "can you trust me with all your heart." I said to him yes, for I had no other choice. I was dying and would trust him with any experiment he had in mind. He said I can't promise you a miracle as you know your cancer is far spread throughout your body, but it has not reached your spine yet. Once it does we will not be able to do anything for you, but the cancer is still about one inch away from your spine. I would like to do 24 treatments of radiation and I think we can help you and extend life for you. He warned that I would get very sick with vomiting, hair loss and nausea from the radiation. I said that would be a small price to pay for any kind of cure.

So I go to the radiation clinic and begin the treatments. I go five days a week, every morning for my radiation treatments. Funny thing is I don't get sick, no nausea, no vomiting and no hair loss. As a matter of fact I continue to go to work every day while I undergo the radiation treatments. Everyone is in shock that I can still go to work. At the end of the 24 treatments, my doctors asks me if I would go through 24 more treatments, to insure they destroy every bit of cancer and with that pretty much insure that it never returns. Well for me that was a no brainer, I said yes right away. It's now over six years that I remain in remission and my PSA tests are constantly less than 1. Isn't God wonderful, you bet he is.

It wasn't my intention to use myself as the main example of faith and positive thinking. However just about everyone knows the story of Abraham, Moses, Noah, Lot and all the other prophets of God. What's sad is they seem to have little effect on people. Most people just shrug the stories off as religious hog wash or they say that was then and God doesn't work that way anymore. Well you are wrong and guess what God still does those miracles today. I am proof of it, I am your modern day Abraham, your modern day Noah, Moses, whatever you want to label me. I have been put through the fire over and over and every time came out with my faith intact and standing firm on the word of God, believing God for everything. So can you, they weren't special, I am not special, we are all special to God and he will do for you just as he's done for me and for all those who believe without a shadow of doubt. There's that word again, doubt. You must remove it from your life and substitute it with faith, belief and a positive mind.

All I can say to you the reader, you need to believe, you need to have faith and be positive about the things of God. Trust him and he will deliver you from all and anything as he did me. I am a living testimony of the power of God in the world today. I am a modern day Peter, Paul, whatever you want to call me, but I am a messenger of God bringing you the Good News of Jesus Christ. I was a worst sinner than most of you, and more lost the most of you. I had divorced myself from God for over twenty five years. I was an atheist and in the twinkling of an eye Jesus turned my life around, and he will do the same for you. I am one person who can say without equivocation, beyond a shadow of doubt that Jesus Christ is the savior of the world, the messiah. I live because of him and his love for me otherwise the heart attack or one of the two cancers would surely have killed me. To live in Christ one needs to remove all doubt, for doubt is the enemy of man. Nothing good will come to you when you are in doubt. God can't bless you when you doubt in him, after all God cannot bless a mess.

You can search the prophets of the bible who were all just ordinary men just like me until God touched them. Once touched of God, they instantly became men of faith with a positive mind free of all doubts. You can check it out for yourself with the life of Abraham, Moses, Lot, Noah, David, Jonah, Elijah, John the Baptist, the Apostle Paul and the list goes on. All of these men were touched and tested by God, and every one of them became men of faith with a sound positive mind and free of all doubts. They knew that they knew that God was their father and there could be no other. They dedicated their lives from that very moment to believing in God, in following God and serving him with the rest of their lives.

This is what happened to me when I first met with Jesus. I went from an atheist to a man of God instantly, for all my doubts and fears were instantly quenched when Jesus called me out. I went from feeling alone and neglected and frustrated living in a world where I was an oddball to society being gay and could not fit in with the rest. I was bitter over the sexual child abuse I had to endure for ten years leaving me with very serious questions as to who I was and was I a mistake living in this world. I was hated by many when I was born and through my youth. Evidenced by the way I was sexually child abused. I had thirty eight years of bitterness and hate built up inside me that it would take an act of God to heal me and bring me back to life. And that is exactly what happened. Jesus came to me with his love and simply asked me to follow him. I knew instantly in my heart that God had not forsaken me and I gave my life to Jesus that very moment. I found my faith and trust in God, and began to develop a positive mind. Before I knew it doubt which was my enemy was now defeated and faith became my new friend. There may not be many in the world today who can claim to have met Jesus, as I have. Why was I chosen remains a mystery to me, but I thank God that Jesus did choose to visit me over and over again. I am sure I would have never made it if he hadn't come to me. Now I give you what was given to me, I give you Jesus Christ, the savior, the messiah, your salvation. Whether you are Christian, Jew, Hindu, Muslim, no matter what you are, you must know Jesus as your Lord and savior. Be a Jew for Jesus, a Hindu for Jesus, a Muslim for Jesus, but be for Jesus. I am living proof that the Lord Jesus Christ is the savior of the world and that through him and him alone, can we save ourselves and in doing so, save the world from an inevitable cataclysm. Amen.

CHAPTER TEN

LOVE IS THE KEY OF LIFE

Right now is a good time to stop and reflect on all that you've read. Ask yourself does any of this make sense to me? Do I believe much of what I've read? Talk to yourself deep in the heart, meditating and praying over it. What you don't understand or believe ask God to help you and shine a light on what you don't understand. Ask yourself do you want to begin a changed new life, one centered in God, living in the spirit? Do you want to be a truly spiritual person, God centered and in control and fully knowledged in who you truly are? To do this you need to get face to face with your demons that constantly tear your life down, make you weak, bring you stress, cause you to be evil and sinful. Demons that cause you to doubt, fear, worry, hate, and so on. You must bring it all out and bear it all to God, including your joys, your sorrows, your disappointments in you life, your bitterness, your hatred, your anger, bear it all and speak it all with God. Praying deep from in your heart and just open up and speak your mind. Then when all is said and done, rest and be quiet and just meditate and listen. Keep doing this everyday and try to do it the same time each day. If morning is best then do it every morning whenever you can be alone, get together with yourself and God.

In time you'll begin to hear a quiet voice inside of you talking to you. Encouraging you, soothing you and caressing your soul. Giving you advice, giving you truth, and giving you love. Some call this voice your conscience, but believe me the one speaking to you is no other than the Holy Spirit of God, reaching out to you. This is where God meets with you, in your soul where the true you are, and not the one outside in the flesh. This is

God's holy temple, your soul (spirit). And as you continue this journey for the truth of yourself and are sincere in your pursuit, God will meet you there in your heart and begin to show you the way back both to him and to yourself, to your healing and to a new spiritual life, a life that is eternal not like the world where everything is temporal.

You'll be able to see everything that is good yourself, and then you'll discover new things about yourself. New talents you didn't know existed in you. You'll be able to face up to the things that tick you off, make you angry and bitter and find a new quiet patience in which to deal with them. You'll be able to see the errors of you ways. You'll come face to face with your addiction or addictions that cause you so much pain and loss in life. Be it drugs, money, greed, lying, cheating, alcoholism, sex, lust, perversion, crime, dishonesty, and so on. God will show you that nothing you are suffering from is beyond His mercy, His healing, or His forgiveness, for God is ready to forgive, to heal all those who admit their wrongs and seek a change in themselves.

These meditation sessions can take weeks and months of soul searching or it can be quick. Everyone is different and we each have our own set of problems and our own set of ways of dealing with them. Here is where God works best, for he comes to each one of us differently, according to what we can handle and understand bringing with him forgiveness and mercy and healing for our troubled souls. As I said it's different for each of us. Some come quickly to God and others take time and God in his love is ready to deal with you and take all the time necessary to bring you back home to Him.

But God needs for us to take control of our lives and stop the massacre of ourselves and of each other. In my case I was so lost that Jesus had to come into my home and talk to me right to my face to stop me from my self destructive way. I will never forget that glorious night of my salvation. He didn't yell at me, or give me warnings of thus says the Lord; you will surely die if you don't stop this wanton lifestyle. No, no on the contrary he said to me what worked best for me, he said: "My son, my son, I love you very much and want you to follow me." I heard that gentile and quiet voice but my heart was refusing to believe it, so he persisted and said "My son, my son, I need to talk to you. I love you and want you to follow me."

It was then that my heart leaped in my chest and a quiet voice within me said to me "it's Jesus Christ, who's come to visit you." I remember how I started to tremble, my lips were quivering and the tears swelled up in my eyes like a hot boiling pot running over. I then fell on my knees, yelling out to him "Lord Jesus, is it really you?" And he replied "Yes, my son it is I and I've come to tell you that I love you and want you to follow me." That was the beginning of my new life in the spirit. I've followed the footprints he left for me and it's been my pathway home. But as I said before, for some of us it comes easy to change and for others it takes lots of healing and time but we all will change nonetheless. In my case it's taken over 26 years, to draw me to this place in time in my life walking with the Lord and culminating with the writing of this book. It's my testimony to you that Jesus Christ is alive and ready to heal and to forgive all that you've done, to bring you to where I'm at along with millions of other believers, to the Son of God and no other. I have no church to coax you into, no ax to grind and I am not asking for your money. I'm no healer, no miracle worker, won't mail you healing crucifixes or blessed cloths dipped in olive oil and I'm especially not asking you to join any religion. What I'm trying to do is open your eyes and your minds to the truth, of which has escaped too many of us for much too many years. Much too many people go through life in death of their sins not knowing or realizing that God is right there ready to forgive, to heal and fix everything in their lives. Ultimately much too many people die in their sins, never knowing the love and mercy of God. There lies the mystery of salvation and spirituality and that it is up to you, for it's by your free choice who you will serve. Will you serve God having total spiritual control of your life or will you choose to continue in the worldly path you're now on leading to your eternal death. You must want a true spiritual life and want to be united in union with God and walk with God. God will never force himself upon you, but you must call out and say yes Lord, be my God. You must make the first move to save yourself by acknowledging Him and calling out to Him in the privacy of your heart. From the reading of this book, you know my truth and what God did for me. I can't promise you that He will visit you like He did me. I believe He meets us where it's best for us, in the manner best suited for us. Whether that is in an actual visit or in the quietness of your heart, he will be there nonetheless. He's not an imposing God, but a loving God. You call to Him and He comes to forgive, to save and to heal all that is broken. I believe God came to me without my calling Him for I was on the pathway to destruction and my ultimate death and separation from God. But somehow deep inside of me there existed a good person unknown to me, but thank God very well known to Him. He knew that with gentle love He I could be reached and saved for the kingdom of heaven. He was so right and why shouldn't He be, for He is God. I had suffered so much in my life and was a most hated and unwanted child from the very inception of my birth. It seemed like death walked alongside of me all my days looking for the day to snatch me from this earth. All too many tried to destroy my life, but for the grace of God they failed. No matter what came against me in life, they or it failed. Illnesses, eight operations in all, a heart attack, two battles with cancer all failed to kill the spirit within me. Evidently God always had plans for my life that I would find out about later in life.

I never knew love and how to love for I was raised a creature to bring sexual pleasure to others. Happiness was a fleeting dream for me as my companion everyday was loneliness. All my relationships in life ended in failure for a multitude of reasons of which when I look back are mostly mine. I wanted to love and be loved but knew not how and the enemy was only too ready to send evil men into my life to destroy me. I was made into a sex machine not a man. As I said I never knew love until Jesus Christ. On that glorious day of his visitation to me I found real love. I found my first love. It was like being born for the first time and coming out of the womb and into the arms of my mother, my father, my God and Savior. For the first time in my life I felt wanted, I felt complete and I felt love. I felt the love of God swimming all over and all throughout my body until I felt drunk in love. Before Christ everything and everyone were dead relationships and experiences for me. Since Christ everyone and everything has been God blessed to me and I'm alive to receive their love and to give it back. Yes I'm alive in Christ and I have love for God first loved me and taught me how to love. I was dead and now today I live in love, I live in Christ.

You too can do as I did, to truly receive him and make him the Lord and the Savior of your life, that they'll never ever be another God before you, no matter what those gods may be whether it is money, power, material possessions, booze, drugs or whatever. That nothing will ever again separate you from God. I made that commitment and promise to myself and it's been the truth of my life ever since. I have been free ever since. One thing I have found true for myself, when I commit I truly commit. I don't cheat God, for He is the one eternal love in my life and in my soul. I have found happiness ever since. I am fulfilled for the first time in my life. The healing and the blessings have been tremendous. I honestly don't know where my life would have ended up without Jesus Christ, without his love, his constant divine love pouring out to me everyday. Love that overwhelmed me, embraced me, held me up when I was down and weak and near death, love that constantly picked me up off the ground every time I fell into sin for my heart was so willing but many times my flesh was too weak. And it's this most wonderful merciful Lord, who awaits you with open arms, to fill you with his unimaginable love. To bless you with healing and forgiveness and anything else you're in need of. You're heart will be flooded with his love, his mercy and healing will begin that very moment you ask him into your life.

That's why love is also the key to our salvation and the key to the life in you, in this world and in the universe. Jesus said the two greatest commandments is one to love God with all our hearts and soul and strength. The second is to love one another as much as we love ourselves, these are the two greatest commandments, on this Jesus said, hangs all the law and all the prophets. On love hangs all the law of God, on love, imagine that something so simple, so pure and so true. The basic key to life is the foundation of God's law, and that is love.

Love is the greatest power in the universe for love is God, and God is love and it is His love that caused Him to create everything that is and ever will be including you and me. Through prayer and meditation you will discover the love inside of you and this love will connect you and God together and begin a healing that will make you a totally new person. You will discover a new revelation about your new life in the spirit and that is that God made us perfect as He is perfect. That when we live in the spirit we will be one with Him made perfect in love with the same powers of love that Christ Jesus has.

Trouble, trials and defeats must come and happen in our lives. They come to test us and cause us to grow more spiritually and successfully in our lives here on earth. Just like the mother bird has to push her young ones out of the nest to teach them to fly or they will die. Along with these trials often comes the problem of stress, worrying, and anxiety. We can worry ourselves and often do into heart attacks, numerous other diseases and body disorders that often culminate in death. Why? What did we gain from worrying or from stressing ourselves out? Nothing but a stack of doctor bills and painkillers and drugs to control what we are unwilling to take control of and that is our lives. Worrying also takes our focus off of God, takes us out of the spirit filled life and directs our lives back to the world, where there is pain and more suffering. We begin to focus on the stresses and fears of everyday living and before you know we're falling back into the world and out of our spirituality. But one must remember this that perfect love casts out all doubt, fears and evilness and brings you always to the creator.

In Matthew 6:25-34, Jesus says about worry and anxiety, *Therefore I tell you, do not worry about your life, what you will eat or what you will drink, or about your body, what you will wear. Is not life more than food and the body more than clothing? Look at the birds of the air, they neither sow nor reap nor gather into barns, and yet your heavenly Father feeds them. Are you not of more value than they? And can any of you by worrying add a single hour to your span of life? And why do you worry about clothing? Consider the lilies of the field, how they grow; they neither toil nor spin, yet I tell you, even Solomon in all his glory was not clothed like one of these. But if God so clothes the grass of the field, which is alive today and tomorrow is thrown into the oven, will he not much more clothe you-you of little faith? Therefore do not worry, saying, 'What will we eat?" or 'What will we drink?' or 'What will we wear?' For it is the Gentiles (the world) who strives for all these things; and indeed you heavenly Father knows that you need all these things. But strive first for the kingdom of God and his righteousness, and all these things will be given to you as well. So do not worry about tomorrow, for tomorrow will bring worries of its own. Today's trouble is enough for today."*

Does this mean we shouldn't save or invest and prepare for the future? No absolutely not! Does it mean we shouldn't prepare for tomorrow, for the education of our children, for building a better community in which to live? Again the answer is no. What the Lord does say is deal with each day one day at a time. For today has enough problems of itself, don't worry about the tomorrows. And if you have made arrangements to save, to invest money for the future for your family or yourself, then relax and let it be. Don't preoccupy yourself with worries of how much the market went up or down each day. Don't be obsessed by it all, for is wealth or money better than your health? Don't the wealthiest people in the world suffer the same pains as we do and die the same as we do and from the same illnesses and diseases as we do? With all their wealth they can't buy their health or buy a cure for the diseases that ravage through their bodies. Neither can they buy peace or happiness or love. Be at peace with your decisions and move on in the love that God has given you. If your investments are such a concern to preoccupy so much of the time, then withdraw the money and put it in savings account. Sure the Dow Jones Index is up today and it's inviting you to buy stock but also beware that it'll be down tomorrow. But in the long haul it usually always balances favorably for the investor. And suppose the market did crash, and everyone lost everything. Would worrying or crying bring it back, of course not? So what do you do and the answer is simply to start all over again, that's what. Bankruptcy and a stock market crash won't kill you or your family and yes it will cause some suffering and a definite lack of material things, but that's about it. The pain and hurt it brings, is brought on by you and your love and obsession with money. When in fact the best thing to know and realize is that it's just material things. Here today, gone tomorrow and before you know it, you'll be back in the saddle again. It's never the end of the world, just a set back. I've been there, done that and believe me I survived bankruptcy, everyone does and so will you. Losing it just means regrouping and getting started all over again. And if you think life has past you by and it's too late to start over, then you surely have lost the message of life and the purpose of your life here on earth. For truly we're not here just to accumulate wealth or beat one another to a pulp or just to become doctors, lawyers or Indian chiefs. We're here for a very short time passing through on an eternal journey through life growing and perfecting the spirit that is in us. We were created to live our lives spiritually but also need to experience life in the flesh for our spirits to grow with a complete knowledge of all life. Life isn't just the 70 or 80 years we live in these mortal bodies on earth, for that's just a thought in the true scope of eternity. The fact remains that there is an eternity for each and every one of us rich or poor, faithful or atheist, child of God or child of Satan, white or black, whole or disabled. No one can escape eternity it's our prime purpose in life to get on with our eternal life. So what then is this mortal life all about here on earth, surely it wasn't meant for destroying ourselves in wars, conquests or to be dominated by one another? Nor was it meant to abuse one another, or to hoard and be selfish and denying your fellowman his share of the pie. Life here on earth I believe was meant for us to grow and to learn about love, wisdom, knowledge and understanding of ourselves, our loved ones and our family, of all humanity, and of God. It is also a place where we can grow and learn to experience and live spiritual lives in a physical environment. Exchanging ideas, feelings, knowledge and understanding with one another. Thus preparing ourselves for the continued journey through eternity when we shed our mortal bodies, in exchange for immortal ones and continue where God wants and needs for us to be. Each one of us learning, growing and applying the new lessons to our lives as we move from one spiritual plane to the next, as we go from glory to glory. People leaving our lives as new people enter into our lives, all part of the process of learning and developing our spiritual selves, creating in us the new man, a new start of life in the spirit.

So the message is stay focused in today, and live today as it was the rest of your life. Be centered in love, in God and love your fellow man. Be filled in his Holy Spirit, leading you in your spiritual life. Let the love of God flow through you each day and spreading it to those around you. Give and when you give do it with love, and it will be given back to you. A good measure, pressed down, shaken together and running over (Luke 6:38). You can't out-give God and you can't out-love God, but you can share the gift and the love of God with everyone as God has given it to you.

I know it sounds corny, but return evil with the good in your heart, with love. I know that it's very difficult to turn the other cheek, but turn it we should and must. For it's not about winning or losing, but about learning and loving in spite of the opposition. Remember that in spite of ourselves, God so loved us that he gave his life for us on the cross so that we could find life and live it more abundantly through him.

Love covers a multitude of sins; love will never surrender but always conquers in the end. Don't let yourself be trapped into doing things in a worldly way, or resolving your disputes and problems with worldly solutions. Be grounded at all times, centering yourself in God's divine love. With this take your time, be patient and pray and meditate for a good answer or resolution to your problem. It may take a little longer to resolve but the resolution will be a permanent one totally satisfying to your soul. You'll walk away totally at ease and very happy with the outcome. Not like rushing to judgment or rushing off an answer or giving a quick fix to a problem as the world does. Only to find a short way down the road, that the resolution didn't quit work out or didn't work well at all. It was only a "quick fix" but the problem still remains. When you operate out of love you are operating out of the fullness of yourself and tapping all the resources within you. No greater gift can one person give another than to give totally of himself in resolving a dispute or problem from the fullness of the love within him. When the problem is resolved it is final and complete and both parties walk away happy and completely satisfied.

Saint Paul gives us one of the best understandings of what love is in his letter to the Corinthians in 1st Corinthians, chapter 13, *If I speak in the tongues of mortals and of angels, but do not have love, I am a noisy gong or a clanging cymbal. And if I have prophetic powers, and understand all mysteries and all knowledge, and if I have all faith, so as to remove mountains, but do not have love, I am nothing. If I give away all my possessions, and if I hand over my body so that I may boast, but do not have love, I gain nothing.*

Love is patient; love is kind; love is not envious or boastful or arrogant or rude. It does not insist on its own way; it is not irritable or resentful; it does not rejoice in wrongdoing, but rejoices in the truth. It bears all things, believes all things, hopes all things, and endures all things. Love never ends. But as for prophecies, they will come to an end; as for tongues, they will cease; as for knowledge, it will come to an end. For we know only in part, and we prophesy only in part; but when the complete (the Lord) comes, the partial will come to an end. When I was a child, I spoke like a child, I thought like a child, I reasoned like a child; when I became an adult, I put an end to childish ways, for now we see in a mirror, dimly, but then we will see face to face. Now I know only in part, then I will know fully, even as I have been fully known. And now faith, hope and love abide these three; and the greatest of these is love.

Saint John writes in John 1:1-5, *in the beginning was the Word, and the Word was with God, and the Word was God. He was in the beginning with God. All things came into being through him, and without him not one thing came into being. What has come into being in him was life, and the life was the light of all people. The light shines in the darkness, and the darkness did not overcome it.*

John goes on to write in John 1:10: Now that is astonishing, amazing and all the other superlatives you can add to it, *The Word (which is Jesus, the promise of the Messiah to come, God incarnate) was at the beginning because he was to bring light to a darkened world. And through God who is love "all things came into being".* You see my friends it's all done by God through love as the two are inseparable. God must be love. He could be no less than the utter fulfillment of love, because for God to be anything less even by the very tinniest measurement of a degree would render all of us without sufficient mercy to save us from our sinful selves. But thanks be that God is the all in all, the completion of everything from the very beginning and completion of love. Before anything was there was God, there was love. Beyond all eternity there is God and there is love. When man needed God the most, God allowed man to crucify him on a cross. This is a love surpassing all the combined imaginations of all of humanity from the beginning of time including all their combined knowledge, wisdom and understanding.

Can any of you name anything in this world so enduring? Do you own anything more complete, more rewarding or more fulfilling? Do any of you have the power to heal the sick, raise the dead, or to extend your life by even one day, one hour, one minute or one second? Can any of you make a fly, make a horse, make a tree, or make a man? Can anyone create life and make it perfect by just the spoken word? No, of course we can't, but God can and did exactly that and more and by just his spoken word. That's how complete and total is the love of God.

God through his love blesses us with miracles in our lives. By just his spoken word to me, he healed my grandmother. He revealed and spoke to me of a home he had for me to buy and showed me in a vision of the woman who would sell it to me a year hence. To the very date I met the woman and she sold me her house at half its valued price as the Lord had promised me. At an Easter party I had prepared for senior citizens at a nursing home, more people showed up than we had planned for. Yet I remained calm and allowed for no panic. I turned and in prayer I asked for the Lords help and he supplied it by multiplying all the food and drinks we had to feed all and there was food left over. Oh, how I pray this message is reaching you down deep into your soul, for love is the conquering force against all of the evil that is in the world and that is in each of us.

1st John 2:5 states: *But whoever obeys His word, truly in the person the love of God has reached perfection,* Imagine we can reach the perfection of love in our lives right now. We don't have to wait; it's already been done for us at the cross. And he that is perfect will make us perfect, and he that is perfect love will make love perfect in us.

So let us turn our lives and our love away from worldliness, for the love of God is not in the hearts and souls of those who love the world. 1st John 2:15-17 says it best, *Do not love the world or the things in the world. The love of the Father is not in those who love the world; for all that is in the world—the desire of the flesh, the desire of the eyes, the pride in riches—comes not from the Father but from the world. And the world and its desire are passing away, but those who do the will of God live forever.* I couldn't say it any better, no one can. The love of the world, the way the world is not the way of God. We need to awaken and get out of the darkness. We need to walk into the light and truly confess ourselves to God so that perfect love can be made perfect in each of us. For without perfect love we can't be with God, we can't know God nor can we share eternity with God, for to do all that we must have what God has and that is perfect love. Why is this so important? Because that which is imperfect cannot dwell with God who is all perfect; which is why he removed Lucifer from heaven and sent him to hell. But God made a plan for us to achieve perfection, and that plan was Jesus Christ, that through his Son, we can all be made perfect in all ways. Perfect in body, perfect in soul, perfect in spirit and perfect in love.

We see this again in 1st John 3:1-3, *See what love the Father has given us that we should be called children of God; and that is what we are. The reason the world does not know us is that it did not know him. Beloved, we are God's children now; what we will be has not yet been revealed. What we know is this; when he is revealed, we will be like him, for we will see him as he is. And all who have this hope in him purify themselves, just as he is pure."*

And for me this is the culmination of everything I've written here. To live in the spirit is to become one with God, and in doing so becoming a child of God's. Nothing could be greater or more important in a person's life, and yet it does get better because John says we do not know what we will be or become but that we do know when he is revealed to us, we will be like him. We will be like Jesus, the completion and the perfection of all life, of all creation, the completion and the perfection of man. Revelations 21:3-4, *And I heard a loud voice from the throne saying, 'See, the home of God is among mortals, He will dwell with them; they will be his peoples, and God himself will be with them; He will wipe every tear from their eyes. Death will be no more; mourning and crying and pain will be no more, for the first things have passed away."* How can that be possible, one would ask? I believe it is because as John said, then we will be like him when he is revealed to us. We will be perfect, and death will have been conquered once and for all, and sin will have been conquered once and for all. Imagine the things we'll be able to do with the power of perfect love in us. I can't wait can you? We will probably discover and answer all the mysteries of science both here on earth and in the universe. Nothing will be unknown to us. I can imagine that somehow through this power of love we will find ways to travel through the universe and see everything there is. We will conquer every known disease to man and eliminate them from the world. One can only imagine and even that can't measure to the real truth of what we will become when he is revealed to us.

I came from the gutters of Brooklyn and Los Angeles, to testify to you of this, for I was there where many of you are today. Lost in the darkness of the web the world had spun for me, my sins worse than most, my bitterness and pain beyond help and measure. I was a street hood, derelict and abuser of myself. I lived in a perverted hell of lust, sex and drugs for more years than I care to remember. I experienced all that hell offered me and found the world empty in its offerings. I always came up short, left wanting, left hungry and thirsty for more and more action. Much too often it brought me to the brink of death and each time Jesus Christ performed a miracle to save my life.

You have the best opportunity in the world to escape the fate that was mine and for some of you a fate worse than that which was mine. You can make a conscious decision to stop and change your life around. Give it to God, before you lose it. Not everyone will make it and that's an unfortunate reality. Many chose to remain in sin. The end of that is death, but believing in God is the beginning of life itself, eternal life filled in truth and perfect love.

And this is the word that God has given to me to give to all. Now is the time to usher in the great revival bringing the call of salvation to all men, for the Lord will give mercy and forgiveness onto to all those who confess and receive Him into their hearts, and when salvation on earth is fulfilled shall He come to gather in His flock. Then shall He usher in the seven great years of tribulation on earth bringing upon man such suffering and pain as has never been seen of the face of the earth. They'll be wars, famine and death throughout the world and all types of diseases to test and try man's soul. For still in His mercy He will save the repented heart, but in those days it will be hard to be saved. For your hearts will grow bitter and hard and you'll ever distance yourselves further from the Lord. But in those days shall Israel, turn back to her God receiving Christ Jesus back into their hearts and then shall come the end and the return of our Lord, Jesus Christ."

Are you hungry, thirsty for something better in your life? Are you dissatisfied with life as it is? Are you always on the short end, left hanging and always losing out in life? Then turn you life around and get yourself back to the Lord, and get centered with him. Jesus says come all who are hungry and thirsty and I will give you living waters and you'll thirst no more. When Jesus came to me, he said "I love you and I want you to follow me." I have done so all these years since and will continue to do so throughout eternity. He came to me with his love, and his love conquered my flesh, nailed it to the cross and saved my life. He left for me his footprints, the pathway home. I've been on the journey ever since. You too can join me in this journey home. I pray for each and every one of you in the world, to turn to God and seek him within your heart. I challenge you to do this for yourselves. To go and find the truth and the love of God that's within you. Give God the opportunity to shine a light on the pathway home for you, to leave you his footprints for you to follow homeward. I pray for the peace of the world and for the salvation of the Lord to be realized by one and by all. May the God that passes all understanding, bless you all and guide you all home safely to Him. With all my love to you all in the name of Jesus Christ, have a safe-journey home, Amen.

Made in the USA
Middletown, DE
06 February 2015